THE ILLUSTRATED TREASURY OF
MEDICAL CURIOSA

Art Newman

McGraw-Hill Book Company

New York St. Louis San Francisco Auckland Bogotá Caracas Colorado Springs
Hamburg Lisbon London Madrid Mexico Milan Montreal New Delhi
Oklahoma City Panama Paris San Juan São Paulo Singapore Sydney
Tokyo Toronto

THE ILLUSTRATED TREASURY OF MEDICAL CURIOSA

1 2 3 4 5 6 7 8 9 0 HALHAL 8 9 3 2 1 0 9 8 7

ISBN 0-07-046301-8

This book was set in Palatino by Monotype Composition Co., Inc.;
The designer was Maria Karkucinski.
Arcata Graphics/Halliday was printer and binder.

Library of Congress Cataloging-in-Publication Data

Newman, Art.
    The illustrated treasury of medical curiosa.

    Bibliography: p.
    1. Medicine—Miscellanea.   2. Medicine—Anecdotes, facetiae, satire, etc.   I. Title.   [DNLM: 1. Medicine—anecdotes. WZ 308 N55li]
R706.N48   1987   610   87-3381
ISBN 0-07-046301-8

The quoted material on the back cover is from G. B. Harrison's *A Second Jacobean Journal*, published by the University of Michigan Press, 1958.

CONTENTS

iii

iv   *Contents*

PREFACE

Dr. Johnson said he loved anecdotes, but "if a man is to wait until he weaves anecdotes into a system, we may be long in getting them, and get but a few in comparison of what we might get." I have not heeded the great oracle's magisterial advice, thinking to construct my "system" of seventeen chapters generously enough to admit any anecdotes likely to tickle, divert, or astound. True, some few didn't quite make it. Where to put that dissolute young rakehell who was so distressed and disquieted by the sight of his would-be mistress's cancerous breast that he forswore his scandalous life? Where to put the spectral ship, the *Rodeur*, with its cargo of slaves adrift on the wide ocean, all on board, human cargo and crew alike, blinded by a mysterious disease of the eyes?

But those were exceptions. More often the problem was how to fit a plenitude of riches into limited space without gleaning too much material from one epoch at the expense of others. Inevitably, however, because I dug wherever gold lay buried, it is the spacious times of Pepys and Boswell, the seventeenth and eighteenth centuries, that provide the lion's share of the book's contents. Then there is the question of familiarity. Oft-told tales are not, strictly speaking, curiosa. But some old favorites proved irresistible, like Mrs. Tofts and her lagomorphic progeny, and wormed their way in by right of oddity. In the main, however, I think the reader will find much that is rare and singular, and perhaps, too, a little

> *. . . of that nature as to make*
> *One's fancy chuckle, while the heart doth ache.*

A.N.

ACKNOWLEDGMENTS

(Numbers in parentheses indicate pages on which the illustrations appear.)

Grateful acknowledgment for permission to reproduce pictorial matter
from art collections and published works is made to

Courtauld Institute of Art, London (91)

Dover Publications, Inc., New York
   The Bizarries and Fantasies of Grandville by Stanley Applebaum, 1974
   (50, 76)
   Callot's Etchings by Howard Daniel (ed), 1974 (202, 231)
   The Graphic Worlds of Peter Breugel by H. Arthur Klein, 1963 (84)
   London, A Pilgrimage by Gustave Doré and Jerrold Blanchard,
   1970 (232)
   The Picture Book of Devils and Demons by Ernest and Johanna Lehner,
   1971 (4, 51, 63, 120, 122, 146, 186)
   A Short History of Anatomy and Physiology by Charles Singer, 1957 (60)

Harper and Row, Publishers, New York
   Illustrations on pages 11, 14, 26, 126, 172, and 174 from *Devils, Drugs
   and Doctors* by Howard V. Haggard, M.D. Copyright 1929 by Harper
   & Row, Publishers, Inc. Reprinted by permission of Harper & Row,
   Publishers, Inc.

The Henry E. Huntington Library and Art Gallery
   Rowlandson's Drawings for the English Dance of Death by Ronald R. Wark,
   San Marino, California, 1966 (40, 220, 264)

Little Brown and Company, Boston
   A Syllabus of Medical History by Fred B. Rogers, 1962 (1)

The Metropolitan Museum of Art
   An Allegory of Sickness by Giorgio Ghisi (54)

The Philadelphia Museum of Art and Dover Publications
   Medicine and the Artist by Charles Zigrosser, 1970 (12, 30, 52, 59, 125,
   254)

Routledge and Kegan Paul, New York
Clean and Decent by Lawrence Wright, 1960 (246, 249)

The Trustees of the British Museum
Anatomist Overtaken by the Watch by Rowlandson (23)
Salus Populi Suprema Lex by Cruikshank (256)

The Wellcome Trustees, London
A Lithotomy (75)

The Yale University Medical Library, New Haven
Gravida (212)

Every effort was made to trace copyright owners. Omissions brought to the attention of the publishers will be corrected in future editions.

The state of the art, the horde of quacks and charlatans who roamed Europe and claimed the title of doctor, the doctor's fee—all tarnished the doctor's image. Listen to troubled Margaret Paston, writing to her husband in 1464: *"Also for Goddys sake be war what medeysyns ye tak of any fysissyons of London. I schal never trust hem because of your fadir and muy onkle, whoys sowls God assoyle."*

A fashionable doctor. By Mary Darley, 1773.

THE DOCTOR'S IMAGE

AS SOME PRACTITIONERS SAW THEMSELVES

A PHYSICIAN WITHOUT ILLUSIONS (c. 1700)

SIR Samuel Garth, a prominent physician in his day, once dallied so long over his wine at his club that a friend was moved to remind him of his duty to his patients. He replied that "it was no matter whether he saw them that night or next morning, for nine had such bad constitutions that no physician could save them, and the other six had such good ones that all the physicians in the world could not kill them."

AN EMPIRIC—UNLICENSED BUT WILLING

FROM an advertisement in a London newspaper: "A likely sober Person . . . has a mind to serve a Gentleman as a Valet de Chambre or Butler; he is known to shave well and can make Wigs; he well understands the Practice of Surgery which may be of great use to a Family in the country or elsewhere; he is a Sportsman, he understands Shooting, Hunting and Fishing . . ."

A QUACK—WITH LICENSE TO KILL

"THOMAS Johnson of Brunswick, who is well known for his Abilities in the Cure of the Flux, gives notice that he also cures the following Disorders, *viz.*, the Spleen, Cholic, Asthma, and any kind of Fevers, lingering Disorders, bad Coughs, Scurvy, and Kind of running Humours or scorbutic Disorders, Yaws and French Disorder, without Salivation, sore Legs, Dropsy, Scurvy in the Gums, and has great reason to believe he can cure the Consumption if timely applied to."

A PHYSICIAN WITH FAITH IN HIS ART (c. 1550)

JEROME Cardan, the celebrated Milanese physician, had profound confidence in himself and a strong belief in the ability of medicine to effect cures. In his autobiography he says, "What of the fact that I was not wont to lose a single fever patient, and of those sick of other ills, scarcely one in three hundred?" Elsewhere he says, "Altogether I restored to health more than one hundred men given up as hopeless, at Milan, Bologna and Rome."

AS OTHERS SAW THEM

THE MAN IN THE STREET

FOUR contending physicians attended Cardinal Mazarin, stricken with what proved to be a fatal illness. Brayer located the trouble in the cardinal's spleen, Guénaut in the liver. Valot insisted there was water in the chest cavity, and Des Forgerais an abscess in the mesentery. One day when Guénaut's carriage was held up in a jumble of vehicles, a cart driver shouted, "Let the Doctor go ahead! He's the one who did us the service of getting rid of the Cardinal."

A TITLED LADY AT COURT

LISELOTTE, duchesse d'Orleans, was the mother-in-law of Louis XIV of France. In a letter written in 1705 she says, "My cough is gone, just as I thought it would. I'm not worried about irritating doctors. When I appointed mine, I told him straight out that he was not to expect blind obedience from me. While I should permit him to state his opinion, he was not to be offended if I took no notice of it. . . . Doctors are scarce able to heal diseases, how on earth could they expect to prevent them. . . . I loathe all medicines, and when I am forced to take any I get no sleep all night long and feel as cross as a cockroach."

A MAN ABOUT TOWN

ACCORDING to Dr. William Ober, James Boswell, the biographer of Samuel Johnson, had nineteen attacks of urethritis, "almost all following sexual exposure, and almost all gonococcal in origin." One such attack brought Boswell to the surgeon Douglas. "I joked with my friend," says Boswell in his journal. "But Douglas talked seriously in the way of business . . . as a friend he is most kind—made me live in his house and suggested every plan of economy. But Douglas as a surgeon will be ready to keep me as long under his hands and as desirous to lay hold of my money as any man. . . . I have not to do with him but his profession."

BEDSIDE MANNERS — STRATEGIES AND PREDICAMENTS

Medicine is a farce performed at the patient's bedside by three players—the doctor, the patient and the disease.

François Rabelais

Dying man surrounded by his attendants.

GUILE AND *ARS MEDICA*

ARCHIMATHEUS OF SALERNO

QUESTION the messenger who summoned you about the nature of his master's illness, advises Archimatheus. Then if examination of the pulse and urine does not enable you to make a diagnosis, "you will at least excite the patient's astonishment and win his confidence because of your accurate understanding of his symptoms."

LLOYD ROBERTS

"ALWAYS take your overcoat off in a patient's home. Even if you are there but a few moments, he will feel you are not in a hurry." Roberts's definition of gynecology: "Anything either curable or lucrative."

GALEN

GALEN tells of a visit arranged by his friend Glaucon to the bedside of an ailing physician. Entering the patient's home, they encountered a servant carrying a basin from the sickroom. A glance and a sniff told Galen that it contained "a thin fetid discharge in which floated excrementitious masses that resembled shreds of flesh—unmistakable evidence of liver disease." Confident of his diagnosis, Galen ticked off the various symptoms the patient must be experiencing, all of which the latter confirmed with astonishment. Says Galen, "Glaucon's confidence in me and the medical art after this episode was unbounded."

BEDSIDE BENEVOLENCE

HENRI DE MONDEVILLE

"**K**EEP up your patient's spirits by music and viols and the two-stringed psaltry, or by a forged letter describing the death of his enemies, or by telling him he had been elected to a bishopric if a churchman. . . ." Mondeville was not as simpleminded as these words would make him appear. "Never dine with a patient who is in your debt," said he, "but get your dinner at an inn, otherwise he will deduct his hospitality from your fee."

CELSUS

FROM Aphorism XX: "An experienced Physician should not, as soon as he enters, go instantly to feel the Patient's pulse; but let him first sit down with a cheerful countenance and ask how he finds himself; and if he finds that he is under Fear or Apprehension, let him endeavor to hearten him by some plausible Discourse, and then he may proceed to feel the Patient's pulse."

ANON (ENGLAND FOURTEENTH CENTURY)

THIS typical recital of do's and don't's stresses neat appearance, clean hands, and well-shaped nails and goes on to offer this sound advice: "If the patient asks how soon a cure may be expected, the doctor should say twice as long as he really thinks . . . for it is better to indicate too long a time than to have the cure drag on. This discourages the patient at a time when faith in the doctor is one of the greatest aids to recovery. . . . It is also useful for the doctor to have a good store of amusing stories to make the patient laugh, both from the Bible and other tragedies. . . ." To avoid distress to the patient, "a doctor should not look too boldly at the lady of the house or her daughters or other fair women, or offer to kiss them, or touch them with his hands. . . . "

THE NO-NONSENSE TACTIC

JOHN RADCLIFFE

RADCLIFFE was personal physician to William III, by whom he was paid 600 guineas per annum. Five years before the king's death, Radcliffe told the royal invalid, "Your juices are all vitiated, your whole mass of blood corrupted and the nutriment for the most part turned to water. But if your majesty will forbear making long visits to the Earl of Bradford [a notable carouser] I will engage to make you live three or four years longer; but beyond that no physician can protract your Majesty's existence." On another occasion, William showed his swollen ankles to Radcliffe. "Doctor, what do you think of these?" "Why, truly," was Radcliffe's answer, "I would not have your Majesty's legs for your three kingdoms!"

A COUNTRY DOCTOR

IN his account of boyhood and youth in French Basque country, P.-J. Hélias records the unorthodox manners of the local doctor, a fine horseman who "would arrive hell-bent for leather and begin by asking the patient, 'Do you sleep well? Do you eat well? Do you shit well?' When the answer to all questions was in the affirmative, M. Neiz would look at the entire household with terrifying eyes and explode, 'Then why in the world are you bothering me?'"

SILAS WEIR MITCHELL

IN England it was called the vapors. Dr. Mitchell, a distinguished Philadelphia neurologist, novelist, and poet, called it hysteria, a female complaint for which he prescribed complete bed rest not to exceed two months. To one young patient who tried to extend her stay under the blankets, Dr. Mitchell gave this ultimatum: "If you are not out of bed in five minutes, I'll get into it with you!" Off came his coat, then his vest, but when he began to remove his trousers, a furious woman sprang out of bed with alacrity.

BEDSIDE FOLLIES

CURE BY LAUGHTER

RADCLIFFE, ordinarily the dourest of men, once staged a pudding-throwing contest in the home of a gentleman ill with a quinsy. When the abscess wouldn't respond to his treatment, he had the lady of the house prepare a hasty pudding. He then had his own servants, already coached in the parts they were to play, set it on a table in full view of the patient. "Come, Jack and Dick," said Radcliffe, "eat as quickly as possible; you have had no breakfast this morning." Both began to ply their spoons, "but on Jack's dipping only once to Dick's twice, a quarrel arose. Spoonfuls of pudding were discharged on both sides, and at last handfuls were pelted at each other." The spectacle induced such a violent fit of laughter in the sick man that the quinsy burst and Radcliffe "soon completed the cure."

DR. RAVENS TRIES HIS LUCK

ACCORDING to a diary of 1628 quoted by E. S. Turner, a certain Dr. Ravens, while in the chamber of "a widow, an alderman's daughter, worth 20,000 pounds, putte his legge into the bedde; she asked who was there; he answered Dr. Ravens; she cried out and company came in." The impetuous doctor was fined 500 pounds and imprisoned.

A NOISE TO WAKE THE DEAD

HORN blowing and electric shock were among the "live tests" introduced in the last decade of the eighteenth century to prevent premature internment. The almost universal fear of being buried alive was fed by the usual hair-raising stories of "actual" cases, a few of them authentic, many of them spurious.

PREDICAMENTS

ROYAL PHYSICIANS AT A NONPLUS

THE staff of royal physicians in attendance on George III was understandably ignorant of the nature of his illness, which we now know to have been porphyria. Royal protocol sometimes made their ministrations even more unlikely of success. Unless first addressed by the king, they could not question him about his symptoms or his state of mind. One woebegone bulletin reads: "His Majesty appears to be very quiet this morning, but not having been addressed, we know nothing more of his Majesty's condition of mind or body than what is obvious in his external appearance."

CROMWELL REFUSES TO TAKE HIS MEDICINE

JESUIT missionaries in 1632 brought from Peru samples of cinchona bark, the source of quinine. Oliver Cromwell, who suffered from malaria a good part of his adult life and who was troubled in his last illness by malarial sweats, refused to take the "Jesuit bark" despite the urgings of his physicians for fear of a Popish plot on his life. By Charles II's time there was a turnabout. Physicians were reluctant to prescribe the bark largely because it had been taken up enthusiastically by the quacks, Sydenham being one of the few physicians of reputation to recommend it. When the king was stricken with a "dangerous ague," his physicians refused to prescribe the remedy. Less hidebound than Cromwell, he ordered them to do so. They did, and he recovered.

AUSCULTATION UNDER DIFFICULTIES

AMERICAN physicians at the turn of the century in country districts were not remarkable for the thoroughness of their physical examinations. Arthur Hertzler, author of *The Horse and Buggy Doctor*, was an exception, but sometimes there were problems. He tells of a large family in which "all the boys were sewn into their clothes in the fall when the cold weather approached. At bedtime blankets were thrown on the floor and the youngsters lay down on them, clothes and all. In the spring the clothes were ripped off and the children saw themselves for the first time in months."

A DIAGNOSTIC DILEMMA

IN 1906, Dr. Edward Hume was called on to visit a Madam Ch'u Changsha of Hunan Province. He found her in an elaborately carved wooden bed hung with heavy curtains. "Gorgeous red embroideries formed a canopy over the curtains. I wondered how in the world I could examine a patient within such an enclosure." Presently the curtains parted. The patient's hand appeared, holding a little ivory figure of a nude reclining woman, marked on the chest and abdomen to show where the pain was located. Madam Ch'u was following the 300-year-old tradition of the diagnostic doll, or "Doctor's Lady." It didn't give Dr. Hume much to go on.

Chinese diagnostic dolls are usually in a standing or recumbent position. In this seated figure, the tiny feet are encased in slippers.

TREATING THE UNSHRIVEN

THE Church's requirement in the Middle Ages that the patient confess before treatment began presented doctors with a dilemma. Would not the obligation, insisted on by the doctor, be interpreted by the patient to mean that his recovery was despaired of? Some doctors, before going to the bedside, would send to ask whether the patient had confessed or at least had promised to do so. Neglecting the clerical injunction could be costly. Ferdinand and Isabella decreed that if a doctor paid two visits to a desperately sick man without persuading him to confess, he was to pay a fine of ten thousand maravedis.

BEDSIDE AT THE HOSPITAL

AN AMERICAN TRAVELER TELLS TWO HORROR STORIES

L. SIMOND, an acute American observer, relates what he saw in a London hospital about the year 1770. "The physician, seated at a table in a large hall, with a register before him, ordered the door to be opened; a crowd of miserable objects . . . pushed in and arranged themselves along the wall." Simond goes on to describe the summary examination of "20 or 30 male spectres," and one particular case of violent palpitation of the heart accompanied by severe shoulder pain. "The unhappy man, thrown back on an armchair—his breast uncovered—pale as death—fixed his fearful eyes on the physicians who palpated and discussed." The patient was already at the door without having heard advice or given remedy when he was called back and cupping prescribed.

Hospital patient in bed with a corpse. A common occurrence in charity hospitals of two or three centuries ago. An etching by Daumier.

ON another occasion, Simond visited a room overflowing with the sick awaiting attention. Accompanied by a group of medical students, a surgeon entered the room carrying a piece of bloody flesh in a dish, apparently the ossified lung of a consumptive who had died the day before. "They handled it, cut it up, and held it between the eye and the light—these almost palpitating remains of a creature who breathed only yesterday. The symptoms of his disorder and the circumstances of his death were freely talked over and described." All this in a roomful of the desperately ill.

TEMPTATION AT THE HÔTEL DIEU

THE Italian priest, Sebastiano Locatelli, traveling from Bologna to Paris in 1664, visited the eight-hundred-year-old Hôtel Dieu, where sick men "lay three or four in a bed, the women too. You can imagine the stench that infects this holy place." Locatelli was shocked to see "some extremely pretty girls" among the nuns attending both men and women. "I presume," says he, "that this holy place, although full of invalids, is not protected against devils; and convalescence, like spring, gives new life to the senses."

Hospital Interior, French School, c. 1500. Reproduced from Medicine and the Artist (Ars Medica) *by permission of the Philadelphia Museum of Art.*

HOW TO PRESCRIBE FOR A CORPSE

ACCORDING to a collection of medical anecdotes told by doctors themselves, a certain Dr. Sutherland while in Paris accompanied a doctor making his rounds at L'Hôpital de la Charité. They rapidly went from bed to bed, pausing only long enough to give an appropriate prescription to the friar who followed behind them. At one bedside the doctor stopped momentarily to repeat his usual questions. "Do you cough? Sweat? Have you used the chamber pot?" Turning to the friar, he said without pausing, "Give him a purge." "But, Sir," replied the friar, "he is dead." "The devil you say! Let us proceed." And off galloped doctor and entourage to the next bedside.

INHUMANITY ON THE WARD

WHENEVER Dr. Mark Akenside entered a hospital ward, he was preceded by patients who cleared his way with brooms so none of ths sick could come too near. On one occasion the finical and irascible Akenside ordered cinchona in boluses for one poor wretch who simply could not swallow the big pills. The sister of the ward was directed to discharge him. Said Akenside, ''He shall not die under my care.'' On the way out, the unfortunate man expired. Akenside was known to discharge frightened patients out of hand if they were slow or indirect in answering his questions.

THE DOCTOR AS A
MAN OF BUSINESS—FEES

IN every age it was the doctor's fee that stained the doctor's image. When William of Harsely was appointed physician to Charles VI of France, Froissart noted that it was decided to "gyve hym that he shulde be content with al, which is the ende that al physisians requyere, to have giftes and rewardes." Was Froissart thinking, too, of his contemporary, John of Arderne, the first great English surgeon and perhaps England's first "fashionable" doctor? Arderne's practice was chiefly among the nobility from whom he expected—and received—exorbitant fees. He is said to have sometimes taken in payment the ransom meant for knights captured during the Crusades. It was even rumored in the Middle Ages that doctors were responsible for spreading pestilences so they could profit therefrom. The libel was still alive in 1849. In that year, with cholera epidemic in England, Cruikshank published his caricature—a doctor eating his fill of "cholera pie."

"Cholera pie." A caricature by Cruikshank indicating a popular belief of the past that physicians became wealthy as a result of epidemic pestilences. Rowlandson drew a similar cartoon showing physicians paying homage to influenza.

THE FASHIONABLE LONDON PHYSICIAN

The office of physician can never be supported but as a lucrative one.

Thomas Percival

THE archetype of the princely practitioner was Sir Astley Cooper, called by his contemporaries "the Wellington of British surgery." Cooper literally caught his biggest fee from a patient who made his fortune in the West Indies. The bedridden nabob, convalescing from a lithotomy performed by Cooper, threw his nightcap at the surgeon. In it was a draft for 1000 guineas. One of the most successful physicians on record, Cooper made 21,000 pounds in a single year, and for many years his income was over 15,000 pounds. His servant was said to pocket 600 pounds yearly just by showing patients in out of turn.

It was an era when the rich and famous were paid handsomely. For vaccinating Empress Catherine of Russia and her son against smallpox, Dr. Thomas Dimsdale received a 10,000 pound fee, 2,000 pounds for expenses, and a life annuity of 500 pounds and was made a baron of the empire. French royalty was equally openhanded. Felix, chief surgeon to Louis XIV, was given a country estate, 300,000 livres, and a patent of nobility

for curing the king's anal fistula. Rewards could be transferable. When Dr. Warren was offered a peerage by Lord North, whom he had successfully treated, he responded, "My Lord, I do not aspire to the honor you have been pleased to tender me, but if you will place my brother on the bench of bishops, I shall consider it an indelible obligation." Warren's brother was accordingly made bishop of Ely.

THE RICH COUNTRY DOCTOR

ERASMUS Darwin, grandfather of Charles, traveled about thirty miles daily, or 10,000 miles a year, while making his rounds. His horse was trained to follow his master's carriage. When roads were more than usually bumpy and rut-ridden, Darwin would leave his bone-shaking coach and complete the journey on horseback. When roads were impassable, he would refresh himself from the hamper of delicacies that always accompanied him. His fees were determined by the length and difficulty of his journey and the prosperity or lack of it of his patient.

THE COUNTRY DOCTOR IN THE COLONIES

The poor are my best patients because God is their paymaster.
Boerhaave

BENJAMIN Waterhouse, first professor of medicine at Harvard Medical School, complains in a letter, "I have no taste for the practice of physic as it is practiced in this country. . . . I know how a London Physician gets his bread, but with us it is widely different: a man like me of weakly frame, addicted to study, is liable to be called out five or six miles on horseback in a severe winter night, and to remain out all night, and to receive in the course of a year a guinea for it! We are obliged to be physician, surgeon, apothecary and tooth-drawer. . . ."

Things did not improve much in time for country doctors. In her autobiographical work, *Images and Shadows*, Iris Irigo tells of a local doctor in Tuscany "attempting to reach a child stricken with diphtheria in the ox cart which had been sent to fetch him. He sat upright in his dark brown suit in a kitchen chair, while the oxen ploughed on in deep mud and the distracted father urged them on."

THE ENGLISH PARISH DOCTOR

AMONG the practitioners outside the metropolis, fees were likely to be small and long in coming. Here is the text of a receipt signed by a doctor practicing in a country parish:

> *Jan^{cy} 12 1781. Rec^d of Mr. Clark overseer of ye poor the sum of five shillings and sixpence for Doctoring pims Leg thirteen years ago and in full payment of all Demands by me.*
> *Stephen Dumleo*

FEES AND THE LITERATI

JOHNSON PAYS WITH AN OPUS

SAMUEL Johnson, a confirmed hypochondriac, gloried in the company of medical men. While attended by Drs. Pott and Cruikshank in London, he would be corresponding with Dr. Mudge in Plymouth. But fees for the impecunious Johnson were no problem. When Dr. Richard Warren, who was to treat him in his last illness, came to see him, Johnson said, "You have come in the eleventh hour, but you shall be paid the same as your fellow laborers. Frank, put into Dr. Warren's coach a copy of *Lives of the Poets* [Johnson's last major work]."

GOLDSMITH LOSES A FEE

FORTUNATELY for literature, Oliver Goldsmith, who studied at Edinburgh and Leiden, had a short and unprofitable medical career. Once, visiting one of his very occasional patients, he found her apothecary at her bedside, and a loud and prolonged squabble ensued concerning the proper course of treatment. The two contestants decided at length to ask the patient, a Mrs. Sidebotham, whose advice she would prefer. She chose the apothecary.

EDWARD GIBBON PAYS AND PAYS

"IN the list of my sufferings from my birth to the age of puberty few physical ills would be omitted," says Gibbon. "From Sir Hans Sloane and Dr. Mead, to Ward and Chevalier Taylor,* every practitioner was called to my aid; the fees of Doctors were swelled by the bills of Apothecaries and Surgeons: there was a time when I swallowed more Physic than food; and my body is still marked with the indelible scars of lancets, issues and caustics."

SLIM PICKINGS FOR ANTON CHEKHOV

EVEN after his first not inconsiderable successes as a writer, Chekhov did not give up the practice of medicine. In 1892 he was asked to help contain an epidemic of cholera in a country district outside Moscow. He found the peasants "crude, unsanitary and mistrustful." He might have added poverty-stricken, and here as elsewhere his treatment in most cases was given without remuneration. He said of himself, "Of all the doctors here I am the most pitiable; my carriage and horses are mangy, I don't know the roads, I can't see anything at night, I have no money, I tire very quickly, and most of all—I can't forget that I ought to be writing."

---

* Ward and Taylor were empirics, both of whom had won the patronage of the king.

HOW TO AVOID A FEE

BE POOR

JOHN Hunter, founder of modern experimental and surgical pathology, adjusted fees to the pocketbooks of his patients. Nobody was turned away, and nonbeneficed clergymen, authors, and artists were not required to pay at all. Working men were always seen first, while persons of rank and fortune were obliged to cool their heels in the waiting room no matter how early they had arrived.

ACT POOR

IN 1840 a London physician speaks of the "encroachments of well-to-do people on the gratuitous relief afforded at London hospitals and dispensaries. "Rich women drive in their carriages to a convenient distance from the hospital whence they walk and shortly present themselves in plain attire to receive advice of the duped and unsuspecting physician." Wives and daughters of the wealthy were known to borrow their servants' clothes and call at the hospital in the character of outpatients. It appears the practice was not confined to women.

When Patients come to I,
I physics, bleeds and sweats 'em;
Then if they choose to die,
What's that to I? I Lettsom.

SO went the contemporary rhyme, but it was scurrilous, for John Coakley Lettsom, a Quaker, offered his services free to the poor—fully half his labors were said to be gratuitous. One visit took him to the hovel of an impoverished widow. After inquiring into the case, he wrote his prescription directed to the overseers of the parish: "A shilling per diem for Mrs. Moreton. Money, not physic will cure her."

QUIZ A FELLOW SUFFERER

ONE of the earliest efforts to determine the value of therapeutic procedures is recorded by Herodotus. It was the custom of the Babylonians to exhibit their sick in a public place so that passersby who had had similar illnesses could impart to the sufferers the nature of their own successful treatment.

MAKE THE PHYSICIAN PAY

JAMES IV, grandfather of Mary, Queen of Scots, was an amateur physician, surgeon, and dentist. In the account books of his lord high treasurer appear the entries that indicate his subjects made the king pay for his hobby: "17s to allow the King to let blood . . . 18s for allowing the King to pull a tooth . . . 13s to a blind woman to have her eye shorn" [an operation for cataract].

PUBLIC RELATIONS AND THE M.D.

A BOOST FROM THE PULPIT

DR. Meade, an able practitioner of the early nineteenth century, was the son of a minister. Whenever he was called out of his father's church to attend the sick (a frequent occurrence), the Rev. Dr. Meade would interrupt his sermon to say, "Dear brethren, let us offer a prayer for the safe recovery of the suffering patient to whom my son has gone to administer relief."

THE CURTAIN FALLS ON A DOCTOR'S PLAYGOING CAREER

DURING the playgoing season, a certain Dr. Kennedy could be found in his box at Covent Garden or Drury Lane several times during the week. Between acts he would have people in his pay enter the theatre and call loudly, "Dr. Kennedy! Dr. Kennedy!" Kennedy would bow, take up his hat and cane, and depart. One night a malicious wit in the gallery suddenly shouted, "Dr. Kennedy! Dr. Kennedy! Call for Dr. Kennedy!" The cry went from throat to throat until the entire theatre was rocking with it. And so ended the theatrical career of Dr. Kennedy.

DR. VAN BUTCHELL'S SIDESHOW

WHEN Dr. Van Butchell's wife died he had her body embalmed. Shortly after, London papers carried an advertisement informing the public that "his dear departed could be seen in his sitting room, where she is preserved in a glass case dressed in a fine gown of linen and lace, any day between 9 and 1 o'clock, Sundays excepted." Poor Mrs. Van Butchell remained on display until her husband married again, at which time the remains were banished to John Hunter's museum.

A QUACK FILLS HIS WAITING ROOM

QUACK doctor "Spot Ward," notorious purveyor of Ward's Drop and Pill, advertised that he "performed many marvelous and sudden cures on persons pronounced incurable in several hospitals." He did in a way—by the simple expedient of hiring "patients" at half a crown a week and instructing them in the symptoms they were to simulate. A better-dressed group, paid a crown each, arrived in coaches and sat in Ward's consulting room as his private patients. Ward paid the coach fare.

WINNING OVER THE CARRIAGE TRADE

SIR Edward Hannes was another early public-relations genius. He would send liveried footmen into the streets with instructions to pop their heads into every coach they encountered. They were to ask urgently whether Dr. Hannes was a passenger!

A FAMOUS PHYSICIAN ADVERTISES HIS COMPETENCE

JEROME Cardan declared publicly in Bologna that he would cure every sick person "who would come into my hands who was not more than seventy years old and not younger than seven." The offer also excluded those whose disability was caused by a wound, a blow, an accident, fright, or poison, as well as those with epilepsy, consumption, schirrus livers, deep ulcers, and large bladder stones. Cardan issued another challenge, of which he says circumspectly, "I was free to take up the hazard or not." It was to the effect that "if anyone fell sick unto death," he would show where the seat of the disease was, and if after the patient's death, it was found that he was in error, Cardan was to be held for one hundred times the moneys taken in stake. It appears the offer brought on a rash of autopsies, but Cardan was never found to be in error.

DOCTORS AND RESURRECTION MEN

IN the last decades of the eighteenth century and the early decades of the nineteenth, dissection gave the medical profession a bad name. No man wanted to rise from the grave at the Resurrection minus an organ or a limb, or to be anatomized when he might still be alive. To the man in the street, all doctors were suspected clients of the corpse snatchers.

John Hunter (1728–1793) is shown in his celebrated museum at the Resurrection besieged by anatomical specimens. Hunter's collection of over 500 dissections is now in the Hunterian Museum of the Royal College of Surgeons.

EIGHTEEN CADAVERS "WASTED"

VESALIUS obtained his cadavers by cutting them down from the gallows tree. Felix Platter in the sixteenth century dug up corpses in the cemetery of St. Denis with his fellow medical students. Two centuries later, when instruction in anatomy was available in most European universities, demand for cadavers exceeded the ability of professors and students to supply them, and the golden age of the body snatcher began. One hardened resurrectionist testifying about his activities said he had sold 305 adults and 44 children to London medical schools, and had shipped another 37 to Edinburgh. The latter were packed in salt after pickling in brine. One horrifying statistic appearing in the testimony concerned "wastage," which accounted for the loss of eighteen cadavers.

WERE DOCTORS ACCESSORIES BEFORE THE FACT?

SIR Astley Cooper, President of the Royal College of Surgeons, in his testimony before a Parliament committee in 1828 stated that "There is no person, let his station in life be what it may, who, if I were disposed to dissect, I could not obtain." Cooper had a huge army of body snatchers at his disposal and paid them well, as much as seventy-two pounds for six cadavers. It is Cooper who is mentioned in Hood's satiric ballad, *Mary's Ghost:*

> The arm that used to take your arm
> Is took to Dr. Vyse;
> And both my legs are gone to walk
> The hospital at Guy's.

> The cock it crows, I must be gone!
> My William, we must part!
> But I'll be yours in death, altho
> Sir Astley has my heart.

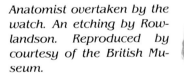

Anatomist overtaken by the watch. An etching by Rowlandson. Reproduced by courtesy of the British Museum.

BODY SNATCHING IN OLD NEW YORK

100 DOLLARS REWARD

Whereas one night last week the grave of a person recently interred in Trinity Churchyard was opened, and the corpse, with part of the clothes carried off. Any person who will discover the offenders, so that they may be convicted and brought to justice, will receive the above reward from the Corporation of Trinity Church.

by order of the Vestry
New York   Feb 21, 1788

THE culprits were not likely to have been anatomy students. Their favorite hunting grounds were Potter's Field and a cemetery for blacks. But the methods of the grave robbers were everywhere the same—dig a hole down to the head of the coffin and then break through enough of the lid to permit hauling the cadaver out. The corpse had to be disrobed and the clothes replaced to avoid the charge of stealing. The richer ones among the students could hire others to do the dirty work. One dodge was to engage a pair of accomplices who would turn up at an almshouse or inn where a death had occurred and claim the body of the dear departed as that of a relative.

THE DOCTORS' RIOT OF 1788

"WE have been in a state of great tumult for a day or two past," wrote an observer of the so-called Doctors' Riot in New York. What had inflamed the minds of the public was the discovery of the "Corpse of a Young gentleman from the West Indies, who was lately taken up—the grave left open, & the funeral clothing scattered about. A very handsome and esteemed young lady of good connections was also recently carried off." It needed only a spark to ignite a blaze that was not quenched for forty-eight hours. It was provided when some citizens noticed a human limb hanging out of a hospital window. A mob gathered, stormed the hospital, and destroyed a great number of anatomical preparations. Two students were cornered and their lives threatened, but by the mayor's intervention they were lodged in jail. The enraged populace would not be put off. They stormed the jail, the militia was called out, and when all was over, five members of the mob were dead and ten were wounded.

A MALEFACTOR ESCAPES DISSECTION

IN the eighteenth century, one of the chief sources of cadavers for dissection was the gibbet. When Dick Turpin, the notorious highwayman, was hanged in 1739 at York, his corpse was interred "in a grave made remarkably deep." Despite other measures taken by the mourners to secure the body from the depredations of grave robbers, it disappeared during the night. The aroused populace found the missing remains in a garden belonging to one of the surgeons of the city. They carried it in triumph through the streets to the burial ground, where they filled the coffin with unslaked lime and buried it in the grave from which it was stolen.

A VERY LITERATE CRIMINAL WRITES A LETTER

A surgeon received this letter from James Brooke, jailed and under sentence of death: "Sir: Being informed that you anatomize men; and being under the present unhappy circumstances, and in a very mean condition, would gladly live as long as I can; but by all appearances I am to be executed next March, having no friends on earth that will speak a word to save my life, nor send me a morsel of bread to keep life and soul together until that fatal day; so if you will vouchsafe to come hither, I will gladly sell you my body (being whole and sound) to be ordered at your discretion; knowing that it will rise again at the general resurrection, as well as from your house as from the grave."

"LIVE TEETH" FOR A GUINEA

JOHN Greenwood, who was to become George Washington's dentist, openly paid one guinea apiece for "live teeth," that is, teeth taken from cadavers. The year 1815 was to prove a banner one for dentists like Greenwood. In that year, Waterloo furnished a bumper crop of teeth stolen from the corpses of the slain.

AFTER THE **BATTLE OF WATERLOO** (1815), LONDON DENISTS WERE PLENTIFULLY SUPPLIED WITH NATURAL TEETH BY **GHOULS**

CORPSE SNATCHER TURNS CORPSE MAKER

HOW "BURKING" BEGAN

Down the close and up the stair,
But and ben wi' Burke and Hare.
Burke's the butcher, Hare's the thief,
Knox's the man who buys the beef.

Children's rhyme, Edinburgh, c. 1830

IN 1827 William Burke and his partner in crime, William Hare, sold sixteen cadavers to Dr. Robert Knox, whose school of anatomy "always had a well-kept table." Their fiendish career began when an old army pensioner expired in Hare's run-down lodging house. His corpse was sold to Dr. Knox for seven pounds, ten shillings. Hare and friend Burke, scenting the unlimited financial possibilities, decided that waiting for normal dissolution was a mug's game. They began luring their victims—prostitutes, the friendless and penniless—to Hare's place, where Hare would restrain them by lying on them while Burke pressed murderous hands against nose and mouth. The last victims of a total of sixteen smothered—a popular prostitute, an old drunken harridan, and an imbecile youngster—were all well known in the neighborhood. Their disappearance was noted, and when the trail led to Burke and Hare, all Edenburgh was aroused. Burke was hanged, but Hare, who turned state's evidence and implicated Burke and Burke's mistress, was freed, much to the outrage of the populace. In response to an incensed public, the burning of dissecting rooms, and the mobbing of anatomists, a lethargic Parliament finally bestirred itself, but failed to pass a bill that would have given recognized schools of anatomy bodies unclaimed by relatives at hospitals and workhouses. The bill died in the Lords because "it would have favored the rich over the poor."

William Burke in Chains. Burke enriched the language with the word "burking," which now signifies "to suppress or hush up."

HOW IT ENDED

THE methods adopted by Williams and Bishop, felonious Londoners both, were more murderously refined than those of Burke and Hare. Instead of strangling the victim, they first put him to sleep with a tumbler of rum laced with laudanum. After stripping him, they would suspend him head downward in a deep well behind a house they owned in a London slum. There he was left to dangle and die, with a rope tied to one ankle. In the meantime, the partners made the rounds of the dissecting rooms until a bargain was struck, usually for the going rate of nine guineas. Their last victim, a young boy, put up a struggle, and the gash on the head he was given proved their undoing. The wound was noted by the lecturer in anatomy with whom they were negotiating. He asked that Williams and Bishop wait while he changed a bank note. He returned with the police. This last atrocity was too much even for Parliament, and the bill providing for a legal supply of cadavers was introduced again and passed. The terrible nightmare of Burking and grave-snatching was finally over.

IN PURSUIT OF GIANTS

CORNELIUS McGrath, who died in 1760, was seven feet, nine inches tall—a prize no self-respecting anatomist was inclined to overlook. Four anatomy students disguised as mourners joined the giant's wake, and having doped the freely flowing whiskey with laudanum, carried off the cadaver under the noses of McGrath's senseless friends.

IRISH GIANT

*To be seen every day this week
in his large elegant room at the cane-shop
next door to the late Cox's Museum, Spring Gardens
Mr. Byrne, the surprising Irish Giant, who is allowed to be the tallest
man in the world; his height is 8 feet two inches, and in full proportion
accordingly; only 21 years of age.
Hours of admittance every day, Sundays excepted, from 11 till 3,
    and from 5 till 8, at half a crown each person.*

THE skeleton of the Irish Giant, Charles Byrne, is now in the Hunterian Museum of the Royal College of Surgeons in London despite Byrne's strict deathbed injunction that his body be sunk at sea in a leaden coffin. He knew he was on Hunter's list. He was shadowed wherever he went, and his pursuers were on the spot when death struck. They bribed the undertaker's watchers, and Hunter had another subject for his dissecting table and another specimen for his museum.

Cotter, another victim of giantism (eight feet four inches), one night terrified a watchman who saw him reach up to a street lamp, remove its cover, and light his pipe. It was his pleasant custom when appearing on stage to reach up and extend his hand to the spectators in the upper boxes.

DOCTORS AT BAY

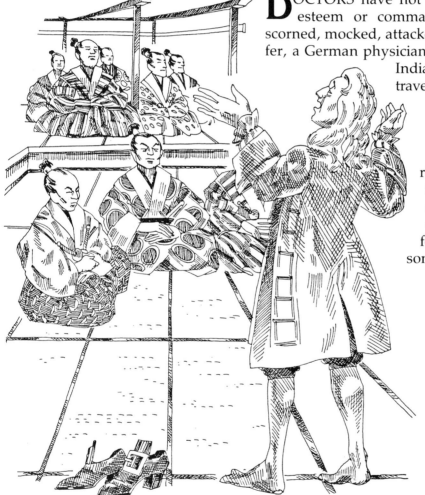

DOCTORS have not always and everywhere enjoyed esteem or commanded respect. They have been scorned, mocked, attacked—even slain. Engelbert Kaempfer, a German physician who served with the Dutch East India Company from 1690 to 1692 and traveled extensively in Japan, was given an audience by the Shogun. Compelled to approach the royal personage on hands and knees, and forced to answer "a thousand ridiculous and impertinent questions," he was then ordered to dance. Despite the humiliating commands of the despot, Kaempfer was undaunted and sang a love song on his own to prove it.

PUNISHMENT BY WHIM

- The doctor as healer was often betrayed by the state of the art. Sometimes he had to pay for his failures with his head. In the year 580, the daughter of King Guntram of Burgundy and Orleans lay dying despite the desperate efforts of her physicians, Nicholas and Donato. She asked her father to have them beheaded. He did.

- Guntram's contemporary, the Frankish King Chilparic of Neustria, had his chief physician beaten, divested of his property, and enslaved because his remedies had proved ineffectual.

- Gabriel Zerbi, professor of anatomy at Bologna in the second half of the fifteenth century, was called to Constantinople to treat a personage of rank at the court. He apparently cured his patient and was richly rewarded. On the eve of his departure, his patient suddenly died. Relatives of the deceased seized Zerbi and his son and executed both.

- While still a newcomer to Capri—she was to administer to the people of the island for forty years—Dr. Elisabeth Moor was called on to assist in the intubation of a child stricken with diphtheria. When her colleague made the incision in the larynx, the little patient suffered a heart attack and died. Pulling a knife, the frantic father went for the doctor. "I held his wrist," says Moor, "with all my strength, hanging on so Dr. Procillo could duck out the door."

PUNISHMENT UNDER THE LAW—MALPRACTICE

Heelmeester. Engraving by Johann Georg Hertel after Cornelius Dusart, 1695.

THOMAS WOMBE VS. THOMAS LECHE (1381)

"THOMAS Wombe of London, taverner, in his own person offered himself against Thomas Leche of London in a plea why, whereas the same Thomas undertook well and sufficiently to heal the left arm of the same Thomas Wombe of a certain infirmity whereof it was held, the aforesaid Thomas Leche so negligently and unduly cared for the healing of the arm aforesaid, through the fault of the same Thomas Leche is incurable, so that the same Thomas Wombe cannot in any way work or make his due profit with his arm aforesaid, and Thomas Leche committed other enormities against the said Thomas to his damage in forty pounds."

WILLIAM GOODNEP VS. WILLIAM CLOWES (1575)

"HERE came one William Goodnep and complained of William Clowes for not curing his wife *de morbus gallico* [the French disease; i.e., syphilis] and it was awarded that the said Clowes should either give the said Goodnep XXs or else cure his said wife, which Clowes agreed to pay the XXs and so they were agreed and each of them made acquittance of the other."

FIVE MALPRACTICE CASES—FOUR GUILTY VERDICTS

ONE scholar has compiled seven major malpractice cases dating back to 1354. Here are the charges and dispositions in five:

Maiming and neglect of jaw wound
Verdict: Guilty

Endangering leg
Verdict: Guilty

Deceit and falsehood in treatment of a woman patient
Verdict: Guilty

Failure to cure and excessive fees
Verdict: Guilty

"Iatrogenic sequelae," maimed hand
Verdict: Not Guilty

PUNISHMENT UNDER THE LAW

In Egypt. In the first century of our era, Egyptian doctors, who were paid by the government, prescribed according to written rules set down by committees of medical men of the highest reputation. If the treatment recommended by them was followed and the patient nevertheless succumbed, the physician was free from blame; but if he should depart from the written instructions and the patient died, he was liable and could face the penalty of death.

In Babylonia. From the Code of Hammurabi: If the doctor has treated a gentleman for a severe wound with a lancet of brinze and has caused the gentleman to die, or has opened an abscess of the eye for a gentleman and has caused the loss of one eye, one shall cut off his hands.

In Rome. According to Roman jurisprudence, a doctor who operated on a slave but did not properly follow up the convalescence was obliged to pay the price of the slave plus the amount lost by his master during the period of illness. Later, the Cornelian laws decreed punishment for neglectful doctors and those whose skills were questionable. Those guilty were deported if they were of noble blood or affluent, but guilty physicians of low degree were put to death.

In England. Jews in the Middle Ages were confined by law largely to the practice of lending money, but a few among them became medical men. Their religion exposed them to the hatred of the mob and the prejudice of the courts. In one case, a Jewish doctor having lost a patient, the Jews of London were collectively fined the not inconsiderable sum of 2,000 pounds because of "a sick man whom they killed."

MEDICAL MEN IN JEOPARDY

RADCLIFFE HOLES UP

FEELING somewhat queasy, Princess Anne sent a royal messenger to fetch her physician, gruff and tough John Radcliffe. Snug and happy over a bottle of wine in his favorite tavern, Radcliffe banged his fist on the table and exclaimed, "Tell her Royal Highness that her distemper is nothing but the vapors!" A second messenger failed to budge him. The next day he was dismissed from his royal post. When the princess—now so obese as to be almost immobile—died soon after, the rumor went round that Radcliffe had refused to treat her, and the public blamed him for her death. In great trepidation, Radcliffe gave up his practice and retired to the country, not daring to leave his residence for fear of the aroused populace.

OSLER KEEPS HIS DISTANCE

WILLIAM Osler, practitioner, teacher, and medical historian, tried to obtain the consent of Alexis St. Martin's family for an autopsy in order to preserve the most celebrated stomach in medical history. The answer he got was a wire, reading, "Don't come for autopsy. Will be killed." Alexis's relatives buried him eight feet deep and are said to have stood guard over his grave.

DR. KNOX'S ARMAMENTARIUM

PUBLIC feeling ran so high against Dr. Robert Knox, receiver of graveyard goods from the notorious resurrectionists, Burke and Hare, that he went about London in a military cloak under which he carried a sword, a pistol, and a dirk.

RHAZES TAKES A LONG CHANCE

THE Amir Mansus, unable to walk because of a rheumatic affliction, was placed in a hot bath on orders of the great Rhazes, his physician. Nearby a fleet horse was tethered. Standing over his patient, Rhazes proceeded to insult and abuse him, even going so far as to threaten him with a knife. When the outraged amir leaped out of his bath and went for him, Rhazes vaulted on his horse and from a safe distance wrote explaining the medical grounds for his conduct. Now much improved because of his activity, the amir responded with a gift of female slaves, a yearly pension, and 200 ass-loads of corn.

ON THE TRAIL OF TYPHOID MARY

TYPHOID Mary (Mary Mallon), an itinerant cook, was officially credited with at least ten outbreaks of typhoid including fifty-one cases, three of which were fatal. Within seven years she was employed in eight households; in seven there was an outbreak of the disease. The doctor investigating the case for the New York Department of Health followed the trail and at last ran down his quarry in a Park Avenue kitchen. When the doctor tried to explain his mission, Mary went for him with a meat cleaver. He returned with the police, and Mary's fatal career was over at last.

DR. MEADE TANGLES WITH THE REDOUBTABLE SARAH CHURCHILL

MEADE was in attendance at the bedside of the duke of Marlborough when her grace, the celebrated Sarah, flew into a violent rage at some remark Meade had dared to make. Meade fled from her down the grand staircase while the duchesss pursued him, threatening to pull off his wig and throw it in his face.

IN RUSSIA, BAD HAND—DIRE FATE

RUSSIAN doctors in the eighteenth century were, for the most part, government employees, and were overworked and poorly paid. Fees were set by czarist law, and doctors were required to attend a patient whenever service was requested—this in a country in which the ratio of physicians to population in 1857 was 1 to 9,000. A harder restriction to live with may have been the regulation permitting prosecution of physicians who failed to write their prescriptions legibly.

CRANKS, ECCENTRICS, AND ORIGINALS

CRANK, eccentric, original—most nonconformists in the medical profession have been a little bit of all three. A few, like Messenger Monsey, were simply *sui generis*. This accomplished doctor, wit, and friend of Swift's, invented a remarkable procedure for extracting teeth, which consisted "in fastening a strong piece of catgut around the affected tooth; the other end was, by means of a strong knot, fastened to a perforated bullet." When the bullet was discharged from a pistol, its propulsive force tore the offending tooth from its roots and gave the sufferer immediate relief.

HUNTER FANCIES A POLYP

JOHN Hunter had a purely clinical interest in his social visitors. Haydn, at the height of his fame in London, was unfortunate enough to be the object of Hunter's attention because of a polyp on his nose. Hunter lured the composer into his surgery with a trumped-up message while two assistants dragged Haydn to an operating chair. Hunter advanced with scalpel at the ready, but his reluctant patient tore himself free and escaped.

BOORDE NEGLECTS TO PUT NETTLES IN HIS CODPIECE

ANDREW Boorde, doctor, roisterer, and sometime priest, published the first medical book in English, the *Breviarie of Health*. He repeatedly warns against "venerious actes," especially in summer and on a full stomach. In 1549 he was charged with "keeping a brothel for his brother bachelors," and the Bishop of Worcester testified that he had found three loose women in Boorde's chambers. Despite his office—he was physician to Henry VIII—he was convicted and died in jail. Boorde's cure for satyriasis: "leape into a great vessel of cold water or put nettles in the codpiece."

BROUSSAIS DEPLETES THE LEECH POPULATION

TO François Broussais (1772–1838) there was only one disease—inflammation of the gastrointestinal canal. All other disorders were merely varieties of gastroenteritis, and the same treatment—diet and bleeding—was therefore suitable for all. Application of leeches was the favored method of bloodletting, and with the Broussais doctrine as popular as it was, demand continually outran supply. According to Stieglitz, the number imported in 1824 (the French supply was soon exhausted) was 2 or 3 million. By 1827, it had increased to 33,000,000. As one opponent of Broussais put it, vampirism had got control of the healing art.

HAHNEMANN ADMINISTERS A MINUSCULE DOSE

SAMUEL Hahnemann held that the doctor should employ "that medication which is able to produce another very similar artificial disease." Cinchona, for example, produces a fever in the healthy and cures it in the sick. Called upon to treat a 10-year-old, he decided that her symptoms were similar to those caused by belladonna—pain in the abdomen, itching, restlessness, headache, pain in the throat, great weakness, and dull and staring eyes. He therefore administered belladonna in a homeopathic dose of 1/432,000 part of a gram. According to Hahnemann she was remarkably improved and shortly after was completely well.

JOHN BROWN TAKES A DOSE OF HIS OWN MEDICINE

BROWN proclaimed that all ailments were produced by one of two circumstances—either too much excitement of the vital force or too little. To treat the former, Brown prescribed opium; to treat the latter, alcohol. So simple and attractive a course of treatment was bound to be popular. Doctors by the hundreds used it, so did Brown—on himself. He died of opium and alcohol abuse.

AN M.D. SMASHES FRYING PANS

BECAUSE of the ease and speed with which it produced cooked food, the frying pan was a popular utensil in England before World War I. Doctors, however, thundered against the deleterious effects of fried foods. Robert Salford, who spent his boyhood in the slums of Salford, tells how "One local doctor whenever he called on our humbler neighbors with stomach trouble would demand the family frying pan, then go outside and smash it against the wall. . . . Doctors were demi-gods in those days, and no housewife dared protest."

HUMPHREY HOWATH, SURGEON, AVOIDS SUPPURATION ON THE FIELD OF HONOR

SAMUEL Rogers, in his *Table Talk*, relates how Howath appeared on the field of honor stark naked when challenged to a duel. His flabbergasted opponent demanded an explanation. "I know," said Howath, "that if any part of the clothing is carried into the body by a gunshot wound, festering ensues; and therefore I have met you thus." His adversary made it clear that dueling with a man in the altogether would be utterly ridiculous, and with that the antagonists retired from the field.

DR. WEINHOLD MAKES A MODEST PROPOSAL

DR. Karl A. Weinhold, professor of medicine and surgery at the University of Holle-Wittenberg, published a pamphlet in 1827 advocating obligatory infibulation of all beggars and indigent unmarried persons, all the chronically ill, all male servants, journeymen and apprentices, and all military personnel of lower rank. Instead of the usual solid ring or padlock device, Weinhold proposed soldering the ends of a wire together by means of a state seal. Tampering with the seal could be detected by periodic inspection.

DR. DUKE SAYS IT LIKE IT IS

DR. O'Connor Duke was a well-known and flamboyant seamen's medico in Buenos Aires when windjammers plied the seas. "Doctor Soda Water" as he was called, would stand on the wharf when ships dropped anchor and shout, "Is there anybody on board to be killed?"

M. DE L'ORME DODGES DRAFTS

M. DE L'ORME, a physician at the court of Louis XIV, was convinced that fish lived to a great age because they were never subject to drafts. Accordingly, he wore six pairs of stockings and four head coverings and slept in a kind of brick oven furnished with hot water bottles. When out of doors, he was carried in a fur-lined sedan chair. Nancy Mitford, in her *Sun King*, reveals some other astonishing eccentricities. He kept a bit of garlic in his mouth and put incense in his ears and a stick of rue in each nostril. He never touched vegetables, raw fruit, jam, or pastry and lived chiefly on sheeps' tongues and the syrup of greengages. At eighty-seven he married a young wife "and wore her out." She died within a year, while de l'Orme lived to be ninety-four.

DR. ROBERTS LAUNDERS HIS FEES

BORN in the 1830s, Roberts served his native Manchester for many years as "a general practitioner with a leaning towards women." In his consulting room "amongst the instruments on the mantelpiece there were walnuts which he cracked at intervals with explosive violence. These served for lunch. Then there was a bowl in which all the filthy lucre he received must be washed before he would put it into his pocket en route to the bank."

A DOCTOR FROM CINCINNATI ADVISES ON WHERE TO HANG THE SHINGLE

FRANCES Trollope, mother of the novelist, toured America in 1827. In her *Domestic Manners of the Americans,* she tells of a Cincinnati physician who gave her his prescription for finding a neighborhood most likely to furnish a lucrative practice. "He would walk through the streets at night, and if he saw the dismal watchlight twinkling from many windows, he could be sure that disease was busy in that neighborhood, and there the location would suit him well."

SMELLIE INVENTS A TEACHING AID

WILLIAM Smellie taught midwifery at his own London residence with the aid of manikins constructed with human bones and leather. Fetuses were "little stuffed babies." Teacher of many a male midwife, Smellie was in bad odor with the females of the profession. A well-known midwife, Mrs. Elizabeth Nihell, called him "a great-horse-god-mother of a he-midwife."

SANTORIO SPENDS A LIFETIME IN HIS WEIGHING CHAIR

SANTORIO Santorio (1561–1636) spent a good part of his life in his celebrated weighing chair. Suspended from a steelyard and furnished with a calibrated scale, the chair was used by Santorio before and after eating, sleeping, and sexual activity. His careful measurement made him a pioneer in the modern science of metabolism.

SHEN NUNG ANTICIPATES BEAUMONT AND ST. MARTIN

THE probably mythical Shen Nung, reputed to be the founder of the Chinese pharmacopoeia, made an incision in his abdominal wall into which he fitted a window. With the aid of a mirror, he was able to follow the action of his remedies at leisure.

"Clysterum donare, postea saignare, ensutta purgare"—so sings the mocking chorus in Moliére's La Malade Imaginaire. *Bleed, purge, clysterize, take the pulse, and cast the urine—these pretty much exhausted the doctor's resources from antiquity to the end of the eighteenth century.*

Death and the Doctor Leaving the Sickroom. *From Thomas Rowlandson's* Drawings for the English Dance of Death.

II

THE DOCTOR AS HEALER

A ROYAL DEATH BED

WHAT KILLED THE KING—AN EMBOLISM OR HIS DOCTORS?

BEFORE the advent of modern medicine, it was the great and powerful who were best able to afford the multiple bleedings, the exotic remedies, and the fearsome surgery of earlier centuries. A doubtful blessing. On his deathbed Louis XIII turned to Bouvard, his chief physician, and exclaimed bitterly, "It is because of you that I am in this state!" Charles II of England had even more reason for resentment. In the thirty-seventh year of his reign, while being shaved, he suddenly cried out and fell to the floor in convulsions. His treatment by no fewer than a dozen desperate doctors is notorious

and serves to throw a grim light on the medical practice of the time. In his memoirs Dr. Scarburgh, one of those attending the royal patient, gives a dismaying account of the particulars, which are enumerated here:

1. Bled
2. Shoulder cut into and incised area cupped for an additional eight ounces of blood
3. Emetic and purgative given
4. Second purgative given
5. An enema containing antimony administered
6. Enema repeated in two hours, together with purgative
7. Patient's head is shaved and a blister is raised on his scalp
8. A sneezing powder is given "to strengthen his brain"
9. Cathartics repeated at frequent intervals
10. A soothing drench of barley water, licorice, and sweet almonds given in between times
11. A plaster of Burgundy pitch and pigeon dung is applied to the patient's feet
12. Bleeding and purging continued
13. The king's condition worsens. Forty drops of human skull is given
14. Bezoar stone given
15. Raleigh's antidote given (a prescription containing an enormous number of herbs and animal extracts)
16. Grand finale (or coup de grâce?): another dose of Raleigh's antidote mixed with pearl julep and ammonia

THE BLOODY REIGN OF VENESECTION

THE seventeenth century was drenched in blood, blood drawn from the veins of high and low, young and old, the sick and the sound. Employed by the Jews in Biblical times and by Hippocrates, venesection was sanctioned by 2,000 years of history. In feudal times some abbeys had special "houses of bloodletting," where monks were bled for their health's sake "to the strains of psalmody." But bleeding, once practiced in moderation, often as an annual rite, became in time a universal medical sine qua non, to be prescribed repeatedly and intensively for every ill.

Bleeding and scarification in sixteenth-century Germany.

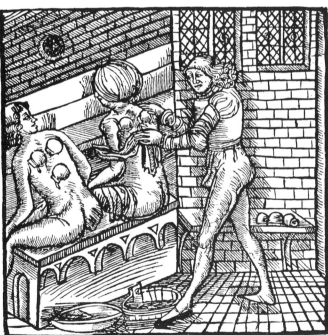

A BLEEDING ENTHUSIAST CURES A TOOTHACHE

"**O**BONNE, O saincte, O divine saignée!" cried Guy Patin and meant it. "I had a bad toothache yesterday," he says, "which obliged me to have myself bled from the same side [as the pain]. The pain stopped all at once, as by a kind of enchantment, and I slept all night. I had the other arm bled and was cured right away. I am, thank God, free of pain." Patin, Dean of the Faculty of Medicine at Paris, bled his aged mother four times for pleurisy, his father-in-law eight times for inflammation of the lungs and delirium, himself seven times for a cold. But his chef d'oeuvre was the bleeding of an infant three days old for "erysipelas of the throat."

BLOODLETTING BY SCARIFICATION

In Tudor England. Scarification—drawing off blood by making superficial punctures in the skin—was facilitated by cupping. The social historian Alston quotes a London man-about-town who visits a bagnio and has himself cupped. "The operator began to Scarifie my Skin as a Cook does a Loin of Pork to be Roasted; but with such Ease and Dexterity that I could have suffered him to have me Pink'd all over as full of Eyelet holes as the Taylor did the Showmaker's Cloak . . . when he had drawn away as much Blood as he thought Necessary for the removal of my pain, he covered the Places he had Carbonaded with a new Skin provided for that purpose and healed the Scarifications he had made in an Instant."

Among the Amerindians. Venesection, scarification, and cupping were practiced in the Americas in pre-Columbian times, and are not unknown even today among some tribes. Among the Cherokees of North Carolina, scarification with as many as 300 long scratches on the skin of arms, thighs, chest, and back was customary before participation in ball games. The coagulated blood was scratched off repeatedly so the blood could flow unimpeded. Loss of the "bad blood" was thought to strengthen the body part from which it flowed. Scarification wounds were made with rattlesnake rattles or with combs fashioned from turkey bones. In cupping, a small skin area was scarified and oral suction used to draw the blood through a cup of bison or cow's horn.

BLOODLETTING WITH LEECHES

WHEN in doubt, doctors in Victorian England prescribed leeches. They were kept in jars, and doctors carried them about the countryside when visiting the sick in their phaetons. Many a poor cottager welcomed the opportunity to wade into ditches of stagnant water with his legs exposed. A morning's catch could mean the difference between subsistence and penury. Because of the great demand for leeches, they were costing Nottingham Hospital fifty pounds per annum.

BLEEDING PHILADELPHIA

WHEN a yellow-fever epidemic held Philadelphia in its grip in 1793, it was Benjamin Rush, signer of the Declaration of Independence and the first American doctor to achieve an international reputation, who sounded the battle cry, "Bleed and purge! Bleed and purge!" At his home, between the eighth and fifteenth of September, he bled 100 to 120 patients daily, and nonetheless had to turn away 50 or 60. His house was "saturated with infection." When there were not enough bowls for his helpers, patients would be bled in Rush's front yard on Walnut Street. "Blood flowed freely on the ground, dried and putrefied there, stank hideously and drew flies and mosquitoes." Rush thought the blood supply was equal to at least five pounds— twice the actual weight. Perhaps that is why his colleagues took such heroic measures when they themselves fell ill. Dr. Physick was bled twenty-two times, Dr. James Mease lost 162 ounces, and Dr. Griffits had seven bleedings in five days.

A ROYAL PASSION FOR PHLEBOTOMY

GEORGE IV, who suffered from a multiplicity of ills from the age of twenty, seems to have a weakness for venesection. It is said that he was bled over one hundred times before he reached his thirtieth year.

BLEEDING EN BLOC

THE brothers Taylor, physicians practicing in Yorkshire, bled the indigent free of charge every Sunday morning. Seated on benches in the surgery, the patients bared their arms while the brothers passed along; one, "deftly applied a tourniquet above the elbow to control the flow of blood while the other opened the vein. The crimson stream was directed into a wooden trough that ran around the room in which the operation was performed."

BLOODY FIRST AID

ENTERPRISING surgeons were on hand in large numbers when the last state lottery was held in London in 1826. Lancets at the ready, they were prepared to bleed anybody so shocked, overwhelmed, or paralyzed by good fortune as to need a quick pick-me-up.

THE BLOOD STOPS FLOWING

THE bloody reign of venesection was to continue well into the nineteenth century. Maxime du Camp, a journalist friend of Flaubert's, tells us that doctors were never without a lancet. "At college we were bled for a headache; once in a case of typhoid fever, I was bled three times in a week and had 60 leeches applied to me. It was a miracle I survived. . . ." Louis (1787–1872), founder of medical statistics, helped mightily to dam the river of blood with his study of pneumonia cases treated with and without bleeding. The difference was nil.

WHEN TO BLEED

Must the earth of necessity be sad because some ill-natured starr is sullen?
Fuller

ASTROLOGY is as old as the Chaldeans. The Romans practiced it. For the influential Regimen Sanitatis, astrological conjunctions for prescribing for human ills were all-important. For Andrew Boorde, a more or less typical physician of the sixteenth century, the authority of the heavenly bodies was absolute. In his *Breviarie of Health* he says, "Also every chirurgeon ought to know the complexion of his pacient . . . and that they may be circumspect in incisions and scarifications and flebotomy, and sure in anathomy, and in no wise to let blud in any particular place, ther wher the signe hath any dominion."

By the seventeenth century, astrological medicine was on the wane, although still very popular, as shown by the many almanacs and calendars of the time. One such manual, *The British Merlin* (1677), says of January, perhaps with tongue in cheek, "In this month let not Blood nor use Physick unless necessity urge thee. . . ." And again, in August, "Beware of Physick and bloodletting in the dog-days, if the air is hot, otherwise, if necessity require, you may safely make use thereof. . . ." On the Restoration stage, allusions to astrology are almost always facetious. In Act V of Marston's *The Malcontent* an old pander is made to say, ". . . court any woman in the right signe and you shall not misse, but you must take her in the right vein then; as when the signe is in Pisces, a fishmonger's wife is very sociable; in Cancer, a precisian's [Puritan's] wife is very flexible; in Capricorne, a merchant's wife hardly holds out; in Libra, a lawyer's wife is very tractable . . . only in Scorpio 'tis very dangerous meddling. . . ."

Harvey's great discovery cut the ground from under the astrological determination of optimal bleeding times. Said Sir Thomas Browne: "All which with many respective niceties, in order unto parts, sides and veins, are now become of less consideration by the new and noble doctrine of the circulation of the blood."

*Zodiac man with favored venesection points,
c. 1480, Munich.*

THE PREVALENCE OF PURGING

English doctors are like bishops that have the
power of binding and loosing, but no more.
Francis Bacon

YOUNG Edmund Verney's bodily aches and pains are preserved in
the family memoirs. Ruefully he writes to his father in 1657, "Truly
I might compare my afflictions to Job's. I have taken purges, vomits,
pills and potions. I have been blooded and I doe not know what I have
had, I have had so many things." Purging and bleeding had been
mainstays of treatment long before poor Verney's time and were to
bedevil patients for two centuries more. Many purged themselves for
minor ills and often, for prophylactic reasons, would go off into the
country or shut themselves up at home for "a course of physic."

A sixteenth-century Italian majolica jar. A
drawing by Emily Holt from a reproduction,
courtesy Cottura, Los Angeles. (Malva is the
mallow plant, used here as a demulcent.)

CLYSTERS FOR THE COMPLEXION

THE palm for enema taking must go to Louis XIII of France, who was subjected to dozens of purges and clysters in the space of six months. Enema fever infected the French court of his successor, where the use of the clyster was reputed to impart fresh and healthy complexions.

PURGING SUGARPLUMS FOR THE LITTLE ONES

FROM the *Flying Post* of January 1705: ''Purging sugar plums for children . . . nothing differing in taste, colour, etc. from sugar plums at the confectioners, having been experienced by thousands to sweeten and purify the blood to admiration, kill worms, cure the green-sickness in maids, pale looks in children, rickets, stomach pains, King's Evil, scurvies, rheumatisms, dropsies, scabs, itches, tetters, etc. . . . . Price 1s the box.

Good in all cases where purging is necessary, being the cheapest, safest, and pleasantest purge in the world.

To be had only at the Golden Half-Moon in Buckle Street.''

LOUIS XI IS CLYSTERIZED

WHEN an Italian physician, Angelo Cato, attended the sick Louis XI, he ordered the tightly shut windows to be opened and prescribed an enema. The clyster did so well for His Majesty that he awarded Catho a 60,000-franc pension and became a confirmed enema addict. So convinced was he of the virtues of bowel cleansing that he had enemas administered to his dogs. When ill, they were placed on a small feather bed and treated with a copper syringe.

ALL-PURPOSE PURGING

FOR TRAVELERS

IN the fifteenth century William Wey published a guide for pilgrims going to the Holy Land. Among his recommendations: "comfortatyves, laxatyves, restoratyves."

FOR INVALIDS

GANDOLFI, a traveler in France in 1644, was bled 22 times and given enemas morning and evening at a Paris hospital as long as his fever lasted. "The strength of the invalid is maintained by giving him veal and chicken soup every three hours. He may drink as much lemonade and other refreshing waters as they like (especially liquorice-water if the patient is poor). . . ." Mirabile dictu, Gandolfi recovered.

FOR THE OBSESSIVE-COMPULSIVE

ARTHUR Throckmorton, a hypochondriacal Elizabethan gentleman, left a diary of his day-to-day activities in London. Recorded in detail are his very frequent physicking and the results thereof. "Brought from Oxford an electuary to take before I sweat, 2s; three purging potions, 7s 6d; bottles of small and strong diet drink, 7s for each lot; four purgations, 12s." He dosed himself with the diet drink at four, at supper, and at bedtime. He was very ill "in his stomach" at night, so he took a purging potion which gave him "twelve stools."

FOR THE HAUTE MONDE

LISELOTTE, sister-in-law of Louis XIV, records the following in a letter dated 9 August 1714: "Last Thursday and Friday my doctor gave me a purge which was so effective I had to retire to my close-stool no less than thirty times." Her medicine, she says, is new, "but so à la mode that all Paris is using it now. It is a salt from England called here *du sel d'Epsom*. You dissolve it in water. The first day I was given three large beer glasses full, and the next day two. The taste is not too bad—only bitter."

UROSCOPY—THE URINE TELLS ALL

"**P**ISS-prophets," as they were called by their contemporaries, flourished in medieval times, but visual examination of the urine has a history going back to Babylon, Egypt, and India. For a long time, the study of the pulse, the presence of pain and fever, and physiognomic signs, while still a part of the doctor's practice, all took second place in diagnosis and prognosis to uroscopy, and with sanction of the authorities it might be added. The Jerusalem Code of 1090 provided that any physician who failed to examine the urine of his patient be publicly scourged. In time the urine flask—often cradled in a wicker basket—became the badge of the medical man and the symbol of his profession.

Doctor and Lover. From La Danse Macabre des Hommes, *printed by Guyot Marchant.*

BRING YOUR OWN OR HAVE IT SENT

CHARLATANS had a field day when the practice of sending a urine flask by messenger took hold. In 1580 a Dublin physician advertised his rates in the following fashion: "Looking at eche passientes uryn without visitation of such passient, six pence sterling for every visitation of such passient and view of his water twelve pence sterling."

The London College of Physicians condemned the practice of uroscopy "by messenger," and a sixteenth century statute forbade it. The law was not strictly observed in Shakespeare's time:

Falstaff: Sirrah, you giant, what says the doctor to my water?

Page: He said, sir, the water was a good healthy water; but for the party that owned it, he might have more diseases than he bargained for.

DIAGNOSIS BY TASTE

BEFORE the advent of chemical methods of urinalysis, it was not uncommon for the late-nineteenth-century physician to detect the presence of glycosuria by taste. In an earlier age tasting the urine seems to have been *infra dig.* Groenveldt's *The Grounds of Physick*, published in 1715, poses this question and reply:

Q. Is it not proper that the Patient or a Servant should taste the urine?

A. It is below the dignity of the Physician to do it, but it may be done by the Patient himself, or his Servant, who may give an account of it to the Physician by which he may obtain some light into the Distemper—if he cannot do that he had better enquire nothing about it."

A fifteenth-century miniature. Brussels, Bibliothèque Royale.

GIVING THE DOCTOR THE URINE TEST

JUDGING from the cautionary statements written for doctors by doctors, many patients tested the competence of their physicians by substituting animal or another's urine for their own. Sometimes the dodge was employed out of malice. To guard against deception, water-casters would try astute questioning or employ confederates who pumped patients or their messengers for information. Water-casters were known to furnish their walls with spy holes to be used while their confederates were at work. One famous case in which a hoaxer got his comeuppance concerns Notker, a monk of St. Gall and a doctor of considerable reputation with particular skill in uroscopy. Notker's liege lord, Duke Henry of Bavaria, substituted a pregnant woman's urine for his own and sent it to Notker for analysis. "God is about to produce an unheard of miracle," announced Notker, undoubtedly with a straight face, "for within 30 days our Duke will be suckling a child born of his own belly."

RADCLIFFE ON UROSCOPY

A WOMAN carrying a flask of her husband's urine came to see John Radcliffe. "Taking the vessel, and casting an eye on its contents, he enquired of the woman what trade the patient was of; and, learning he was a bootmaker, 'Very well,' replied the doctor; and having retired a moment to make the requisite substitution, 'Take this home with you; and if your husband will undertake to fit me a pair of boots by its inspection, I will make no question of prescribing for his distemper by a similar examination.'"

Despite the fact that many judicious members of the profession like Radcliffe rejected water-casting out of hand, Dr. Lettsom was able to say as late as 1787 that "No modern imposters have been more successful than water-conjurers, with which this nation still abounds."

THE LAST OF THE "PISS-PROPHETS"

IT was Lettsom who was chiefly responsible for the fall of England's last fashionable uroscopist, Dr. Myersbach, holder of a doubtful degree from Erfurth, Germany. He was making chamber pots of money, as somebody said, until he collided with Lettsom. Lettsom and some colleagues submitted port wine masquerading as a urine sample to Myersbach. His diagnosis: a severe disease of the womb. Cow's urine was proclaimed to be that of a young man too much inclined to venery. Said Lettsom, "Myersbach knows less about urine than a chambermaid, and as little of medicine as most of his patients." Myersbach left town.

THE ANIMAL POULTICE—
PIGEONS, HENS, MULES, AND COWS

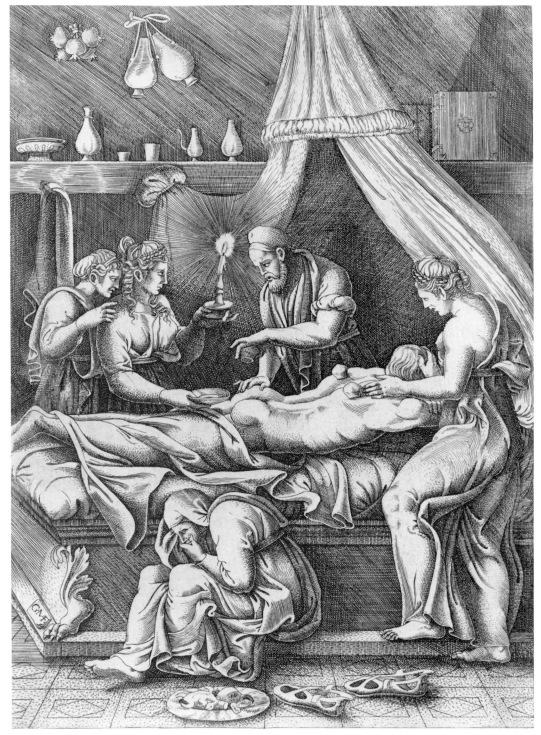

In this engraving by Ghisi, a sick man is being cupped. He has already undergone a favored treatment—application of the entrails of a hen or pigeon to his feet or to a wound. The discarded halves of a fowl can be seen in a dish on the floor in the foreground.

PIGEONS FOR PLAGUE

THERAPY took a new and imaginative direction in 1603, when Dr. Thomas Lodge popularized the concept of disease transfer. He placed live pullets from which the tail feathers had been plucked on plague sores, and as each fowl became infected and died, another was substituted until the last bird escaped contagion, a sure sign that the patient would recover. The treatment caught on, and when the great plague of 1665 raged in London, the customary treatment was to cut pigeons in two and place them on the buboes to draw out the infection.

HENS FOR A HEAD WOUND

JOHANN Dietz (1665–1738), a barber-surgeon in the army, was called on to attend a general who had sustained a head wound falling backward from a height. "In the first place I opened a vein in the right arm and let the blood flow freely. After this I shaved his head and bandaged his wound; and they had to bring me living hens, in which I made a long incision and then tore them clean in two; and these I laid with blood and all on his head, and this I did so often as the hens grew cold. I also gave him several doses of spiritum salis ammoniaci. . . . Finally I made frequent applications of a poultice of cabbage boiled with wine."

An observer writing in 1850 says that application of fowl freshly cut open to cure erysipelas and other diseases was practiced in the Ohio Valley and probably elsewhere "within memory." "I have never heard of but one person bitten in Pennsylvania and New Jersey with the rattlesnake," he says, "and he was kept of it by two chickens slit asunder and apply'd to the place, which drew out the Poyson."

PIGLETS FOR BODY HEAT

AN early treatment for restoring normal temperature to intestines exposed by sword wounds involved slitting a piglet, a fowl, or a cat down the middle and applying it to the break in the abdomen.

A COW FOR A DRUG OVERDOSE

WILLIAM Butler (1535–1618) was called on to attend a parson who had overdosed himself with opium taken to cure wakefulness. Butler had a cow killed and opened, "and the parson to be taken out of his Bed and putt into the Cowes warme belly, which after some time brought him to life, or els he had infallibly dyed."

. . . AND FOR A PROGNOSIS— THE BUSTARD

IN medieval times the stone curlew, or bustard, was thought to have mystic powers of prophecy. When placed on the sickbed, it was closely observed. Prognosis was good if the bird looked at the patient, problematical if the bird looked away from him. Leonardo da Vinci attributed similar prophetic talents to the goldfinch.

A MULE FOR MALARIA

WHEN Cesare Borgia suffered an attack of malaria, his physician tucked him into the skin of a recently disemboweled mule. After a day or two of this all-over poulticing, the great Borgia emerged cured.

A COW FOR SWELLING OF THE HANDS

MADAME de Sevigne, celebrated for her witty letters to her beloved daughter, was affected with a stubborn swelling of the hands. On her doctor's advice, she dipped her hands in freshly passed urine and then plunged them into the warm red throat of a just slaughtered cow.

A SHEEP FOR CHOLERA

JOHN L. Stephens, in his *Incidents of Travel in Yucatan*, describes the character and wanderings of an adventurous doctor named Fasnet. His long residence in South and Central America had familiarized him with the diseases endemic in that part of the world. Called on to attend a sick priest, he diagnosed the illness as cholera "attended with excessive swelling and inflammation of stomach and intestines. To reduce these, Dr. Fasnet had a sheep killed at the door and the patient covered with flesh warm from the animal, which in a very few minutes became tainted and was taken off and a new layer applied; and this was continued until eight sheep had been killed and applied." The inflammation subsided.

THE "PHYSICIAN'S COOKE"

A VADE MECUM FOR APOTHECARIES

WILLIAM Bullen (d. 1576), prominent physician and botanist in the reigns of Edward VI, Mary, and Elizabeth, set forth a number of rules governing the life and conduct of apothecaries. Among them were these:

- That he neither increase nor decrease the physician's bill [prescription], and kepe it for his own discharge

- That he put not in *quid pro quo* [i.e., use one ingredient in place of another] without advysement

- That he do remember his office is only to be ye physician's cooke

BUSY DOCTOR, RICH APOTHECARY

RADCLIFFE was fond of saying that when he was a young practitioner, he possessed twenty remedies for every disease, while at the close of his career he found twenty diseases for which he had not one remedy. Nevertheless, and despite the fact that his favored prescription was fresh air, cleanliness, and wholesome diet, his apothecary, Dandridge, died worth 50,000 pounds.

COFFEEHOUSE RX's

DR. Richard Mead's consulting fee was one guinea and his visiting fee two, but perhaps an even more lucrative source of income was the half guinea he would receive for every prescription he wrote without ever seeing the patient. Like many of his professional colleagues, he would visit one or two favored coffeehouses where he met the apothecaries with whom he habitually consulted. With the apothecary's description of the patient's condition and symptoms as his guide, Mead prepared a prescription in Latin, together with other directions for treatment. Since this was common practice, it was likely the apothecaries saw more patients than did doctors.

KEEPING DOCTORS AND APOTHECARIES HONEST

1224

UNDER Emperor Frederick II a law regulating apothecaries was promulgated, making it a penal offense to substitute one drug for another. The same law forbade physicians to have any pecuniary interest in an apothecary shop, whether directly or indirectly.

The Apothecary. Woodcut by Jost Amman, Frankfurt, 1574. Reproduced from Medicine and the Artist (Ars Medica) *by permission of the Philadelphia Museum of Art.*

1422

IN 1422 representatives of physicians and surgeons petitioned the mayor of London to recognize their newly established guild, the rules of which reflect a sense of serious responsibility. No physician was to take upon himself any "desperate or deadly" cure without first consulting the officers of the guild, and no surgeon was to cut or cauterize without similar notice. Physicians were not to charge fees in excess of ability to pay, and patients too poor to pay could have medical attention by applying to the rector of the guild. A committee of two physicians, two surgeons, and two apothecaries was to search all shops for "false or sophisticated medicines" and to pour all such quack preparations into the gutter.

1540

BY an act of Henry VIII, the College of Physicians was given the right to choose four physicians who would have full authority "to enter into the house or houses of all and every Apothecary . . . to search, view, and see such Apothecary-wares, drugs and stuffs, as the said Apothecaries shall have in their house." After summoning wardens of the apothecaries' guild, the physicians were empowered to destroy all defective and corrupt drugs.

PATIENT CARE THAT WAS

- Pious and ascetic King Louis IX (1214–1270) made a gift of fur capes and felt slippers to the Hôtel Dieu so that patients would not catch cold on their way to the lavatories. He was canonized in 1297.

- Among the courtiers in the English court there was a dignitary who had the job of holding the monarch's head in the event he became seasick when crossing the Channel. We know from Huizinga's *The Waning of the Middle Ages* that a certain John Baker held the office in 1442, and that after his death it was inherited by his two daughters.

- An old inhabitant of the city of Wigdon, England, remembers a more gracious day: "The High Street was cobbled. I remember many and many the time if you lived on the main street and someone in your family was very ill, they used to put bark down on the street so you couldn't hear the horses. Thick bark."

Man is only man on the surface.
Remove his skin, dissect, and
immediately you come to machinery.

W. H. Auden

*Dissection scene from a work printed
by Wynkyn de Worde at London in
1495.*

III

SURGERY BEFORE
ANESTHESIA

THE DOCTOR LEARNS ANATOMY

Despite the threat of excommunication, despite the sanctity of the grave and public condemnation, there was no stopping the dedicated men who performed the first dissections of the human body. Vesalius one night remained outside the city walls, climbed the gallows tree, and cut down the malefactor hanging there. One account says he smuggled the dismembered corpse into the city packed in fruit baskets transported in the carts of peasants. Another dedicated anatomist was Guillaume Rondelet (1509–66) of Montpellier, who, for want of other subjects, dissected, it is said, the body of his own deceased child.

DISSECTION OF A STAND-IN

MONSEIGNEUR du Bouchairge of Meudon was suffering from colic and pain in his side. His physicians appealed to the king for help, saying it was necessary to observe the sites where the disease arose inside the body, "which could not be better accomplished than by opening the body of a living man." The man they wanted was at hand—an archer who had been convicted of various felonies and had been condemned to die on the gallows. Providentially, he had the same symptoms as Bouchairge. The appropriate incision was accordingly made, the necessary observations duly noted, and the archer's entrails replaced. The felonious archer recovered, was granted remission of his crimes, and was given a money reward to boot.

A SEVEN-DAY DISSECTION IN 1505

FROM *A Florentine Diary 1450–1516* by Luca Landucci: "24 January. A young man was hanged; and the doctors and scholars of the University . . . requested the Eight [the governing body of Florence] to allow them to have the body to dissect and it was granted them. And they did this work in some of their rooms at Santa Croce, and it lasted till the first of February, 1505, their meetings taking place twice a day."

DISSECTION BY ROYAL COMMAND

IN the early sixteenth century, Cosimo de'Medici, Grand Duke of Tuscany, had two condemned malefactors delivered to Fallopius, anatomist and professor of surgery, anatomy, and botany at the University of Padua. "Kill them," said the grand Duke, "in any manner you wish and then dissect them."

Septima etas mūdi   CCLXIII
Imago mortis

Dance of Death. This wood-cut illustrates some of the errors of pre-Vesalian anatomy. Inaccuracies are readily evident in the pelvic bones and leg joints.

DIVISION BEFORE DISSECTION

IN 1694 the Edinburgh Town Council granted the ten members of the university's medical faculty the corpses of foundlings, suicides, and homicides for dissection. Each cadaver as it became available was to be divided in ten parts and distributed among the faculty members for their edification.

CHOICE CADAVERS

WHEN the regular study of human anatomy began in most European universities at the outset of the eighteenth century, the corpses of those of the Jewish faith were preferred to others by the anatomists. An anonymous tract of 1829 informs us that "as the Jews bury early, their cemetery produced the best and freshest subjects, equal to the bodies sent to venal undertakers," that is, undertakers who sold corpses in their care to anatomists for dissection.

COUNTING GALEN OUT

UP to the time of Vesalius (1514–1564), it was believed that men had one rib fewer than women because the Lord had used one of Adam's original set in the creation of Eve. Vesalius simply counted the ribs of the male and female cadavers he had dissected and came to an incontrovertible conclusion. By the same method of clinical observation, he corrected dozens of errors in Galenic anatomy in his revolutionary *De humani corporis fabrica.* It is startling to note that nobody had thought of challenging Aristotle's assertion that women have fewer teeth than men until Vesalius did so—by counting them!

SLIGHTLY DELAYED DIAGNOSIS

THE child King Henry I of Castile (c. 1204–1217) died at the age of thirteen after a reign of barely three years. His cranium, preserved for eight centuries, shows a wound directly above the sagittal venous sinus. Apparently, a trepanning operation had failed to correct a local depressed fracture on the median line sustained while the king was playing in the palace garden.

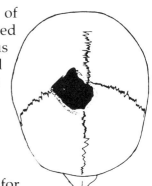

SERVING MEDICAL SCIENCE AND THE PUBLIC WEAL

UNDER British rule no provision was made in the colonies for furnishing cadavers to the medical profession. After the Revolution, Massachusetts passed an act giving surgeons the right to dissect the bodies of slain duelists, "more to inhibit the practice of duelling than to further the art of anatomy."

SURGICAL INGENUITY—LOCALIZATION BEFORE ROENTGEN AND PERCUSSION

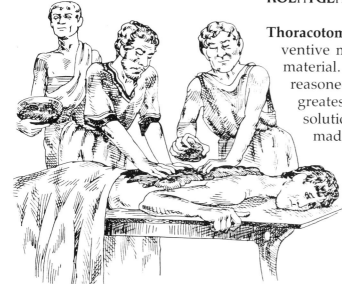

Thoracotomy in Empyema. Early surgeons employed an inventive method for determining the location of pathogenic material. Since empyema is an inflammatory disease, they reasoned, the pus would be located where heat was at its greatest. Mixing fine clay with water, they smeared the solution on the patient's back. The incision was then made where drying first occurred.

Locating an Embedded Bullet. The celebrated surgeon, William Clowes (1544–1604), tells of a soldier who was suffering from the effects of a bullet that had entered near the left hip. At that point a deep sinus or fistula had developed. Clowes filled a long tube he had inserted in the sinus with a solution of alum and silver. In the course of a single day a painful swelling appeared on the right buttock, locating the end point of the sinus and the exact location of the bullet, which Clowes then easily removed.

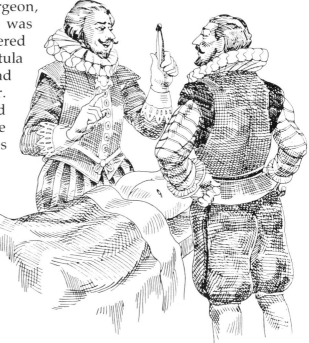

SURGICAL INGENUITY—SUTURING WITH ANTS

As practiced in East Africa and Brazil, the suturing of wounds involved drawing the edges of the break close together. Leaf cutter ants are then allowed to unite the edges by biting through them with their powerful jaws. Once the stitch is made, the ant's body is cut off.

SURGICAL MISSTEPS— THE PERSISTENCE OF ERROR

Fifty years after Harvey's discovery of the circulation of the blood, the medical faculty of Paris petitioned the king to prohibit its propagation as a doctrine contrary to the authority of Aristotle. In America, Harvey's discovery, first expounded in 1616, was still in question at Harvard in 1699. Here are three examples of the persistence of error in surgical practice.

FORGETTING ARDERNE

JOHN Arderne successfully cured fistula in ano and invented the procedure that is now universally followed. Norbury in the *Annals of the Royal College of Surgeons* says that Arderne's "principles and practices" had been forgotten fifty years after the surgeon's death in 1380. He quotes Hume, who asserts in his *History of England* that Henry V (d. 1422) suffered from an anal fistula "which surgeons at that time had not the skill to cure."

FORGETTING PARÉ

THE *Diary of a Surgeon in the Years 1751–52* contains the description of a leg amputation in a London hospital: ". . . there was considerable trouble from the mass of muscle to find the great arteries, which the surgeon wished to ligate with cords, though I learn in such institutions it is quite common to cauterize them only, with a hot iron or boiling tar."

FORGETTING LISTER

JOSEPH Lister, founder of modern antiseptic surgery, proved the effectiveness of aseptic precautions in 1865, but his teaching in some quarters took time to take hold. Consider Dr. Alexander Mott about to operate at Bellevue Hospital: "Spruce in his Prince Albert coat, with his white cuffs showing," the surgeon places his scalpel in his mouth, along with several strands of waxed silk. The operation is about to begin.

THE SURGEON AT WAR

Baldwin, who joined the First Crusade, sustained a deep penetrating wound in battle. The attending leech asked the stricken knight to have one of the Saracen prisoners* wounded in the same place and fashion and afterwards slain so that he might examine the wound at his leisure. This the good prince refused to do and suggested a bear for the experiment. Baldwin survived to become King of Jerusalem.

A similar empirical approach was adopted by the surgeons treating Henry II of France, who had been wounded in the eye by a lance splinter passing through his visor. To help determine the nature of the injury, they had four criminals beheaded and then thrust broken truncheons into the eyes of the corpses at the appropriate angle of penetration.

* "... for it would have been wicked to ask it of a Christian."

"I CUT AND SLASHED FOR 36 HOURS"

BEFORE retreating from Yorktown, the British blew up their magazine, leaving the Continental Army with over 300 wounded and 60 dead. A doctor describes the nightmarish scene in his journal: "The surgeons waded in blood, cutting off arms and legs and trepanning heads, while the poor sufferers cry, 'O, my God! Doctor, relieve me from this misery! I cannot live!' Imagine the shocking scene, where fellow beings lie smashed and mangled, legs and arms broken and sundered, heads and bodies bruised and mutilated to disfigurement! I cut and slashed for 36 hours without food or sleep."

AN ARROW AND A SURGEON DO IN A KING

AT the siege of Limousin in 1199, King Richard was struck in the upper arm by a crossbow arrow. The surgeon "taking in hand to pluck out the quarrel [arrow], drew forth only the shaft at first and left the iron still within." He so mangled the arm with incisions and "butcherly handling" that the King in anguish died "the eleventh day after."

ASEPSIS IN THE CIVIL WAR

UNDER battle conditions, aseptic procedures went by the board. Wrote one doctor, "We operated in old blood-stained and often pus-stained coats . . . with undisinfected hands . . . We used undisinfected instruments and marine sponges which had been used in prior pus cases and only washed in tap water." Surgeons probed chest and abdominal wounds with their fingers, so it is not surprising to learn that among Union soldiers the average mortality in cases of abdominal wounds was eighty-seven percent.

"SPIT, MAN, SPIT!"

TWO centuries ago, when a soldier sustained a gunshot wound in the chest, the doctor would say, "Spit, man, spit!" If the sputum came up tinged with blood, he simply plugged the bullet hole and left the wretched soldier to his fate.

HE DIDN'T MAKE A MOVE

THERE is a painting by Kuniyoshi (1892–1953) depicting the legendary physician Hua T'o (b. A.D. 190). He is operating on General Kuan Kong, who, though wounded in the arm by a poisoned arrow, nevertheless played chess until Hua T'o arrived and continued to play without flinching while the surgeon pulled out the arrow, scraped and cleaned the wound, and sewed up the incision.

CAUTERY FOR A CONQUISTADOR

RENAISSANCE surgery prescribed cautery for all penetrating wounds with either scalding oil or searing iron. Wounded soldiers of the time had no recourse but to suffer the procedure as best they could. It took an uncommonly brave man to prescribe it for himself. Bartolomeo de las Casas, in his *History of the Indies,* tells how Alonso de Ojeda, wounded by an arrow, ordered the torn muscle to be cauterized with white-hot irons. When the doctor attending him hesitated, Ojeda threatened to have him hanged. The reluctant doctor having done his work, Ojeda wrapped himself in bedsheets soaked in vinegar and lay down to await the fever, inflammation, and swelling that would inevitably follow.

AN AMPUTATION EVERY EIGHT MINUTES

LARREY, Napoleon's friend and favorite physician, performed 200 amputations in twenty-four hours at Borodino alone. At the Berezina during the disastrous retreat from Russia, he performed 300 more. Larrey was revered by the men in the ranks. At the almost impassable Berezina River they passed him to safety over their heads from man to man.

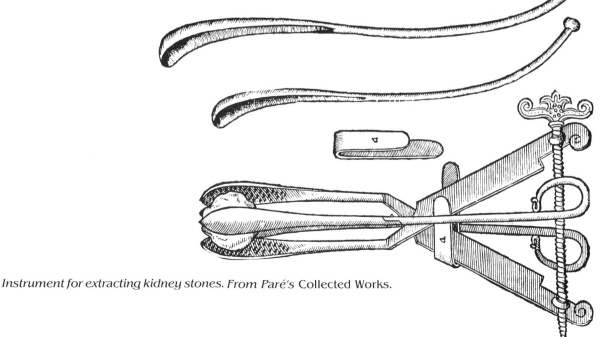

Instrument for extracting kidney stones. From Paré's Collected Works.

PROSTHESES—MARTIAL AND OTHERWISE

AN INCREDIBLE FEAT FROM THE PAGES OF HERODOTUS

HEGESISTRATOS was imprisoned by the Spartans and condemned to die. Chained by his foot in his death cell, he cut off the limb and fled thirty miles to the city of Tigea. There, after the wound healed, he provided himself with a wooden leg and medical history with one of its earliest references to prosthesis.

IRON HANDS FOR A GENERAL AND A FREEBOOTER

PLINY the Younger mentions General Marcus Sergius, who suffered the loss of his right hand during the Second Punic War (218–201 B.C.). He had an iron hand made, which he employed with great dexterity in battle.

Götz von Berlichingen (1481–1562), one of the last of the freebooting knights of the Middle Ages, had his arm shattered and his hand cut off at age seventeen by a sword stroke. Fitted with an iron hand, he waged wars, fought feuds and engaged in quarrels for nearly sixty years.

TWO HANDS FOR A PADUAN

AN article on artificial limbs in the *American Journal of Surgery* of January 1929, cites the case of a patient observed by John Minador, surgeon at Padua. He had lost both hands, but by means of an iron apparatus he could take off his hat, open and shut a purse, and sign his name.

CUTTING FOR THE STONE

There are three sorts of diseases to escape any of which a man has good title to destroy himself; the worst of these is stone in the bladder when the urine is suppressed.

Pliny

"I am in conflict with the worst, the most sudden, the most painful, the most mortal and the most irremediable of all diseases," wrote Montaigne of his bladder stones. His torture was so acute and renal colic so frequent that at one point he even considered suicide. He never seems to have considered lithotomy, and not solely, we may believe, because of his well-known doubts about the competence of the medical profession. Cutting for the stone before the advent of anesthesia was a truly formidable operation. Like Montaigne, some men chose to tolerate the maddening pain, some entrusted themselves to the knives of the surgeons, and a very few, grown desperate and unwilling to seek the dubious treatment of the professionals,* operated on themselves.

The physician has just performed a lithotomy and is holding the bladder stone in his hand. From Hortus Sanitus, *Mainz, 1485.*

* Said Thomas Hollyer, who cut Samuel Pepys for the stone, "I cut 30 of ye stone in one year and all lived, and afterwards cut four and they all died."

SELF-TREATMENT FOR BLADDER STONE

FOUR CASES

- The earliest reference to self-treatment for stone in the bladder concerns a Cistercian monk of Citeaux who guided a catheter into his urethra until it met the stone. He then pushed a thin chisel through the tube, and by careful blows against the stone, succeeded in the course of a year in breaking up the concretion.

- In torment because of the intolerable pain caused by his bladder stone, a Dutchman named Jan de Doot one day in 1651 sent his wife to market so he could make a desperate effort to operate on himself. He cut into the bladder through the perineum, enlarged the wound with his fingers, and dug out the stone. He survived. This almost incredible episode is described in *Observationes Medicae* by Nicolaas Tulp, the Dutch anatomist immortalized by Rembrandt.

- Thorwald, in the *Century of the Surgeon*, tells of a similar operation undertaken by a cooper's apprentice in 1701. This intrepid soul washed the incision out with beer and "actually got up and looked into his mother's sewing basket for a needle, thinking to sew himself up again." Thorwald cites K. L. Walther's *Thesaurus medico-chirugicarum observationum curiosarum* as his source.

- An article appearing in the *British Medical and Physical Journal* of April 1799 describes the heroic efforts of a Colonel Marin in the employ of the East India Company in Lucknow, India. Attempts to dissolve his bladder stone with various mixtures having failed, Martin had a steel probe made. Ridged at one end, it was no thicker than a straw. After distending his bladder by injection of warm water via the urethra, and using a wall to support himself, Martin would bend forward so that the stone slid to the front above the bladder's neck in position for a stroke of the probe. Months of filing reduced it to fragments, and the pieces were voided naturally.

THE LITHOTOMY THAT FAILED

THOUGH only an empiric who had learned to perform lithotomies during an apprenticeship to a roving Italian surgeon, Frère Jacques had a considerable reputation. His operations were often successful, and often disastrous. They were performed before great crowds of admiring onlookers. Jacques rarely asked for fees, contenting himself with food and lodging and a certificate attesting to the success of his ministrations. In 1703 he was summoned by the Marechal de Lorges. Before submitting to surgery himself, De Lorges had twenty-two patients with bladder stones lodged in his mansion and watched Frère Jacques operate successfully on all. Then it was the Marechal's turn. He went under the knife and expired. Frère Jacques left town.

PARLIAMENT BUYS A SECRET FORMULA

FEAR of surgery offered the vendors of lithotriptics a golden opportunity. Mrs. Joanna Stevens enjoyed an international reputation because of the presumed effectiveness of her famous solvent for the stone. Her bona fides was considerably improved by Cheselden, who performed an autopsy on a man who had taken the Stevens solvent for six months. To his great surprise, "I found a stone which had been considerably eroded and destroyed to the extent of one third. . . . it looked like a carious bone." Impressed, Parliament authorized purchase of the secret formula for 5,000 pounds. It was found to contain calcined eggshells and snails, soap, herbs, and seeds. Sir Robert Walpole used it for four years and claimed a cure, but at his postmortem, three vesical calculi were found. During the course of those four years he imbibed pounds of soap and gallons of lime water.

OVERHEAD LITHOTOMY

JOHANN Herman Francken, a Dutch lithotomist of the early eighteenth century, strapped his patients with kidney stones to a ladder slung overhead when operating *supra pubis*.

AN UNLOOKED-FOR CONSEQUENCE OF LITHURESIS

LORD Edmund Howard to Lady Lisle: "Madame, so it is I have this night taken your medicine, for the which I heartily thank you, for it hath done me much good, and hath caused the stone to break, so that now I void much gravel. But for all that, your said medicine hath done me little honesty, for it hath made me piss in my bed this night, for the which my wife hath sore beaten me, and saying it is children's parts to bepiss their bed . . ."

A LITHOTOMY PROVOKES A TRIAL FOR LIBEL

How brutal an operation for the stone could be can be read in the proceedings of *Cooper vs. Wakely.* Cooper had performed a lithotomy at a London hospital that lasted fifty-eight minutes and had a fatal result. A suit for libel was brought by Cooper against Wakely, the editor of the medical journal *The Lancet,* in whose pages a highly critical appraisal of the operation had appeared. Wakely conducted his own defense at the celebrated trial, which drew to its sessions almost every hospital surgeon and eminent practitioner in London. The testimony quoted here throws a revealing light into the operating rooms of the time (1829). At this point in the trial Wakely is questioning a witness. Lord Tenterden is the presiding judge.

Wakely: Was this the position of the patient?
  (*Wakely used a plaster cast of a lithotomy patient to illustrate his points.*)

Witness: The hands were tied to the feet.

Wakely: And the knees were tied to the neck in this way?

Witness: Yes.

Wakely: And in this position the patient remained for nearly an hour?

Lord Tenterden: No; you are to ask how long he remained in that position.

Wakely: How long did he remain in that position?

Witness: It must have been nearly an hour from the notice I took of the clock in going in and coming out.

Wakely: During that period was a sound repeatedly introduced?

Witness: Yes.

Lord Tenterden: That's an instrument, is it?

Wakely: An instrument, my Lord.
  (*Wakely exhibited the instruments as he proceeded.*)

Wakely: Several of these staves or one of them?

Witness: One—several times; I could not say exactly which one.

Wakely: Were several attempts made to enter the bladder with a knife of this description?

Witness: Yes, certainly.

Lord Tenterden: Several cuts were attempted with a knife?

Witness: Yes.

Lord Tenterden: Into the bladder?

Witness: Yes.

Wakely: Into the bladder my Lord.
Was this instrument pushed through the wound—the cutting gorget?

Attorney for Plaintiff: These are leading questions, but I shall not make objection to them now.

Wakely: I shall put the question any way you please.

Lord Tenterden: The proper form of the question is to ask what was done.

Wakely: Was a cutting gorget introduced?

Witness: Yes

Wakely: Was a blunt gorget introduced?

Witness: Yes.

Wakely: Was the scoop introduced?

Witness: Yes.

Wakely: And were several of these forceps introduced or several pairs?

Witness: I noticed two pair—straight and curved.

Lord Tenterden: You noticed the introduction of two pairs?

Witness: Yes.

Attorney for Plaintiff: You don't mean at the same time, I suppose?

Witness: No.

Wakely: One pair at a time is enough for any patient, Sir John.

Cooper had asked damages of 1,000 pounds. He was awarded a mere 100. Even the jurymen knew he should have done a better job.

A lithotomy operation. An engraving by Lalouette, from François Tolet: Traité de la lithotomie, *1708. Courtesy of the Wellcome Trustees.*

Lalouette del et sculp

A SURGICAL OMNIUM-GATHERUM

The introduction of anesthesia brought its own problems—what was called "chloroform poisoning," for example. When the great gynecologist J. M. Sims operated on a French countess, she apparently expired under the combined effects of shock and anesthesia. One of the French physician observers was heard to comment, "Yes, your operation is successful, but your patient is dead!" What happened then is related by Dr. J. T. Johnson. Stung to the quick, "Sims dropped his knife and sprang upon the operating table, exclaiming, 'No, she shall not die!' He seized her by the feet and swung her, head downward, until the anaemic brain, with the aid of gravity, was supplied with blood." The countess recovered.

An etching by Grandville. The Surgeons are a shark and swordfish, the medical students, rats, ravens, and vultures.

THE CONSEQUENCES OF BREAKING A LEG IN THE FOURTEENTH CENTURY

FROM the Calendar of the Coroner's Rolls (London) 1322: "Robert, son of John de St Botulph, playing with others, several pieces of timber fell on Robert and broke his right leg. He lingered from May 19 to July 20 and died of the broken leg and of no other felony."

LIMB REDUCTION AMONG THE INDIANS

AMONG the Hopi especially there were medicine men who had considerable skill in the treatment of fractures and dislocations. An eighteenth-century observer describes one emergency technique: "If an Indian has dislocated his foot or knee when hunting alone, he creeps to the nearest tree and tying one end of his strap to it, fastens the other to the dislocated limb, and lying on his back, continues to pull it till it is reduced."

FRACTURE REPAIR UNDER DIFFICULTIES

ERNEST Henry Wilson, explorer, was struck by a boulder during a rock avalanche while traversing a gorge in the Chinese interior at the turn of the century. His leg was broken in two places below the knee. While his men improvised splints from the legs of his camera tripod, another mule train approached. There was no room to pass, and it was far too dangerous a place at which to stop. There was nothing for it but to place Wilson across the path and let the train pass over him. Nearly fifty mules stepped over his prostate body and not a hoof touched him, although, as he afterward remarked, "each one looked as big as a plate."

TEACHING ANATOMY FROM THE GROUND UP

SANTIAGO Ramon y Cajal, the Spanish histologist and Nobel Prize winner, with his physician father robbed a neighboring cemetery of skeletal remains—crania, ribs, pelves, and femurs. The bones were needed by the elder Cajal for teaching his son the fine points of anatomy.

USEFUL TO THE END

JEREMY Bentham, the founder of utilitarianism, provided in his will that his body be dissected for the benefit of anatomy students, and that all but his head be reduced to a skeleton. The head was to be fitted with glass eyes, and the skeleton was to be dressed in Bentham's usual apparel and be placed on exhibit at every meeting of the Utilitarian Society. For over a century after his death in 1832, Bentham duly made his appearance before his fellow utilitarians.

LONDON SURGEONS TAKE ON AN ELEPHANT

CHUNEE, a five-ton elephant on exhibition at London's Exeter Change in 1826, became ungovernable, threatened to break out of his cage, and with his mad trumpetings set the whole exhibition of ferocious beasts into an ear-splitting cacophony of roars and screams. Civilians and a detail of soldiers fired 152 balls into his body, and the coup de grâce came when a keeper thrust a harpoon into his vitals. Nine butchers worked for twelve hours to flay the hide of the huge beast. When their work was done, "a dozen or so surgeons, watched by a corps of medical students, dismantled his innards," a procedure that occupied them for the better part of a day. The 10,000 pounds of elephant remains were carted away amid an all-pervasive stench.

REDUCTION IN THE LECTURE HALL

COLIN MacLaurin, distinguished mathematician and professor at Edinburgh University, was likely to dislocate his jaw whenever he yawned. Lecturing before his class, he would sometimes throw his jaw out and stand speechless with his mouth agape till his servant, standing by in an adjoining room, was called in to set his jaw again.

LEARNING PHARYNGOLOGY

VIENNA'S Allgemeine Krankenhaus in the 1880s employed in its throat clinic a one-eyed woman between seventy and eighty years old who was paid to permit students to examine her throat. One of them, J. B. Wheeler, in his memoirs recalls her rare talent. "She knew the anatomy of the throat perfectly and could tell you exactly the locality you touched with your probe and give the correct anatomical name for it—left arytenoid cartilage, epiglottis, posterior pharyngeal pillar, uvula, etc. Years of practice had given her such perfect control of her reflexes that I never saw her gag or wince under the manipulations of the clumsiest bungler. Her throat was her fortune."

POSTSURGICAL FUN AND GAMES

MAJOR General Daniel E. Sickles, U.S. Volunteers, left the battlefield at Gettysburg with his right leg shattered by a twelve-pound cannonball. The amputated limb was sent by Sickles to the medical museum of the Armed Forces Institute of Pathology. Attached to the rough coffin conveying the leg was a card reading, "With the compliments of Major Gen. D. E. D., U.S. Vols." From time to time after the end of hostilities, the general would pay the museum a visit to see his leg on display.

DISSECTION ENCOUNTERS A SNAG IN CHINA

FOR most Chinese bodies of the dead are considered sacred. According to Bertrand Russell, a French surgeon commissioned by the Chinese to teach Western medicine requested that he be furnished with corpses for dissection. He was assured that he could have an unlimited supply of *live* criminals, but his request for cadavers was greeted with horror. His Chinese employers found his protests incomprehensible.

IN THE SPIRIT OF VESALIUS

DR. Samuel Gross (1805–1884) was the greatest American surgeon of his time. In his autobiography he tells how he "created at the foot of my garden . . . a little building as dissecting room and obtained a subject from Pennsylvania, going there myself in a buggy for the purpose. I dissected generally several hours a day as long as the material lasted . . . performing the more important operations unmolested."

A SURGICAL PATIENT BETWEEN TWO FIRES

THE first recorded amputation in Pennsylvania was performed by Griffith Owen under rather peculiar circumstances, for "some Spirits in the Bason happened to take fire, and being spilt on the Surgeon's Apren, set his cloathes on fire; and there being a great crowd of spectators, some of them in the Way and in Danger of being scalded, as the Surgeon himself was upon the Hands and Face. . . ." All ended well. The fire was put out and surgery proceeded.

A KING DISSECTS

PEPYS records in his diary that "a child was dropped by one of the ladies [of the court of Charles II] in dancing; but nobody knew who, it being taken up by somebody in their handkercher." Rumor had it that the king had the stillborn infant brought to his chambers where he dissected it. Charles, like so many of his contemporaries, was caught up in the wave of scientific experiment that swept the Continent in the seventeenth century. He had a chemistry laboratory in his private apartments and an herbal garden on the royal grounds.

"HOLDERS DOWN"

BEFORE anesthesia, surgery was an unimaginable purgatory for the patient, who was either strapped to the operating table or forcibly restrained by brawny attendants. The London Hospital still has in its possession the bell that was rung to summon the holders down to duty.

"GUILLOTINE" AMPUTATION—LISTON

THE greatest boon a surgeon could offer his patient was speed. Robert Liston, fastest surgeon in nineteenth-century England, could amputate a leg in two and one-half minutes. On one sanguinary occasion, he was so intent on breaking his own record for speed that in amputating a leg, he sliced off one of his patient's testicles and two of his assistant's fingers. One of his famous cases involved a scrotal tumor, which he removed in four minutes. The possessor of this phenomenon had to carry it around in a wheelbarrow.

SURGICAL TRIALS—CHESELDEN

EQUALLY dexterous was William Cheselden, who was able to extract a stone from the bladder in less than a minute. He said of himself, "If I have any reputation, I have earned it dearly, for none ever endured more anxiety before an operation than I . . . ." One of the French surgeons who came to England to observe Cheselden's technique laughed at this disability. Cheselden said nothing but arranged for the Frenchman to be his guest at a boxing match and thoroughly enjoyed his discomfiture as the two pugilists battered each other to a pulp. Those were the days of bare fists, when victory belonged to the contender who remained on his feet longest.

HELP FOR THE SQUEAMISH SURGEON TO BE

In the 1840s at the Massachusetts General Hospital a bed was kept in constant readiness just outside the operating room. Students showing any signs of weakness were ushered out by attendants and placed on a bed with their heads lower than their feet.

THE OVARIAN TUMOR THAT WASN'T

NINE years after McDowell's historic ovariotomy in Danville, Kentucky, in 1809, Dr. James Overton set out to perform what he thought would be the first such successful operation in the state of Tennessee. Something of a showman, Overton decided to operate in the open in front of the patient's home and in full view of a large crowd of onlookers. He made his incision, revealing what appeared to be an outsize tumor. He was about to enlarge the incision when the tumor moved. Without further ado, the embarrassed Overton quickly closed the abdomen. Shortly thereafter, the patient gave birth to a healthy infant.

A CASE OF BOTCHED CASTRATION

CASTRATION of captives to be sold into slavery took a heavy toll, but the supply, chiefly from the Sudan and Abyssinia, was plentiful and the demand for eunuchs great. The surgical procedure was bloody and clumsy, and sometimes the job was botched. We learn of a Sudanese chief eunuch to the grand sherif of Mecca who seems to have enjoyed every houri in the harem before he was found out—a blonde Circassian having presented the sherif with a mulatto son. The harem was sewn in sacks and drowned, while the eunuch was dispatched to the sultan for sentencing.

A HERNIOTOMY—OPERATING TIME ONE AND A HALF HOURS

JOHANN Georg Zimmerman, a prominent eighteenth-century physician, describes his operation: "June 24 was the day that decided whether life or death awaited me. . . ." In attendance were two surgeons general of the Prussian Army, and "a number of skilled and also very famous men, one of whom directed the work of the surgeon. The operation lasted 1½ hours during which the knife was continuously in my body. According to the surgeon general, I received 2000 cuts with the knife. For three hours after the operation it was touch and go—will I live?" Zimmerman spent twelve weeks recovering, with his wounds frequently requiring the application of silver nitrate, which caused him the utmost torture.

BEFORE ETHER AND AFTER

BOCCACCIO'S "CERTAIN WATER"

BOCCACCIO in 1V, Novel 10, speaks of a doctor who is to operate for the removal of "a decayed bone" from a patient's leg and who prepares for this procedure "a certain water to be distilled which, being drunk, would throw a person asleep." Was this the famous "soporific sponge" described by Teodorico Borgognoni (1205—1298)? According to Borgognoni, who inherited the formula from his father, the founder of the surgical school of Bolgona, the sponge was soaked in a liquid mixture of opium, henbane, and mandrake and left to dry in the sun. It was applied to the nostrils after steeping in warm water for an hour. Apparently the liquid was taken by mouth as well.

A BIZARRE ANODYNE

BEFORE the introduction of ether and chloroform, favored anodynes in surgery were alcohol, opium, and cocaine. In her *Victory over Pain*, MacQuitty reminds us that nicotine was used for this purpose. Smoke was either blown into the rectum or a cigar was inserted in the anus.

JAMES YOUNG SIMPSON THROWS A CHLOROFORM PARTY

CHLOROFORM had been discovered simultaneously in 1831 in the United States, France, and Germany, but none of the three chemist discoverers knew how to use it. It occurred to Simpson that here was an anodyne without the disadvantages of ether that might be useful in childbirth. To test its properties, he organized a "chloroform party," inviting two assistants and some family members. "As they began to inhale, all sense of fatigue vanished; all became lively and over-talkative; a few seconds later all were dumb and flat on their faces."

MINOR SURGERY ON THE PRAIRIE

AMY Laucks and her husband moved to Laken, Kansas, in 1879. With the nearest doctor some seventy-five miles away, Mrs. Laucks often served as the local surgeon, midwife, and nurse to the surrounding frontier community. On one occasion a man left for dead on the prairie by Indians was brought to her home for whatever succor she could provide. His scalp had not been entirely removed, but was pulled down over the eyes. Mrs. Laucks replaced the scalp, stitched it in place with a fiddle string and common needle, and nursed him back to health.

Pilgrimage of the Epileptics to the Church of Moelenbeek, by Pieter Brueghel.

UNORTHODOX THERAPIES, DESPERATE MALADIES

Extreme remedies are very appropriate for extreme diseases.
—Hippocrates

FOR EVERY ILL A REMEDY

FOR DYSENTERY, WARM BODIES

THOMAS Sydenham, the ablest physician of his time, treated a woman patient "very ill of the cholera morbus" by having her husband lie naked against her back and her son of twelve against her belly. We are told that the convected heat resuscitated the patient. Here in Sydenham's own words is the account of a similar case. Treating a patient for dysentery, Sydenham first had her son, "a plump lad of thirteen, and her nurse's son of six or seven, to go to her bed naked and to lie the one close to her belly, and the other close to her back, which they did, and so long as they continued with her she had no stools; but the boys rising at any time the looseness would immediately return. I commanded that she should persist in her course till her cure should be complete (the boys relieving one another by turns in the daytime) and so she fully recovered."

FOR STRANGULATION, A "WARM WOMAN"

SIR William Petty, a founder of the Royal Society and inventor of a double-keeled vessel, was celebrated as well for his exploit in cutting down a malefactor from the gibbet and reviving her by "putting her to bed with a warm woman," after having her bled and given a draught of spirits. She lived to marry and have children. Both Sydenham and Petty could cite a Scriptural precedent. When King David was "old and stricken in years," his doctors counselled that a young virgin be found "to cherish him and lie in the bosom of the King so that he may get heat." Or as Byron put it in *Don Juan:*

'Tis written in the Hebrew Chronicle
  How the physicians leaving pill and potion,
Prescribed, by way of blister, a young belle,
  When old King David's blood grew dull in motion,
And that the medicine answered very well.

TEMAZCALLI FOR RHEUMATISM, ETC.

IN many Indian villages of Mexico a century and more ago, a kind of sauna called a temazcalli was reckoned a certain cure for fever, bad colds, poisonous bites, and rheumatism. In form like a baker's oven, it was made of unbaked bricks and measured eight feet in width and six in height. After making his way inside, the patient poured water on a pile of stones that had been heated to red-hot intensity. While luxuriating in the steam, he applied wetted herbs and maize to the affected parts.

MUSIC FOR WHAT AILS YOU

FROM ancient Greece to our own day, the therapeutic value of music has everywhere been acknowledged. The Greeks chose specific modes, rhythms, and instruments to produce a particular effect on the listening patient, and developed a rationale to explain music's effectiveness. "Pain is relieved by causing a vibration in the fibers of the affected part," wrote Coelius Antipater. Auslis Gellius (c. A.D. 130–180) held that the music of the flute was a specific for the bite of a viper. It was the viper's bite that presumably caused the tarantism of seventeenth-century Italy. Victims fell into a stupor from which they could only be aroused by music to which they responded by whirling in a frenzied dance. Shakespeare sounds a cynical note: "Others, when the bagpipe sings i' the nose, cannot contain their urine."

FLAGELLANTS AS HEALERS

WHEN the Black Death pandemic of 1348 decimated Europe, it gave new life to the flagellant movement. Bands of 50 to 500 and more, wearing white robes emblazoned with red crosses, roamed across western Europe, lacerating themselves with leather scourges fitted with iron spikes. The flagellants claimed their wounds absolved them from sin and made salvation sure. They believed they were powered to drive out devils, heal the sick, and even raise the dead.

BEN FRANKLIN PRESCRIBES A COLD-AIR BATH

FRANKLIN, always a strong advocate of fresh air, was a devotee of the cold-air bath. He thought it less a shock to the system than cold water. "I rise almost every morning," he wrote, "and sit in my chamber without any clothes whatever, half an hour or an hour according to the season, whether reading or writing. This practice is not in the least painful, but on the contrary, agreeable." People do not catch cold from exposure to cold and damp, he told Dr. Rush, but because of the lack of fresh air, too rich a diet, and too little exercise.

CURE BY LAUGHTER

FROM a book of sketches of seventeenth-century notables comes this bizarre tale. Romaineville, a notorious blasphemer, was lying at death's door. A Franciscan came to hear his confession. A friend of the dying man, the Chevalier Roquelaure, took up a gun and, aiming it at the priest, cried, "Stand back, Father, or I'll kill you! He has lived like a dog; he must die like a dog!" This made Romaineville laugh so heartily, he recovered.

WRESTLING ONE'S WAY TO MENTAL HEALTH

IN her diaries, Etty Hillesum tells of her love affair with Julius Spier, a student of Carl Jung's. He had a clinical practice in Amsterdam consisting largely of women, and it was here that Ms. Hillesum visited him as a patient. His treatment was based on the theory that "body and soul are one," and accordingly would insist that sessions begin with a wrestling match between analyst and patient. At her first session Etty won.

A SCREW LEVER FOR TETANUS

KILVERT in his *Diary* records a visit to "young Meredith who has had his jaw locked for six months, a legacy of mumps. He has been to Hereford Infirmary where they kept him for two months, gave him chloroform and wrenched his jaws open gradually by a screw lever. But they could not do him any good."

A MAGNETIC NOVELIST TRIES HYPNOSIS

CHARLES Dickens was attracted to hypnotism after witnessing an eminent practitioner of the art, Dr. John Elliotson, hypnotize a patient in 1838. During his first American tour, Dickens used hypnosis to arrest his wife's headaches and insomnia. "In six minutes," he wrote, "I magnetized her into hysterics and then into magnetic sleep." Later, Mrs. Dickens had reason to become painfully jealous of Dickens's attentions to a lady friend of the family who suffered terribly from hallucinations and who became highly dependent on Dickens for relief. Serious consequences were avoided when Dickens undertook to teach the lady's husband his hypnotic skills.

MALINGERING BEFORE THE MAST

- Edwin Pulver, third mate of the *Columbus*, relates in his diary for 1851 how his rough-and-ready captain cured two men of "sogering." He gave one "a heavy dose of saults," and another "a blister of Spanish flies mixed with pepper sauce. The two were cured in six hours."

- John Knyveton, surgeon's mate, left a record of his experiences on board the *Famillies*. His captain employed a novel if irrational diagnostic procedure undoubtedly devised to discourage malingerers. If the pain was above the string he tied around a seaman's waist, he would administer an emetic; if below, a purge.

FOR RABIES VICTIMS—EUTHANASIA

CELSUS recommends drawing out the venom of mad-dog bites by cupping and the application of corrosives and cautery. Others offered equally ineffective cures, but in the rational eighteenth century a quick death was seen as the only merciful way to shorten intolerable suffering. Not infrequently, the unfortunate victim was smothered by his friends.

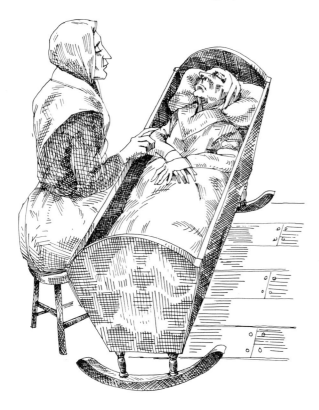

CRADLES FOR THE SICK

ASCLEPIADES of Bithynia practiced medicine in Rome in the second century A.D. He treated some of his patients by placing them in a kind of huge cradle operated by slaves. The early Shakers used similar adult-sized cradles to rock the superannuated ill and senile from this world into the next.

GUARANTEES FOR THE SOUND

DURING the first Babylonian dynasty the owner of a slave had to guarantee that he was the absolute property of the seller and was not suffering from any incurable disease. For epilepsy and leprosy, the guarantee held good for one hundred days.

In A.D. 151 a Greek from Alexandria purchased a girl in an Anatolian slave market and took the girl back to Egypt with him. The bill of sale, written in Greek and Latin, was still legible when discovered at the end of the nineteenth century. It reads, "Sambatis, by nationality a Phrygian, about 12 years of age . . . in good health as required by ordinance, not subject to any legal charge . . . is free from the sacred disease [epilepsy]." The seller guaranteed all this under oath and assumed a penalty of twice the purchase price should his guarantee prove false.

RUBRICITY FOR SMALLPOX

JOHN of Gaddesden, physician to Edward II, recommends in his *Rosa Anglica* that the smallpox sufferer be wrapped in scarlet cloth. "I did this," he says, "when the son of the illustrious King of England suffered from smallpox . . . I took care that all about his bed should be red, and the cure succeeded very well."

HANGING IS GOOD FOR YOU

ALPHONSE DAUDET (1840–1897), the French novelist, confided to his friend Jules Goncourt that he was undergoing a new treatment for ataxia imported from Russia by the celebrated physician Charcot. According to Goncourt, "for one full minute the patient is suspended by the neck and dangles in the air."

MARIA Edgeworth, who in later life became a widely read novelist, was of very short stature. In the establishment for young ladies that she attended, her instructors lifted her off the ground by the head and "swung her by the neck to draw out the muscles."

WHEN "A Gent. with a red ugly, pumpled face" came to see William Butler, the doctor said, "I must hang you. So presently he had a device made ready to hang him from a Beame in the roome, and when he was e'en almost dead, he cutt the veines that fed these pumples and lett out the black ugley Bloud, and cured him." So says Aubrey in his *Brief Lives*.

ERASTUS Root (1789–1829), an obscure New England physician, is noteworthy because his diary contains much information about the medical practices of the period. One case concerns a child with a buckshot wound in the trachea. She was hung by the ankles and pressure put on the trachea without result. The next day she coughed up the shot.

BISHOP Berkeley of Cloyne, the enthusiastic promoter of the cure-all tar water, once went to see a malefactor hanged. His curiosity piqued, he induced his friend Contarini to hang him so he could experience at first hand the sensations associated with gibbeting. When he was cut down, nearly senseless, he exclaimed, "Bless my heart, Contarini, you have ruffled my neckband!"

A sketch by Rowlandson. Courtaude Art Institute, London.

TESTING FOR LIFE ON BOARD

DEATH from ship fever (typhus), dysentery, malnutrition, scurvy, and falls from aloft were not uncommon in the days of sailing ships. On board English vessels, the sailmaker would sew up the corpse in the dead man's hammock. In the merchant service it was customary to put a stitch through the lobe of the left ear in the belief that the ear, being near the heart of the seemingly dead man, the pain of the needle would stimulate cardiac response and cause some kind of reflex action.

HOW TO AVOID DEATH FROM EXPOSURE IN AN OPEN BOAT

IN his account of his 3,618-mile odyssey in an open boat, Captain Bligh records the following sagacious maneuver: "With respect to the preservation of our health during the course of 16 days of heavy and almost continual rain, I would recommend to everyone in a similar situation the method we practiced, which is, to dip their clothes in the salt water, and wring them out as often as they become filled with rain: it was the only resource we had, and I believe it was the greatest service to us, for it felt more like a change of dry clothes than can well be imagined."

HEALING BY TRANSFUSION

IN 1667 Jean Denis of Paris transferred nine ounces of blood from the carotid artery of a lamb to a sixteen-year-old. His second case involved a man of forty-five who was first bled ten ounces and then given twenty ounces from a lamb's crural artery. Following the procedure, the recipient wasted no time in killing and dressing the lamb, after which he went off to a tavern to drink up his fee. In the same year, Samuel Pepys witnessed a similar transfusion from sheep to man. "The subject," says Pepys "finds himself much better since, and as a new man, but he is cracked a little in the head, though he speaks very reasonably and very well."

A LIGHTNING CURE

IN Calderon de la Barca's *Life In Mexico* we read this account of serendipitous electrotherapy. One hot July day a man far gone in consumption was struck down by a thunderbolt. A ball of fire ran through him, emerging at his arm, where an enormous ulcer formed. When it disappeared, "he found himself in perfect health."

MILK FOR AGUE

THE celebrated diarist John Evelyn (1620–1706) had a heroic recipe for attacks of ague. Wrapping himself in blankets, he would sit with his legs soaking up to the knee in milk "as hot as could be borne." All the while he would take repeated drafts of a posset of curdled milk. When his milk bath cooled, Evelyn got into bed and sweated.

GIVE THE PATIENT AIR!

OUR ancestors didn't consider fresh air salubrious for the sick. Colonial physician Lemuel Hopkins, finding the windows of a sickroom tightly closed and curtained, carried his patient out of doors. He stood over her, fending off the pokers and staves of the angry and fearful parents and relatives until the child recovered in the fresh air.

"A CUSTOME LOATHSOME TO THE EYE"

WHEN first introduced into Europe, tobacco got a mixed reception. King James I in his *Counterblast to Tobacco* (1604), summed up for the opposition, indicting the habit as "a custome loathsome to the Eye, hatefull to the Nose, harmfull to the Braine, dangerous to the Lungs, and in the black stinking fume thereof neerest resembling the horrible Stigean smoke of the pit that is bottomlesse." A death penalty was imposed on smokers in Turkey, and the czar of Russia decreed that tobacco users were to be whipped and exiled after having their noses slit. Snuff takers were no more exempt from censure than smokers. In 1624 the pope threatened them with excommunication. Despite denunciations from throne and pulpit, tobacco was in general use by 1700, not only as a pleasurable diversion, but also as therapy. The *London Daily Advertiser* of 15 October 1742, ran an advertisement for "The Famous Cephalic and Ophthalmic Tobacco which by smoking a Pipe of it is good for the Head, Eyes, Stomach, Lungs, Rheumatism, Gout, Thickness of Hearing, Head-ach, Tooth-ach, Vapours, etc. Price 4s a Pound."

EARTHWORMS SAVE THE DAY FOR PARACELSUS

THE father of a youngster whose hand Paracelsus had treated brought judgment against the doctor when the wound failed to heal and became infected. Paracelsus, hoping the inflammation would subside, pleaded for postponement of the judicial proceedings and ordered application of earthworms. The treatment worked.

RX FOR DIABETES: A POUND OF SUGAR A DAY

PHOSPHATE of iron was a favorite prescription for what was once called "the pissing evil." It supposedly inhibited excessive action of the kidneys. As late as 1855, a pound of cane sugar was being given daily to diabetic patients in Guy's Hospital, London, to compensate for the severe depletion of body sugar caused by loss in the urine. Grape sugar was substituted for the cane with no better success, and after a time the sugar diet was altogether abandoned.

A REMEDY SIXTY CENTURIES OLD

REMAINS of mice were found in the alimentary canals of children buried in a predynastic cemetery in upper Egypt. Apparently mice were administered as a last resort to the moribund youngsters. The practice of swallowing skinned mice was known in classical and medieval times and had its adherents as recently as the turn of the century in the British Isles, where it was given as a remedy for whooping cough and other childhood ailments.

BLOOD FOR EPILEPTICS

PLINY describes how Romans afflicted with epilepsy were accustomed to rush into the arena to drink the freshly spilled blood of vanquished gladiators. Blood drinking survived into our own century. Sufferers from tuberculosis and epilepsy were known to visit slaughter houses to obtain fresh blood. Among the ancient Egyptians, baths of fresh blood were employed to invigorate debilitated members of the royal family.

CURATIVE AGENTS

MOTH

"IN shaving my face this morning," says Parson Woode-forde in his diary, "I happened to cut one of my moles which bled much, and happening also to kill a small moth that was flying about, I applied it to my mole and it instantaneously stopped bleeding."

LOUSE

AVICENNA advised insertion of a louse into the urethral meatus of patients with urinary retention. This novel form of stress therapy was followed for centuries. It was recommended by Guy de Chauliac, eminent French surgeon.

LEMON SHERBET

LAWALL tells us that lemonade was used as an antiscorbutic by Italian and French physicians and was dispensed by pharmacists. In 1660 a Florentine pharmacist conceived the idea of freezing the lemonade to make it more attractive as a dosage form. In effect, the product was lemon sherbet, though still called lemonade by the people of the time. It became a popular dessert, losing for the pharmacists a profitable source of revenue.

MOTHER'S MILK

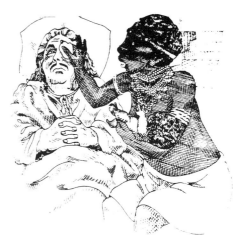

THE slaver Captain Conneau, whose eye was injured in an attempted mutiny, describes his treatment and recovery: "That afternoon the Black Doctor came on board, and after examining my eye, recommended woman's milk fresh from the breast. . . ." A woman who was suckling an infant was sent for with orders to remain with Conneau and bathe his eyes with her milk every half hour. Says Conneau, I know not if nature or this remedy cured me, but in a few days the broken flesh consolidated and the inflammation from the eye disappeared."

Brantôme, author of *Lives of Fair and Gallant Ladies*, had a similar and seemingly more romantic experience. Wounded by an arrow that almost deprived him of his sight, he was strangely healed: "Une fort belle dame de la ma jettait dans les yeux du lait ses beaux et blanc tetins."

PLAYING CARDS

IN many parts of Spanish-speaking America, fortune-telling cards (*naipes*) are employed by faith healers to identify for the sick those who, driven by envy or malice, have caused their illness. According to Marlene Dobkin de Rios, an anthropologist who has observed Peruvian faith healers at first hand, use of the cards also helps elicit important data and develops rapport by endowing the healer with an aura of omnipotence.

HOLY PICTURES

RIGHT up to the nineteenth century, sick cows and sick peasants were given holy wafers to swallow. On them was printed a scriptural subject, usually a crucifixion. Similar pictures were printed on linen strips used as bandages for wounds and skin eruptions.

GARLIC

JON Hartop, one of Fuller's "worthies," joined Sir John Hawkins in 1567 as chief gunner on the *Jesus of Lubeck*. "Long and dangerous was his journey; eight of his men at Cape Verde being killed, and the general himself wounded with poisoned arrows, but was cured by a native drawing out the poison with a clove of garlic, enough to make nice noses dispense with the valiant smell for the sanative virtue thereof."

WATER—PROPHYLACTIC AND CURATIVE

A PREXY-TO-BE TAKES A MATUTINAL PLUNGE

IN a Draconian rite that was celebrated winter and summer, little Josiah Quincy was carried down to the family kitchen where a tub of pump water, fresh and frigid, waited and into which Josiah was plunged three times, held no doubt as Thetis held Achilles—by the heels.* John Locke's *Some Thoughts Concerning Education*, popular in Colonial America, probably encouraged Josiah's parents in their Spartan views. "Wash the child's feet daily in cold water," wrote Locke, "and have his shoes so thin that they might leak and let in water." Quincy lived to become president of Harvard College, and by his own testimony never suffered the usual consequences of wet feet.

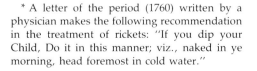

* A letter of the period (1760) written by a physician makes the following recommendation in the treatment of rickets: "If you dip your Child, Do it in this manner; viz., naked in ye morning, head foremost in cold water."

FOR AN OBSTINATE FEVER, SALTWATER

ON a voyage from the island of Jamaica to Liverpool, Dr. William Wright came down with a fever. When all else failed to reduce it, he was encouraged "to practice on myself what I had often wished to try on others with fevers similar to my own." He stripped on the ship's deck and had three buckets full of saltwater thrown over him. "The shock was great but I felt immediate relief. The headache and other pains instantly abated and a fine glow and diaphoresis succeeded."

MORE HYDROPATHY

V. G. Korolenko, in his autobiography, *The History of My Contemporary*, tells us that his father often got a bee in his bonnet. One was hydropathy. One morning Korolenko and his brother were brought to their father's room. "In it stood a wide tub filled with cold water, and father, who had previously gone through the whole procedure himself, made us stand in the tub in turn and, scooping up the water in a pewter mug, began douching us all over." They became so hardened to cold that barefoot and in their nightshirts, they would hide mornings "in an old carriage where shivering with cold (it was autumn, the time of morning frosts), we waited until father went to work. My mother promised him each time that she would dutifully perform the act of douching when we came back,—but God will forgive her, of course— she sometimes deceived him."

DARWIN TAKES A WATER CURE

DARWIN was chronically ill—or thought himself to be—and fell easily into the clutches of Dr. James Manby Gully, author of *The Water Cure in Chronic Diseases*. Gully treated a number of prominent Victorians—Carlyle and Tennyson, among others. Here is Darwin's own description of the hydropathic torture he was made to undergo. "At a quarter to 7 get up, & am scrubbed with a rough towel in cold water for 2 or 3 minutes, which after the first few days, made and makes me very like a lobster. I have a Washerman, a very nice person, and he scrubs behind while I scrub in front. Drink a tumbler of water & get my clothes on as quickly as possible & walk for 20 mintues . . . at same time I put on compress which is a broad and wet folded linen covered by a mackintosh & which is refreshed, i.e., dipt in cold water every 2 hours & I wear it all day except for 2 hours after midday dinner. I don't perceive much effect from this of any kind."

COLD WATER FOR ASTHMA

JOHN Floyer (1649–1734), himself an asthma sufferer for thirty years, recorded the first anatomical account of emphysema (in a horse with heaves). In his *Essay to Prove Cold Bathing Safe and Useful,* he says, "I am certain no Hot Regimen can be proper for Asthma, but the Cold is very useful, viz., to drink Water in the Morning, to shave oft, and wash the Head every Morning, and to Cold Bath once in a Month or fourteen Days." Not unexpectedly, Floyer attributed the rise in the incidence of rickets in Europe to the decline of baptism by total immersion!

A TEAKETTLE SHOWER FOR ARTHRITIC PAINS

CHARLOTTE Wright, whose husband was a physician, wrote to her sister in the year 1800: "I am surprised you do not use cold water showering . . . some nights after going to bed my shoulder pained me so I could not sleep for hours. I would waken Thomas and go out of doors, out of a warm bed, take all my clothes off—he high up on a ladder pouring cold water from a tea kettle on my shoulder—so cold that the spatters would freeze on my hair in solid ice. After the operation the pain was no more for the night."

HARVEY TRIES A FOOTBATH

THE discoverer of the circulation of the blood was in the habit of immersing his gouty and arthritic legs in a pail of cold water while sitting atop his London dwelling, even "if it were a Frost."

CURATIVE WATERS

HYDROTHERAPY on a grand scale came with the rise of the great spas like Tunbridge Wells and Bath. Queen Catherine of Braganza, consort of Charles II, visited both in a vain effort to overcome her sterility. Lesser folk came to cure everything—obstructions, dropsy, black and yellow jaundice, venereal disease, "weakness of Erection and general disorder of the whole Codpiece Oeconomy." The curative waters were drunk as well as bathed in, but no strict provision was made to keep the bathwater separate from the potable, so that ". . . while little Tabby was washing her rump, the ladies kept drinking it out of the pump," as a rhyme of the day had it. Seawater drinking was popular too. In 1750 Dr. Richard Russel wrote his *Dissertation of the Use of Sea Water in Diseases of the Glands,* in which seawater is touted as a beverage. An advertisement of the time reads, "TO BE SOLD, at the Talbot Inn, Southwark, Sea-Water from Brighthelmstome, in Sussex, took off the Main Ocean by T. Swaine."

An early spa.

CURE BY SHOCK

DR. BUTLER'S LITTLE SURPRISE

AUBREY, in his *Brief Lives*, relates that when Dr. William Butler, physician to James I, was "lyeing at the Savoy in London next the water side, where there was a balcony look't into the Thames, a Patient came to him that was grievously tormented with an Ague. The Doctor orders a boat to be in readinesse under his windowe, and discoursed with the patient in the balcony, when, on a signal given, two or three lusty Fellowes came behind the Gentleman and threw him a matter of 20 feete into the Thames. This surprize absolutely cured him."

DON CARLOS HAS A RUDE AWAKENING

THE practice of shocking the sick into normalcy may have begun at the court of King Philip II of Spain. In a desperate effort to cure Don Carlos, the king's invalid son, his doctors had the hundred-year-old bones of holy man Fra Diego dug up and placed in the bed of the sleeping heir to the throne.

PARSON WOODEFORDE TRIES BUTLER'S MANEUVER

WOODEFORDE notes in his diary of 1779, ''My boy Jack had another touch of Ague about noon. I gave him a dram of gin at the beginning of the fit and pitched him headlong into one of my ponds and ordered him to be immediately put to bed and he was the better for it and had nothing of the cold fit but was very hot.''

DR. RUSH'S "BATH OF SURPRISE"

THIS device for the treatment of the mentally ill featured a trap door that opened without warning and dropped the shocked patient several feet into a pool of chilly water.

THE PARTURIFACIENT THAT FAILED

THE fear and fright caused by vicious whipping was once thought to accelerate birth in women whose labor was protracted. Martin Luther is the putative source of a story concerning a gravid German petty princess for whom whipping was, of course, out of the question. A number of surrogates were therefore brought into the lying-in chamber and soundly flogged. Two died, but labor continued slow and protracted.

Fustigation (flagellation) was considered a sovereign remedy in the ancient world. Antonius Musa employed it to cure Octavius Augustus of sciatica.

THE FRANKLINISM VOGUE

"WAS YOU EVER ELECTRIFIED?"

ELECTRICITY, generally thought of as a modern phenomenon, was advocated in medical treatment as early as the eighteenth century. John Wesley had a "galvanic apparatus," which he used in treating his followers, and Benjamin Franklin had noted the effects of electricity in cases of paralysis as early as 1757. A letter quoted in Bayne-Powell's *Eighteenth Century London Life* reads, "Was you ever electrified? We have an itinerant philosopher here who knocks people down for the moderate consideration of 6d., and men and women and children are electrified out of their senses."

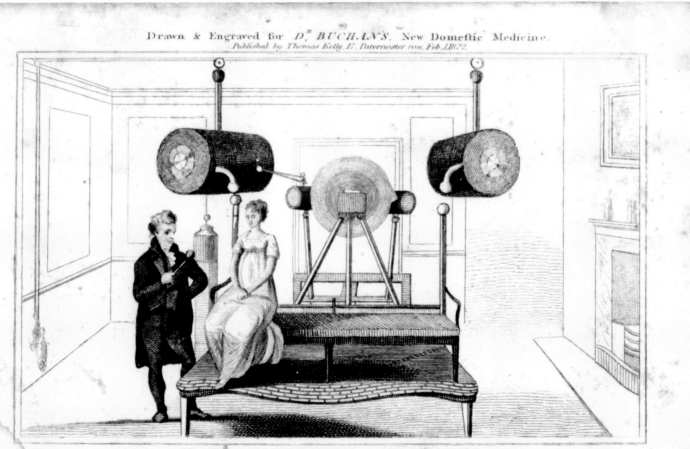

Drawn & Engraved for DR BUCHAN'S New Domestic Medicine.
Published by Thomas Kelly, 17, Paternoster row, Feb. 1, 1822.

GRAND ELECTRICAL APPARATUS,
In the possession of Mr F. Lowndes Medical Electrician, St Pauls Church Yard. This Machine, esteemed the most complete and powerful in Europe, has established the Medical character of the Electric fluid as an efficient remedy in many of the most obstinate diseases.

ELECTRIC SHOCK FOR INSANITY

A FRIEND of Franklin's, Dr. Johannes Ingenhousz, physician to the Austrian court, accidentally received a severe shock. When he recovered, he "felt the most lively joy in finding my judgment infinitely more acute. . . . I found moreover a liveliness in my whole frame, which I had never observed before." This incident led him to suggest to the "London mad doctors" similar shocks to the insane at Bedlam. They were not persuaded.

ERASMUS DARWIN ELECTRIFIES A ONE-YEAR-OLD

WHEN one-year-old Mary Anne suffered alarming convulsions and paralysis, her famous father, Josiah Wedgwood, called in his friend Erasmus Darwin. "Dr. Darwin ordered our little girl to be electrified two or three times a day on the side affected, and to be continued for some weeks. We are willing to flatter ourselves that she will receive some benefit . . . as she begins to move her arm and leg a little." But improvement was short-lived. Franklin was not overly impressed by electric therapy in cases of paralysis. While "paralyzed limbs seem to have recovered strength and be more capable of movement," he wrote, "I never knew any Advantage from Electricity in Palsies that was permanent."

TREATING OLD AGE—SOME ANTIDOTES FOR SENESCENCE

CULTIVATE THE COMPANY OF THE YOUNG

PHILIP Thicknesse, ex-apothecary's apprentice, in his *The Valetudinarian's Bath Guide* (1780), compares the sweet and wholesome breath of the young to that of cows, and offers this prescription for longevity: "Partake of the breath of young virgins . . . the brisk and lively motion of the blood in young people is the cause of their health, vigor and growth." Reinspiring their breath quickens geriatric circulation. Schoolmasters are therefore fortunate, as are Frenchmen who are known to seek the company of young women.

Inspired lunacies of the past sometimes anticipate the science of the present. According to one study concerning the factors influencing the life span of inbred mice, aging mice survived longer than expected if young female mice were introduced into their cages. This study would have delighted Roger Bacon, who reasoned that if disease could be contagious, so should vitality.

IMMERSE YOURSELF IN A BARREL OF WINE

IN a letter to a friend, Ben Franklin remarks, "I should prefer to any ordinary death, the being immersed in a cask of Madeira wine with a few friends . . . to be recalled to life by the solar warmth of my dear country." He concludes wistfully, "In all probability we live in an age too early and too near the infancy of science to see an art brought in our time to its perfection."

PURCHASE A VILLA IN THE EUGANEAN MOUNTAINS

THE Renaissance man most celebrated for his longevity was Luigi Cornaro of Padua. From his thirty-fifth to his ninety-first year he survived on a diet of twelve ounces of food and fourteen of wine daily. In his autobiography, written at age eighty-three, he attributes his long life and sound health to his diet and to country life at his villa: "In the spring and autumn I go to my hills in the most beautiful part of the Euganean mountains, where I have fountains and gardens and a comfortable house."

TRY ANIMAL TESTES

AT age seventy-two physiologist Brown-Sequard (1817–1894) cut dog's testicles into small pieces, mashed them in water, filtered the juice, and injected it into his blood stream. He repeated the process with the testes of guinea pigs. Called on to address the Societé de Biologie in Paris, an audience largely comprising of septuagenarians and octogenarians, he startled his geriatric hearers by announcing, "Today I was able to pay a visit to my young wife!"

Serge Voronoff, a Russian émigré doctor practicing in France, had been physician-surgeon to Abbas II, khedive of Egypt. He had observed that eunuchs guarding the king's harem were more subject to the diseases of senescence than uncastrated men, and concluded that the absence of testicular hormones was responsible. Voronoff's agents shipped thousands of chimpanzee and other anthropoids from the forests of Africa to his villa-clinic on the Italian Riviera. There the aging rich were given monkey gland grafts at a cost of about 5,000 dollars each, making Voronoff a millionaire many times over.

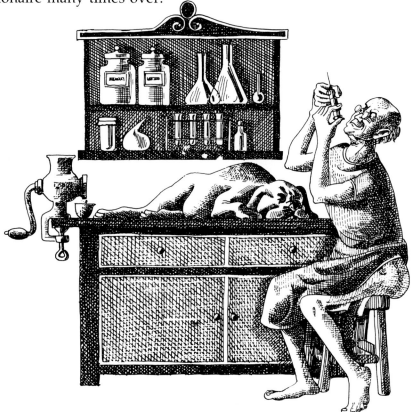

SELF-TREATMENT

ROUSSEAU CATHETERIZES HIMSELF

ROUSSEAU, who suffered from urinary retention, gave up doctors and treated himself with probe and dilator. On one occasion, James Boswell was admitted to the philosopher's presence for an interview. He found Rousseau "sitting in great pain," the instrument just used or actually *in situ*. The author of *Confessions* told Boswell he needed a chamber pot "every other minute."

HENRY VIII DABBLES IN PHYSIC

ONCE handsome and athletic, Henry VIII was moribund at age fifty-six. Gluttony and drink had made him so corpulent that "three of the biggest men that could be found could get inside his doublet." A great dabbler in "physic," he concocted an ointment that included, inter alia, ground tiger's teeth, ground pearls, guaiacum, spices, and incense. These ingredients were to drive out the moist humors from Henry's ulcerous leg. He tried it out on others too, and the "King's own Plaister" ("verrie good against sores on the legs and the lykes") was offered for sale everywhere in England.

REACHING FOR AN ABSCESS

FOLLOWING an attack of erysipelas, Dr. A. E. Hertzler, author of *The Horse and Buggy Doctor*, developed an abscess of the neck. He prepared an anesthetic and hunted for the abscess with the aid of a looking glass tilted upright on the kitchen table. "I bored a dissecting scissors into the depth of my neck until the abscess was reached, hooked an index finger into each handle of the scissors and gave a violent jerk." He then made an opening as wide as the spread of the scissors and inserted a rubber tube. Complicating the procedure was the fact that Herzler had to work with only one eye, the eye on the abscess side being swollen and completely shut.

SURGERY AT SEA

IN American sailing vessels, ship's officers were often called on to perform surgical operations. In 1890, H. H. Bodfish, first mate of the *Mary D. Hume*, performed the first of a twenty-year-long series of operations—on himself. A falling topmast block had crushed a toe. A survey of the damage convinced him he'd have to lose it, "so I sent the steward for the captain to do the job, but he was busy and asked me to wait. I knew the longer I waited the more painful the operation would be, so with the steward and cabin boy looking on and groaning, I whetted my knife and cut it off myself. The way it was injured made it necessary for me to unjoint the bone from the foot too, but I did it and there was considerable satisfaction in having performed my first surgical operation."

SELF-TREATMENT IN NO-MAN'S LAND

ROBERT Graves, in his World War I reminiscences, quotes an officer in the medical corps who was shot in the stomach while bandaging a wounded soldier. Experience had taught him that with stomach wounds lying absolutely still for as long as possible offered the best chance of survival. He crawled into a shell hole, and when the stretcher-bearers reached him, they were met by a drawn revolver. He kept everyone at bay for forty-eight hours until he felt that healing had proceeded far enough to risk the bumpy journey back to the field ambulance.

SEWING UP A SWORD WOUND

FROM an account recorded in 1610: "Last week M. Hall, cupbearer to the King, coming to Sir Everard Digby's house, quarreled with the Steward about certain words spoken to the disgrace of one of the gentlewomen of the house. The Steward cut the guts out of his belly; but he being a strong-hearted man and his bowels not being pierced, he gathered them into his belly and put his hand into his body to make room for the stowage of the tripes and sewed up the wound with pack thread, and may live."

SELF-CIRCUMCISION

LUIS Zacuto, the son of Marrano parents, was a trader in the Indian villages of colonial Mexico. He tells how he returned to his ancestral faith: After reading Genesis 17, with its warning that the soul of him who is not circumcised will be erased from the Book of Life, "I became so frightened . . . that I immediately proceeded to carry out the divine command. I took some scissors and went over to the ravine of the Panuco River. There, with a longing and vivid wish to be inscribed in the Book of Life, I sealed it by cutting off almost all of the prepuce and leaving very little of it."

AUTOVENESECTION

PRESIDENT Andrew Jackson would often call for a servant to hold a bowl while he opened a vein in his arm. Bleeding was part of a desperate effort to ward off a pulmonary hemorrhage.

POTT TAKES COMMAND

DR. Percival Pott suffered a compound fracture of the leg when thrown from his horse. A coach was brought, and bystanders prepared to lift him in. Despite the bitter cold, Pott insisted on lying where he was and arranged for the purchase of a door from a nearby house. Torn from its hinges and nailed to two poles, It made a convenient litter on which the resourceful doctor was carried home.

AVICENNA BOWS OUT

AVICENNA took eight enemas in the course of a single day when attacked by the colic that began a series of pathologic events that were to end with his death in 1037. Through it all, Avicenna prescribed for himself, and when at last he knew his constitution to be broken beyond repair, he declared, "The physician who treated my body was not adequate to his task. Now all attempts to cure are useless."

SHELLEY TAKES OVER

WHEN Shelley's wife, Mary, suffered a near-fatal miscarriage in the isolated village of San Terenzo, no medical assistance was immediately available. Shelley took over. "I took the most decisive of resolutions; by dint of making her sit on ice, I succeeded in checking the hemorrhage and the fainting fits, so that when the doctor arrived the danger was over. . . ."

FRANKLIN DOES A HEADSTAND

BEN Franklin often found it necessary to stand on his head. The inversion was required whenever his bladder stone fell into the urethral opening, blocking it. Upside down he was able to dislodge the stone and empty his bladder. Franklin invented an improved catheter, which he used on himself. He had another made for his brother, a fellow kidney-stone sufferer.

SELF-MEDICATION AT SEA

IN the great days of the Cape Horners, the only "doctor" aboard was a wooden medicine chest. A seaman who served on board the German four-master *Passat* reveals its contents. It contained ten bottles of liquids or powders, all plainly numbered. Number one was given for coughs, number two for colds, four for feverish ailments, six for wasting diseases, etc. One day, when number seven was called for, the second mate found the bottle empty. He took bottles three and four and mixed on equal dose from each. We are not told how the recipient fared.

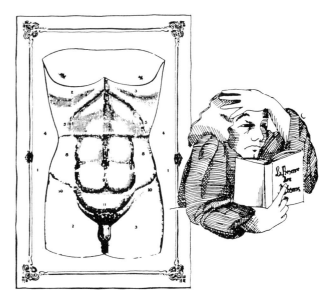

EVERY MAN HIS OWN DOCTOR

POPE John XXI as a young priest wrote his *Thesaurus Pauperum*, or "Treasury of the Poor," a collection of simple remedies for the relief of minor ills by means of which the poverty-stricken could avoid the burden of physician's fees. It was published in 1525.

In 1747 John Wesley, the founder of Methodism, brought out a similar guide—*Primitive Physick*—price one shilling. It featured a series of remedies arranged under various common diagnoses. Once having diagnosed his disorder, the patient tried the recommended remedies until he found the one that worked. The guide advised temperance, moderation, and liberal use of water externally and internally.

EVERY MAN HIS OWN DIAGNOSTICIAN

THEOPHRASTE Renaudot, medical innovator extraordinary, published his sixty-page *La Presence des Absens* in 1642, "a formulary for the use of absent patients." His object was to produce a guide "so simple that not only the country apothecary or surgeon, but also the peasant women with their children, provided they can read, will be able to indicate the condition of a sick person . . . so we can treat him as methodically and well as if he were present." The booklet sold for five sous and carried diagrams of the human body for marking the site of disorders, along with extended lists of symptoms to be similarly marked.

Renaudot was Commissaire des Pauvres at the Bureau d'Addresse in Paris, where free medical treatment was provided as early as 1632. His booklet was a boon for those with "shameful" (*honteux*) diseases like syphilis, who could use the Bureau's services without having to appear in person.

The wise, for cure, on exercise depend, God never made his work for man to men.

John Dryden

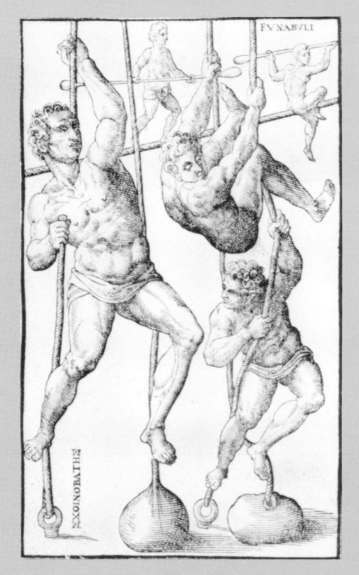

Hieronymus Mecuriale, De arte gymnastica libri sex. *Venice, 1573.*

EXERCISE, INCLUDING FRICASYE

"AN EXCELLENT COMMODITIE"

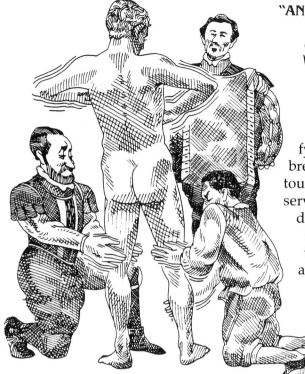

SIR Thomas Elyot's *The Castel of Helth* (1541) is one of the earliest English health manuals. Among its recommendations for exercise is fricasye, to be used "in the mornynge, after thei have ben at stoole. . . . With their shirt sleeves, or if the flesh be tender, with their bare hands, they do fyrste softly, and afterwards faster, rubb theyr breaste and sydes downwarde and overthwart, not touchinge stomack or bealy, and after cause theyr servaunt semblabye to rubbe overthwarte theyr shoulders and backe, and beginninge the neckbone, and not touchinge the raynes of theyr backe, except they doo feele there moche colde and wynde, and afterwards theyr leggs from the knee to the ancle: last theyr armes, from the elbowe to the handwreste. And in this forme of fricasye I myselfe have founden an excellent commoditie."

MORE FRICASYE

FRESH air and exercise were recommended by Bernard Mandeville in his *Treatise on Hypochondria*. His regimen for a young unmarried woman: "Let her be swung for half an hour" in a chair or rope tied to a beam. This was to be followed by two hours of trotting or galloping on horseback. "After let her be undrest and by a nurse be chafed or dry-rubbed till her skin looks red and the flesh glows all over."

HOW TO KEEP THE DOCTOR—
AND EVERYBODY ELSE—AWAY

IN addition to fricasye, Elyot commends gestation (movement provided by coach or boat) and vociferation. This last consists of "syngynge, redynge or cryinge," and is "the chiefe exercyse of the breste and instruments of the voyce. . . . He that intendeth to attempte this exercyse lette hym speake with as base a voyce as he can, and walkynge, begynne to synge lowder and lowder, but stille in a base voyce, and to take no hede of swete tunes or armony."

KEEPING A SOUND MIND IN A SOUND BODY

THE iron discipline that regulates the lives of today's Olympic athletes was equally characteristic of life among the contenders in the Olympic games of ancient Greece. And as is true today, training was in the hands of no-nonsense coaches. One ancient trainer refused to permit his charges to attend dinner parties, maintaining that intelligent conversation would impair their health by causing headaches.

JAMES BOSWELL CUTS SOME CAPERS

"I WOKE as usual heavy, confused and splenetic. Every morning this is the case with me. Dempster prescribed to me to cut two or three brisk capers around the room, which I did, and found attended with the most agreeable effects. It expelled the phlegm from my heart, gave my blood a free circulation and my spirits a brisk flow, so that I was all at once made happy. I must remember this and practice it." So wrote Boswell in his journal for 6 May 1763.

EXERCISE WITHOUT SWEAT

BOSWELL reports that Lord Monboddo woke every morning at four and then for his health's sake, got up and walked through his rooms naked, with the window open. He called it taking an air bath. Having exercised as aforesaid, Lord Monboddo went to bed again and slept two hours more. Ben Franklin observed a similar regimen (see page 88).

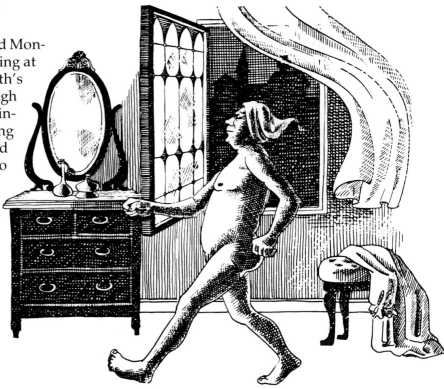

A KING EXERCISES

CHARLES II (1630–1685) had himself weighed before and after his game of tennis. He considered loss of weight evidence of good play. Burton, his great contemporary, would have objected. In his *Anatomy of Melancholy* he observes that sweating "wastes the spirits," and much exercise "consumes the spirit and substance and refrigerates the body."

EMPEROR FREDERICK II ARRANGES A CLINICAL TRIAL

THE emperor had an inquiring mind. According to Salimbene, the medieval chronicler, Frederick had two of his subjects sumptuously fed, after which one was put through a course of vigorous exercise, while the other was permitted to rest. After an appropriate interval, Frederick had them both disembowelled so he could determine which had enjoyed the better digestion.

A ROMAN PATRICIAN HAS A VIGOROUS SESSION OF BALL PLAY

PLINY describes how Spurinna, a retired patrician, spends the day at his country seat: "Every morning he stays in bed for an hour after daybreak. He then calls for his shoes and exercises mind and body with a three mile walk. . . . When bath time is announced (at three o'clock in winter; in summer at two), he strips for a walk in the sunshine if there is no wind; then he has a long and vigorous session of ball play. . . . After his bath he lies down for a brief rest before dinner."

RIDING A CHAMBER-HORSE

BEFORE he converted to vegetarianism and physical culture, Dr. George Cheyne (1671–1743) had been known as "three ells around Cheyne." He weighed thirty-two stone (448 pounds). Diet and exercise slimmed him down considerably. He wrote to novelist Samuel Richardson in 1740, "I wonder you get not the Chamber-Horse which is now so universally known in London. It is certainly advisable and has all the good and admirable effects of a hard Trotting Horse except the fresh Air. I ride an hour every Morning and will do more when Weather will not permit me to walk in my Garden or ride in my Coach."

JONATHAN SWIFT'S HIGH JINKS

WAS Swift's habit when dean of St. Patrick's of chasing his friends around the deanery an idiosyncrasy or a sign of mental aberration? He did have his "fitts" as he called them—attacks of giddiness and deafness. But his high jinks on the grounds of the deanery were attributable to nothing more serious than the delight he took in exercise.

A COLONIAL GENTLEMAN DANCES HIS DANCE

THE diary of William Byrd of Westover reflects the habits of a cultured Colonial gentleman. A typical entry reads: "I rose at 7 o'clock and read a chapter in Hebrew and some Greek in Anacreon. I said my prayers and ate milk for breakfast. I danced my dance."

Medical advice was sought as early as the sixteenth century in cases of abortion, infanticide, malpractice, suicide, and violent death. Doctors were also called on to examine women suspected of witchcraft. Six years after the publication of his treatise on the circulation of the blood, Harvey joined ten midwives, six surgeons, and one anatomist who were to determine whether four accused women had supernumerary teats. They found none. In a celebrated case, Father Urbain Grandier was examined in the presence of two apothecaries and several doctors for areas of insensibility, sure signs of complicity with the Devil. A long sharp probe sealed the priest's fate.

The public burning of Father Grandier. From a contemporary drawing, 1634.

VI

DOCTORS AND THE LAW

MAKING SEPARATION LEGAL

One of the few legal methods for obtaining a marriage annulment in the seventeenth century was demonstrating proof of physical incompatibility. Below are three grounds for divorce set forth by Zacchias in his Questiones Medico-Legalis *(1621).*

Contagious Disease. In his chapter on contagion, Zacchias lists the following as chronic contagious diseases that may be cause for marriage annulment: phthisis, leprosy, syphilis, and alopecia. (Why so trivial an affliction as hair loss? Probably the alopecia of early syphilis is meant.)

Impotence. Zacchias differentiated between natural and unintentional impotence. The latter included impotence caused by witchcraft. ''All witchcraft comes from carnal lust,'' proclaimed witch-hunters James Sprenger and Henry Kramer in their *Malleus Maleficarum.* Girls who have been corrupted turn for help and protection to devils who conspire with them to render their lovers impotent. They may sometimes ''collect male organs in great numbers, and put them in a bird's nest, or shut them up in a box, where they move themselves like living members and eat oats and corn.'' A young man who had been deprived of his member went to a witch to plead for its restitution. ''She brought him to a tree where she shewed him a nest and bade him climb up and take it. And being at the top of the tree, he took out a mighty great one, asking whether he might have it. 'Nay,' quoth she, 'that is our parish priest's tool, but take any other which thou wilt.' ''

A witch enslaving a victim by shooting an arrow through his foot. From a work on witchcraft by Ulrich Molitor, Cologne, 1489.

Obesity. A marriage between two extremely obese persons is dissolvable because it frustrates the procreative goals of holy matrimony. Obesity in only one partner, however, offers "technical solutions that permit fulfillment of the connubial duty to have children."

UNCONSUMMATED MARRIAGE IN FEUDAL TIMES

ALTHOUGH unconsummated marriage was *ab initio* null and void, a decree issued by Hincmar, Archbishop of Reims in the ninth century, offered the impotent a loophole. A man whose marriage had been annulled because of impotence was declared eligible to marry again if his impotence was caused by witchcraft. Inadequacy owing to natural causes, however, was a stringent bar to remarriage.

TALMUDIC LAW AND THE *DEBITUM CONJUGALE*

TALMUDIC law branded as sinners husbands who failed to discharge their conjugal duties, and wives were expected to submit to coitus on demand or risk divorce. Husbands of reluctant wives were allowed an indemnity of seven dinars weekly deducted from the ketubah, a fund set aside for the wife's maintenance in the event of her spouse's death. On the other hand, the wife could ask for a divorce and the entire ketubah too if her husband asked her to avoid conception by jumping or other means. Coitus interruptus and masturbation (committing harlotry with the hand) were under strict interdict.

SEVEN PROOFS OF POTENCY

A CURIOSITY of legal medicine was "congress," the obligation of a married couple to cohabit in the presence of judges and medical men when one partner accused the other of impotence and asked for an annullment. The practice was abolished in France in 1677 after a scandal involving the count of Langey. He produced seven children by a second marriage after he was officially declared impotent.

POTENCY AND VISUAL PROOF

THE duke of Beaufort wished to divorce his wife, whose more than friendly relations with Lord Talbot had become notorious, but the duchesss claimed in opposing his suit that her marriage to the duke had never been consummated. The duke was now obliged to offer legal proof of potency. A committee comprising two physicians, three surgeons, and an ecclesiastical judge waited on the duke at the home of one of the physicians. What followed is recorded by Horace Walpole. The duke agreed to go behind a screen "and when he knocked they were to come to him. He was some time behind the scenes: at last he knocked and the good old folks saw what amazed them—what they had not seen for many a day! Cibber [Colley Cibber, dramatist and wit] said, 'His Grace's p——k is in everybody's mouth.' " The duke wasted no time in suing Talbot for 80,000 pounds in damages.

CERTIFIED FIT FOR TORTURE

THE Empress Maria Theresa in 1766 issued an edict directing the court physician to certify the fitness of male-factors to undergo torture, in order to ensure "healthy" (i.e., factual) testimony. Ivan Illich in his *Medical Nemesis* says it was one of the first laws to establish mandatory medical certification.

CONCEIVING *SINE CONCUBITO*

IN the case of a woman who had borne a child though absent from her husband for four years, a French judge legitimized the infant, ruling that the child owed its paternity to a dream. This was an age when Zacchias, an early writer on legal medicine, believed in the evil eye and Paré in sorcery—an age when doctors could gravely debate the question, Can a woman be made pregnant by the Devil? In an earlier time, Talmudic scholars no doubt pondered the case of Ben Sira, who reported that his mother had told him he had been conceived while she was bathing in a pool in which a male bather had had an emission.

AMBROISE PARÉ SIGNS TWO MEDICOLEGAL REPORTS*

Deadly Wound. I, Ambroise Paré have gone today on the order of the court of parliament to the house of X, Rue St. Germain with the ensign of S, and have found him in his bed having a wound on the left part of his head over the temporal bone with fracture. Several parts of this bone have broken through the two membranes and entered the substance of the brain. Therefore the above-named had lost all consciousness with a convulsion, the pulse is very small, and the sweat cold. He neither drinks nor eats. I therefore certify that he will soon die. Testified by my seal, etc.

Abdominal Wound Resulting in Abortion. I, Ambroise Paré, have come on the order of the great Provost to the Rue St. Houbré, to the house of Mr. M., where I have found a lady called Margaret in bed with a high fever, convulsions, and hemorrhage from her natural parts, as a consequence of a wound that she has received in the lower abdomen situated three fingers below the umbilicus, in the right part, which has penetrated into the cavity, wounded and penetrated the uterus. She has therefore delivered before term a male infant, dead, well formed in all its limbs, which infant has also received a wound in its head, penetrating into the substance of the brain. Therefore the above-mentioned lady will soon die. Certified this to be true in putting my signature, etc.

ANNO·ÆTATIS.
68

Ambroise Paré, sixteenth century. Reproduced from Medicine and the Artist (Ars Medica) *by permission of the Philadelphia Museum of Art.*

* Copyright 1950 CIBA-GEIGY Corporation. Reprinted with permission from CIBA Symposia by E. H. Ackerknecht, M.D.

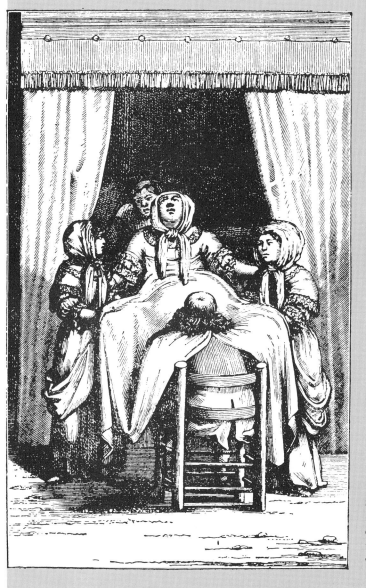

It was in childbirth particularly that prudery was most likely to manifest itself. The Princess of Wales in 1716 was delivered of a stillborn son after four days of excruciating labor. During all that time, her doctor had been kept from her bedside "for reasons of modesty," despite a petition from the cabinet ministers that he be allowed to attend her. The princess's midwife, aggrieved by the insulting petition, at first refused to perform her duties, but in the end resumed her ministrations in time to save her patient's life.

False modesty was not confined to the patient, as this excerpt from Dr. William Buchan's *Domestic Medicine* (1824) testifies: "Besides the indelicacy and immoral consequences which too often attend the employment of men-midwives in this natural occupation of the other sex, females are altogether much better qualified than males. They are more tender, careful, and observant, and to them the patient can more freely disclose her situation. The employment of men is of modern introduction, copied from the manners of the French, where women pay little regard to that delicacy for which British females are deservedly admired."

The height of prudery—a physician operating under the sheet. For thirteen centures the physicians of Europe were not allowed to attend normal cases of delivery, but in the seventeenth century they began to participate to some extent. A woodcut from the works of a Dutch physician, Samuel Janson, 1681.

VII

MEDICINE AND
MRS. GRUNDY

THE BODY TABOO

OBSTETRICS IN THE DARK

IN 1658 doctors were still persona non grata at the parturient patient's bedside. But in that year occurred the famous case of "a great lady of Middlesex," in which the midwife panicked and called for a doctor. A Dr. Willoughby of Derby was sent for. "The resourceful doctor arrived at the door of the lady's chamber, got down on all fours, crept into the room, examined his patient, and crept out the same way."

JACOBA CHAMPIONS MODESTY

"IT is better and more honest that a wise and expert woman in this art visit sick women than a man to whom it is not permitted to see, inquire of, or touch the hands, breasts, stomach of a woman; nay, rather ought a man shun the secrets of women and their company and flee as far as he can. And a woman before now would permit herself to die rather than reveal the secrets of her infirmity to any man . . . and this is the cause of many women and also men dying of their infirmities, not wishing to have doctors see their secret parts. . . ."

So testified the woman empiric known as Jacoba at her trial in 1322. Her crime? Practicing medicine without the sanction of the Dean and Faculty of Medicine of the University of Paris. Not only had she—a woman—treated patients, she had had the temerity to cure many of them, a fact attested to by many witnesses at her trial. Jacoba was forbidden to practice medicine under pain of excommunication and was obliged to pay a fine of sixty Paris pounds.

SMELLIE GETS BOTH BARRELS

THIS venomous attack on Smellie's *Treatise on the Theory and Practice of Midwifery* appeared in 1752: "I know not which to despise most, the professors of this bawdry profession, or the husbands who tamely submit their wives to be so wantonly and unnecessarily handled by them. . . . I desire every man who loves his wife . . . seriously to figure to himself a smart man-midwife, locked into his wife's apartment, lubricating his finger with pomatum, in order to introduce it into his wife's *Vagina!* Nay, if he pleases, two fingers, or one finger in the *Vagina* and the other into the *Rectum,* according to the ingenious Dr. Smellie's direction."

THE BIKE AS APHRODISIAC

CYCLING was opposed by many nineteenth-century American physicians who feared it would "beget or foster the habit of masturbation." Saddles designed especially for men were particular objects of attack because they were more likely when used by women to lead to "friction and heating of the parts where it is very undesirable and may lead to dangerous practices."

SHAME MONEY

IN Talmudic times it was forbidden for a Jewish woman to be examined by a physician. In the event of illness, examination was made by her servants or a midwife who described the nature of her symptoms to a physician or rabbi. A diagnosis was then made and treatment prescribed. The Talmud relates that the physician Samuel ben Abba, wishing to study the anatomical structure of the female breast, "examined a slave, whereafter he gave her four zuz 'shame money' as compensation for the indignity."

If biblical prudery seems excessive, consider the case of Elizabeth Montagu, a noted beauty whose literary salon was frequented by Johnson, Walpole, and Burke. At the age of twenty-one, while staying at the home of the duchess of Portland, she wrote to her mother, "Mary brings me word my bathing tub is ready for use; so tomorrow I shall go in. Pray look for my bathing dress, till then I must go in in chemise and jupon!"

A DIET FOR CHASTITY

DR. Dio Lewis in his *Chastity: Our Secret Sins,* published in1874, offers some suggestions for combatting excessive sexual activity and lascivious daydreams. For breakfast he advises coddled apples, Graham mash and oatmeal crackers, and for dinner, wheat germ, dates and stewed beans. Suppers are to be skipped. Water alone is to be drunk, especially since "coffee . . . taken into the system gives rise to ungovernable salacity."

PRUDERY KILLS A QUEEN

QUEEN Caroline suffered miserably from a mysterious malady. It turned out to be a rupture which she had carefully concealed from her physicians for years. According to the *Dictionary of National Biography,* her fatal illness in 1737 had its origin in the untreated disability.

PRUDERY AND THE STETHOSCOPE

WHEN a buxom lass of sixteen, chaperoned by her father, appeared in Laennec's office, he was faced with the problem of monitoring her heart sounds without causing scandal. In Laennec's words, "The patient's age and sex did not permit me to resort to the kind of examination I have just described [ear to chest]. I recalled a well-known acoustic phenomenon; namely, if you place your ear against one end of a wooden beam, the scratch of a pin at the other extremity is most distinctly audible. . . . Taking a sheaf of paper I rolled it into a very tight roll, one end of which I placed over the heart, whilst I placed my ear to the other. . . ."

DR. DARBY, MEET DR. LAENNEC!

APPARENTLY, Laennec's great discovery (1819) had not found popular acceptance on these shores by 1861, as this excerpt from *A Diary from Dixie* would indicate. Sally was ill with a sore throat, and as she lay on the sofa wrapped in a cashmere shawl, Dr. Darby dropped to his knees by her side. "What is that for?" said the captain [Sally's brother], standing up brusquely. "I mean to try auscultation, percussion, and so on to see if her lungs are affected." "Come, that sort of thing won't do!" "Miss Sally," said Dr. Darby, "this sort of thing is done every day. It is strictly professional. I must rest my head against your chest. It is absolutely necessary for medical diagnosis." The captain cried, "Sir! . . . if you don't want to see a chair smashed over your head, take care not to move a peg nearer!"

Syphilis is a blessing . . . inflicted by the Almighty to act as a restraint upon indulgence of evil passions.*
Samuel Solly, President of the Royal Medical
and Chirurgical Society of London, 1867

The Seven Deadly Sins—the Lustful in Hell. From Le grand Kalendrier et compost des Bergiers, Troyes, 1496.

* When Pope Leo XII banned the condom in 1826, it was not because it prevented pregnancy, but because it prevented God from striking sinners.

VIII

IN THE ARMS OF VENUS

THE CURSE OF THE POX

A LESSON IN EPIDEMIOLOGY FROM CASANOVA

Surgeon: I have made a good deal of money, and it is to you, Captain—may God bless you!—that I am indebted for my present comforts.

Captain: How so?

Surgeon: In this way, Captain. You had a connection with Don Jerome's housekeeper, and you left her. When you went away with a certain souvenir which she communicated to a certain friend of hers, who, in perfect good faith, made a present of it to his wife. This lady did not wish, I suppose, to be selfish, and she gave her souvenir to a libertine, who in turn was so generous with it, that within less than a month, I had about fifty clients.

IN VENERY THERE IS SAFETY IN NUMBERS

JAMES Yonge, ship's surgeon, in his journal describes a visit to a prostitute by five of his shipmates. All five contracted gonorrhea, while two sailors from a sister ship who followed them into the lady's quarters did not. Yonge explains: "The reason I apprehend to be because those who went on first imbibed and absumed the venereal matter in the vagina, and with their own sperm had, as it were, washed it clean against the others that escaped."

LA BELLE FERRONIÈRE GIVES FRANCIS I A LITTLE GIFT

"LA Belle Ferronière," the lovely subject of a portrait by Leonardo da Vinci, caught the lascivious eye of Francis I. The king, exercising his royal privilege, made her his mistress. The enraged husband intentionally contracted syphilis and passed it on to his wife, who in turn passed it on to the king.

MAKING VENERY SAFE

CATHERINE the Great of Russia is said to have had syphilophobia. To enjoy without fear what seems to have been an enormous appetite for sex, she screened her numerous lovers through a committee of six ladies of the court, "les Epreuves" (testers), who were given a period of six months to pass judgment on them.

SYPHILIS AS A WEAPON—1649

IN 1649, when Venice was warring against the Turkish Empire, a Venetian doctor concocted a "plague-quintessence" for use against the enemy. Articles of clothing hawked in the Turkish camps were to be liberally sown with the ingenious doctor's infective invention. It seems doubtful that the scheme was ever carried out.

SYPHILIS AS A WEAPON—1706

WHEN besieged in Madrid by the Portuguese and their English allies in 1706, Philip V of Spain ordered the authorities to permit the city's prostitutes to ply their trade among the besiegers. The expedient nearly saved Madrid—half the besieging army was shortly *hors de combat*.

SYPHILIS AS A WEAPON—1944

BRITAIN'S A-Force in Italy devised a plan for reducing the fighting efficiency of the German army. Having collected a number of attractive Neapolitan prostitutes, all of whom were suffering from venereal disease, they removed them to a guarded villa where they were given "all the army white bread and spaghetti" they could eat and were entertained with a trip to Capri. When told that they would be expected to fraternize with the Germans, they were terrified at the notion of crossing the battle lines, but most of all they couldn't bear the thought of parting from their pimps. The plan was dropped and the girls turned loose on the streets of Naples.

AN EMPRESS RESCUES HER SCARLET SISTERS

THE Byzantine Empress Theodora (d. 548) was an actress and harlot before her marriage to Justinian I. He made her joint ruler of the empire on his accession to the throne in 527. By royal command, 500 women were rounded up from the streets and brothels of Constantinople and lodged in a converted palace. Perpetual confinement did not suit some, and in despair they hurled themselves into the Bosphorus, but according to Gibbon, the rest were grateful for their deliverance from sin and misery.

Frederick the Great's solution to the problem of prostitution was somewhat similar, but more in keeping with German efficiency. Specially trained women were employed to police their erring sisters, and anyone caught plying her trade was delivered to the abhorred Spinnhaus, condemned to spin wool for the prosperous Prussian wool industry. Those found to have venereal disease were turned over to the Charité Hospital in Berlin, where they were subjected to the mercury treatment then in vogue. They were not discharged until apparently cured.

ERASMUS SPOKE TOO SOON

ERASMUS was hard on the victims of syphilis and advocated castration as punishment. He proposed that the marriage contract be declared void if one of the partners had the disease. When his sarcophagus in the Basle Cathedral was opened to permit the construction of a heating system, osseous thicknesses were observed in the skeletal remains, and X rays revealed manifest signs of syphilitic infection.

NO SALVATION IN SALIVATION

THE mercury ointment employed as a cure for syphilis in eighteenth-century England caused constant salivation and inflamed the mouth so badly that speech was often impossible. When he was brought to trial, Jonathan Wild, the notorious thief and thief-taker (i.e., informer), presented a Writ of Salivation to the court on the ground that since he could not speak, he could not defend himself. Postponements were occasionally granted on this pretext, but Wild's petition was thrown out. He died on the gallows.

MERCURY AND VENUS IN STUART ENGLAND

Restless he rolls about from whore to whore,
A merry monarch, scandalous and poor.
               Lord Rochester on Charles II

If we are to believe the chroniclers of the age, venereal disease was rampant at the court of Charles II and among the titled and well-born. We learn from Aubrey's *Brief Lives* that Sir Henry Blount was "called to the barre, for spreading abroad that abominable and dangerous Doctrine that it was cheaper and safer to lye with Common Wenches than with the Ladies of Quality." And Pepys reports a conversation concerning the "vices of the court, and how the pox is so common there, and so I hear on all hands that it is as common as eating and swearing." The promiscuity of the king himself was a byword among his subjects, and his reputation as a prolific progenitor of bastards was a subject of remark and ridicule. In 1675, persons unknown placed a pillion on his equestrian statue "at Stoks Market and on the horse's brest [was] writ on paper, Hast, post-hast, for a midwife."

Though Charles, for all his womanizing, seems to have avoided the venereal taint, hundreds of the best men of the realm were not so fortunate. Among these was the wit, poet, and king's confidant, John Wilmot, Lord Rochester, who "died of old age" at thirty-three. His career tells us much about the temper of the times. At court, the king told the story "of my Lord Rochester's having of his clothes stole, while he was with a wench; and his gold all gone, but his clothes found afterwards stuffed into a feather bed by the wench that stole them." A contemporary says of him, "he was ever engaged in some amour or other, and frequently with women of the lowest order, and the vilest prostitutes of the town."

Inevitably, like so many of London's roistering blades, Rochester was "poxed." We know that he resorted for treatment to the notorious Mrs. Fourcard's "Baths" in Leather Lane, where no doubt he was sweated, fumigated with mercury, and given "dyet-drinks." This last was an infusion of sarsaparilla and sassafras, to which the bark of lignum vitae (guaiacum wood), a frequent ingredient of quack nostrums, was sometimes added. Turpentine pills were popular for a time, and like everything that had to do with the "French disease" were a subject of hilarity on the Restoration stage. Shadwell, in *The Virtuoso*, describes the young fops of the day coming "drunk and screaming into a play-house, and stand upon the benches, and toss their full periwigs and empty heads and with their shrill unbroken pipes, cry, Dam-me, this is a damned play: Prethee, let's to a whore, Jack. Then says another, with great gallantry, pulling out his box of pills, Dam-me, Tom, I am not in a condition; here's my turpentine for my third clap; when you would think he was not old enough to be able to get one."

But it was the box or tub that was *the* symbol of treatment. In it the patient sweated out his pox. At the same time he might be exposed to the fumes of mercuric sulfide. Or he might be covered with mercury ointment. Treatment with mercury could be devastating. Necrosis of the jaw bones, with ulceration of the cheeks, loss of teeth, and uncontrollable salivation were a few of the probable sequelae. It would be nice to think that the survivors took the wise and humanitarian advice of Fracastorius: "Above all, flee the seductions of love, for nothing could be more harmful, and your kisses would taint the tender daughters of Venus with a vile corruption."

"The Spaniard with Naples disease" is undergoing the approved seventeenth-century powdering tub treatment for syphilis. Two chafing dishes provide the fumes of cinnabar (mercury ore), which condense as a powder on the skin.

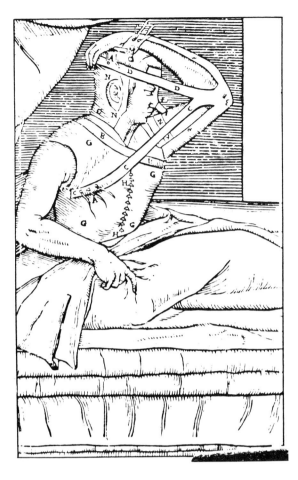

RHINOPLASTY TO THE RESCUE

WHAT must have been a common sight in Restoration England was a flattened saddle nose caused by a gumma of the bony ridge. At least the plays and broadsides of the time have great fun with this souvenir of dissolute sex. A typical victim was Sir William Davenant, Shakespeare's godson, who, according to Aubrey, "gott a terrible clap of a Black handsome wench that lay in Axe-Yard, Westminster . . . which cost him his nose." On the Continent, noses could be restored by the "Italian" method first perfected by Tagliacozzi in 1580. Some regarded the operation as a blasphemous encroachment on the prerogatives of the Creator, a view held by Paré.

HOW TAGLIACOZZI DID IT

THE nose was first scarified with crisscross incisions. A flap of skin of the required shape was then taken from the arm,* and while still attached by a pedicle, was applied to the deformed nose. The arm was then bound to the face. After fourteen days, the pedicle was separated and the flap, now attached securely to the nose, was trimmed and molded into a presentable new nose.

---

* Samuel Butler in his *Hudibras* refers to a more risible part:

> *So learned Taliacotius from*
> *The brawny part of porter's bum*
> *Cut supplemental noses which*
> *Would last as long as parent breach,*
> *But when the date of Nock [porter] was out,*
> *Off dropped the sympathetic snout.*

VENUS AT SEA

'Tween the wind and the water
She ran me ashore . . .
From a sailor's song of 1800

- Aboard sailing ships of the last century, syphilis and gonorrhea alike were called "lady's fever." "There's now more than half our men sick," reported a seaman on board the *Cavalier* in 1850, "most of them with syphilis—blind bubboes abundant. It appears that the Ladies fever has been innoculated into the starboard watch—the mate is but a shell, a mere wreck and most of the men are diseased."

- Eleven days after leaving Tahiti, Dr. George Hamilton, ship's surgeon of the *Pandora*, made an entry in his journal: "We now begin to discover that the ladies of Otaheite had left us many warm tokens of their affection." On the homeward passage the *Pandora* made for the island of Tutuila in the Samoan group. Here, says Hamilton, "One woman amongst many others came on board. She was six feet high, of exquisite beauty, and exact symmetry, being naked and unconscious of being so, added a luster to her charms. . . . Many mouths were watering for her, but Captain Edwards, with great humanity and prudence, had given previous orders that no woman should be permitted to go below, as our health had not quite recovered the shock it had received at Otaheite. . . ."

- Engelbert Kaempfer, a Western medical pioneer in feudal Japan, refers to that country as "the bawdy house of China," because great numbers of Chinese sailors frequented the houses of prostitution that lined the highways of Nagasaki. Forbidden in feudal times, prostitution made rapid strides in China. In 1889 it was reported that "out of 10,000 Chinese houses in the Shanghai foreign settlement, 688 were brothels," many of which made a specialty of entertaining sailors. As many as a quarter of a visiting ship's crew would sometimes be infected.

TREPONEMA PALLIDUM GETS AN ASSIST IN DENMARK

ACCORDING to Parran, free medical advice and treatment were made available for patients with venereal diseases in Denmark as early as 1788. Implementing the new and forward-looking regulations proved onerous, however, as this contemporary account testifies: "We were faced by more than a hundred men, armed with heavy flails, foaming with rage and threatening us; if we did not leave their women and children alone, they told us, they would do us violence."

CONTAGION BY KISS

IN 1579 the London surgeon William Clowes reported that seldom fewer than fifteen out of every twenty patients admitted to Saint Bartholomew's Hospital suffered from syphilis. According to F. E. Cartwright, a possible reason for the extreme contagiousness of the disease may be the fact that syphilis originated in its African analog, yaws, which was then going through a transition phase from the cutaneous nonvenereal stage to the syphilis of today. The primary chancre could have appeared on lip or tongue, and in Tudor times, when greeting was by kiss, not handshake, the disease could have been passed by mouth-to-mouth contact.

CONTAGION BY WHISPER

IT is maintained by some that Henry VIII's cruelty and irrationality late in life can be attributed to general paresis or syphilitic insanity. At least one historian—Hume—believes that the king had Cardinal Wolsey imprisoned because he suspected the cardinal had infected him with syphilis by whispering in his ear.

DR. CONDOM'S SHEATH

To guard yourself from shame or fear,
Votaries to Venus, haste here;
None in my wares e'er found a flaw,
Self-preservation's nature's law.
        From a London handbill advertising condoms

Fallopius in his *De morbo gallico*, published in 1564, wrote the first description of a condom, of which he claimed to be the inventor. For him, the condom was a prophylactic device, and the chapter introducing it is titled "On Preservation from French Caries [syphilis]." The pertinent passage reads, "As often as a man has intercourse, he should wash the genitals, or wipe them with a cloth; afterward he should use a small linen cloth made to fit the glans, and drew forward the prepuce over the glans. . . . I tried the experiment on eleven hundred men, and I call God to witness that not one of them was infected."

In a sense, Fallopius reinvented the condom. Penile protectors were known to the Egyptians, among others. Knowledge of the condom was not widespread in Fallopius's day in Western Europe, and for another hundred years largely ineffective and even magical means were employed

MARY PERKINS, fucceffor to Mrs. Philips, at the Green Canifter in Half-moon-ftreet, oppofite the New Exchange in the Strand, London, makes and fells all forts of fine machines, otherwife called C————MS.
 Dulcis odor lucri ex re quâlibet.
 De quel coté le gain vient.
 L'odeur en eft toujours bonne.
 Alfo perfumes, wafh-balls, foaps, waters, powders, oils, effences, fnuffs, pomatums, cold cream, lip-falves, fealing-wax.—N. B. Ladies' black fticking-plaifter.

WHEREAS fome evil-minded perfon has given out handbills, that the machine warehoufe, the Green Canifter, in Half-moon-ftreet in the Strand, is removed, it is without foundation, and only to prejudice me, this being the old original fhop, ftill continued by the fucceffor of the late Mrs. Philips, where gentlemen's orders fhall be punctually obferved in the beft manner, as ufual.
 N. B. Now called Bedford-ftreet; the Green Canifter is at the feventh houfe on the left hand fide of the way from the Strand.

A seventeenth-century handbill of a maker and vendor of condoms.

to avoid conception and infection. Mme. de Sevigne in a letter to her daughter dated 1671 speaks of a sheath made of gold-beater's skin as "armor against enjoyment, and a spider's web against danger." By the middle of the eighteenth century, sheaths made of animal intestines were being advertised and widely sold in France and England. Mrs. Philips, who did business at No. 5 Orange Court in London, advertised that she had "thirty-five years experience in the business of making and selling machines, commonly called implements of safety, which secures the health of our customers."

Was there a Dr. Condom, reputed inventor of the device that bears his name? The story goes that Charles II, dismayed by the growing number of royal bastards, turned to Dr. Condom for help. The doctor thereupon produced the condom and earned a knighthood. The tale has never been verified.

I looked, and behold a pale horse:
and his name that sat on him was Death, . . .
Revelation 6:8

The Apocalyptic Horsemen. From the Cologne Bible, 1479.

THE FOURTH HORSEMAN

PLAGUE

I buried with my own hands five of my children in a single grave.
Many were buried so superficially that the dogs dug them up and
devoured them. No bells. No tears. This is the end of the world.

Siena 1354

Allegoric representation of the
Demon of the Plague. From H.
von Gersdorf's Feldtbuch der
Wundarzney, *printed by Johann*
Schott, Strassburg, 1540.

QUARANTINING THE BLACK DEATH

And here the Plague began,
  she dying pyson'd many,
Th' infection was so great where it came
  *yet scarce left any.**

Landucci in his diary for 12 May 1498 tells how officers went into the hospitals of plague-stricken Florence and drove the unfortunate sufferers out of the city. "They were actually so cruel as to place hempen rope with a pulley outside the Arte de' Corazzai (Armorers' Guild) to torture those who tried to return. It was a brutal thing and a harsh remedy." When Bologna was stricken, it was surrounded by a virtual *cordon sanitaire*. Guards were posted every three miles around its borders and all those living near were cautioned to be on the alert for strangers crossing unguarded points. They were to "cry in chorus, ring bells and follow the trespassers until their capture."

Houses of the infected were everywhere quarantined. The Lord Mayor of London was directed by the Privy Council in 1630 to "have guard set at the door and a red cross or 'Lord have mercy upon us' writ on the doors to warn passers-by.' " From the archives of Canterbury comes this grim entry: "Gave to Goodman Eccles for watching at Anthony Howe's door in the Morning after the Watch was broken up when his House was first infected with the plague—2d." In Turin, Italy, doors were nailed or bolted on the outside. The rich enjoyed the privilege of guards only if they paid for them. Supplies for these shut up houses were obtained by lowering baskets from windows to the street below.

Defoe in his *Journal of the Plague Year* reports that no fewer than eighteen or twenty watchmen guarding the houses of plague victims were either killed or seriously hurt in the performance of their duties. One family blew up a watchman with gunpowder and escaped through a first-floor window, leaving behind two of their number who were too far gone to flee. Pepys in his diary relates the story of another escape: "a complaint was brought against a man of the town for taking a child from an infected house. It was the child of a very able citizen, a saddler, who had buried all the rest of the children of the Plague, and himself and his wife being shut up

* Lines on Katherine Havitt, died of the plague, 1609, in Bottsford, Leicester.

in despair of escaping, did desire to save the life of the little child, and so prevailed to have it received stark naked into the hands of a friend, who brought it, having put it into fresh new clothes, to Greenwich."

While suspected ships were quarantined, and crew and passengers kept aboard for the required forty days, rats made their way ashore without hindrance. And port officials were often inefficient and corrupt. James Yonge, a ship's surgeon who sailed in the latter half of the seventeenth century, tells how all on board his ship upon landing at Messina in Sicily were directed to a small quadrangle "where an old fellow, perusing a bill of health we had from Genoa, puts on a great pair of spectacles as big as saucers, and, making each man expose his groins and armpits, he looks into them and with a stick thrusts in them, where finding nothing we are allowed prattick,* and then went into town." (At Genoa, not having had a bill of health from their previous port of call, Yonge "drew one up as from the Governor of Newfoundland and signed myself as Secretary.")

Ignorance often went hand in hand with greed. The *Great St. Anthony* had taken on some Turkish passengers in Tripoli, one of whom died. His corpse was taken up with iron hooks to avoid contagion and thrown into the sea. Within days the two sailors who had disposed of the body died. When the ship reached Marseilles, the captain let it be known that they had died of food poisoning, perhaps because the chief magistrate of the city had a considerable investment in the cargo. In any case, the plague brought by the *Great St. Anthony* was to cost 90,000 lives, but the regent's physician insisted when over 500 were already in their graves that the cause of death was merely "a very ordinary malignant fever caused by poor nutrition of the indigent." His remedy: "hire some violinists and trombone players and have them play in every neighborhood to give young people the chance to forget sadness and melancholy."

---

* *Pratique:* permission granted to a ship to call at a port.

FOR A RUTHLESS SCOURGE, RUTHLESS MEASURES

- Archbishop Giovanni Visconti, despot of Milan, took ruthless action to contain the inevitable. When plague was reported in neighboring towns, he commanded that the first houses in which the disease claimed a victim were to be walled up with all the inhabitants inside, enclosing the quick, the dead, and the stricken in one common tomb.

- In Leicestershire, the lord of the manor burned and razed the village of Norelay to the ground when plague occurred there. According to the historian Barbara Tuchman, he apparently succeeded in his object of preventing spread of the disease to the manor house since his direct descendants still occupy it.

- Guglielmo Piazza, Commissioner of Health in Milan, was seen walking down the street one summer evening in 1630. While strolling he made notes in a tablet, using the inkhorn at his belt. Every now and then he paused to wipe his ink-stained fingers on the walls of houses as he passed. Neighborhood women accused him before the City Council of smearing dwellings with plague "poison." He was arrested, his flesh torn with red-hot pincers, his right hand cut off, his bones broken, and his body stretched on the wheel. After six hours of dreadful suffering, he was burned at the stake together with "accomplices" whose names had been elicited by torture.

- In 1633 it was decreed by the seneschal of Champagne that "at the least sign of contagion, beggars and vagabonds must come and report their sickness under pain of being shot down by arquebuses." Paupers who came for food to the gates of convents, hospitals, and great houses were the chief victims of this bloody draconian law.

BACTERIAL WARFARE c. 1350

THE Black Death reached Europe in the autumn of 1348 from a ravaged Middle East. When the city of Caffa was besieged by Tartars, the pestilence seized the invading army and thousands died. The desperate survivors catapulted the putrefying bodies of their fellow soldiers over the battlements. Within the space of days, "the last of the besieged died as horribly as the last of the besiegers."

WARRING AGAINST INFECTION—1585

IN 1585 the magistrates of Aberdeen set up three gibbets "that in case any infected person arrive or repair by sea or land to this Burgh, or in case any indweller of this Burgh receive, house or harbour, or give meat or drink to the infected person or persons, the man be hanged and the woman drowned."

KEEPING THE PLAGUE AT BAY

THE CITIZENRY

- Treatment was useless, and lone survivors watched helplessly as whole families caught the taint and died. Between May and September of 1401, there were 11,000 plague deaths in Florence. The Florentine Goro Dati recalls the horror twenty years later: "It began with the man-servant Piccino . . . within three days our slave Martha died; on the 1 April my daughter Sandra, and on the fifth Antonia. We left the house and went into one opposite. In a few days Veronica died. Again we moved and went to live in Via Chiara. Here Vendecca and Pippa were taken ill, and on 1 August both went to Heaven. They all died of the plague, Heaven help them!"

- In many places the panic-stricken population simply denied the presence of the plague, and few were brave enough to announce the truth. In 1630 a physician in the town of Busto Arizio in Italy was fatally shot for diagnosing plague in his patients and revealing the fact.

- Staffing lazarettos or pest houses was a serious problem; providing them with adequate facilities was another. In the San Miniato pest house at Florence in 1630 there were only eighty-two beds for 412 female patients, so that an average of five women shared a single bed. In the men's section there were ninety-three beds for 312 patients. During the plague of 1630, Cardinal Spada visited the pest houses of Bologna and recorded what he saw there: "Here you will see people lament, others cry, others strip themselves to the skin, others die, others become black and deformed, others lose their minds. Here you are overwhelmed by intolerable smells. Here you cannot walk but among corpses. Here you feel naught but the constant horror of death. This is the faithful replica of hell. . . ."

- In their insane fear, the citizenry turned with vicious ferocity on the Jews. Wherever plague struck in medieval times, the Jews were accused of poisoning the wells. The Chronicle of Jean de Venette records the indiscriminate slaughter of thousands in the plague years 1348–1349. "The unshaken, if fatuous, constancy of the men and their wives was remarkable. For mothers hurled their first into the fire that they may not be baptized and then leaped in after them to burn with their husbands and children."

THE PHYSICIANS

- Doctors—with many honorable exceptions—observed the prescription adopted by the affluent—go quick, go far, and return late. In Prussia a medical ordinance of 1693 forbade doctors from leaving towns where they practiced when plague struck. However, they were excused from entering infected premises if they undertook to prescribe from outside on the basis of information provided by those who had access to the infected. During the plague of 1639, the doctors of Bologna, citing the death of many of their number in little more than two months, suggested in a petition to health officers that patients be treated at a "distance." The barber surgeon officiating in the lazaretto was to shout from the windows the sex and condition of the patient and the stage of illness, while from a safe distance the doctor would shout back the recommended treatment.

- As early as 1460 a treatise on the plague advised doctors to stand as far off from patients as possible with their faces turned toward an open door or window, "especially if it is toward the north." In later centuries physicians adopted protective costumes. The one most favored featured long black robes with pointed hoods, leather gloves, boots, and masks with long beaks filled with begamot oil. At their waists they wore amulets of dried blood and ground-up toads. Before approaching a plague victim, they doused themselves with vinegar and chewed angelica.

- Epidemics have always meant lush times for quack and empiric. Defoe says that during the great London plague of 1665, "the posts of houses and corners of streets were plastered over with doctors' bills." Here is a typical specimen: "An experienced physician who has long studied the doctrine of antidotes against all sorts of poisons and infection, has, after forty years' practice, arrived to such skills as may, with God's blessing, direct persons how to prevent their being touched by any contagious distemper whatsoever. He directs the poor gratis."

THE CLERGY

- The Jesuit bishop of Marseilles, when plague struck in 1720, proclaimed strict safety rules for his priests. They were to turn their backs on parishioners when hearing confession so as to avoid infectious breath. Extreme unction, a sacrament much in demand, was to be delivered at a distance, with the priest extending a rod from which dangled pieces of cotton impregnated with holy oil.

- In southern France mortality from the Black Death was so great in the first half of the fourteenth century that the pope consecrated the river Rhône at Avignon, so that corpses flung into the river might be considered to have had Christian burial.

- An amulet worn by Pope Adrian against the plague contained two ounces of powdered toad, one-half ounce of arsenic, one drachm of pearl, and one-half drachm each of coral, zircon, and emerald, all powdered. The pope at Avignon in 1349 stopped all sessions of court, locked himself in his room, allowed none to approach him, and had a fire blazing before him around the clock.

THE GRAVE DIGGERS

In Italy.   From Luca Landucci's diary: "15 August. The following case happened. At the church of San Pagolo, in the churchyard outside it, the grave diggers were burying someone, and one of them dropped his keys into the grave, and went down into it to get them; but there was such a stench that he died there before they could draw him out again."

In England.   Daniel Defoe tells how country folk disposed of the bodies of those townsmen who, "grown stupid and melancholy by their misery," had crept into hedge or bush to die. With long hooked poles they would drag the corpses into pits, "and throw the earth in from as far as they could cast it, to cover them, taking notice how the wind blew, and so coming on to that side which the seamen call to windward, that the scent of the bodies might blow from them."

In France.   In 1720, nearly one thousand convicts and galley slaves were forcibly freed from chain and cell to act as grave diggers in plague-stricken Marseilles. These "crows," as they were called, were promised their freedom if they survived. About one-third died. Stendhal, in his *Travels in the South of France*, tells of the self-sacrifice of a certain Chevalier Roze, a "plain citizen," who, outraged by the sight of more than a thousand corpses lying exposed for two weeks, led 200 soldiers and 300 crows to the scene. When the latter recoiled, Roze dismounted and picked up a corpse in his arms to encourage them. Of the crows, only two survived. Roze emerged from the experience with only a slight illness.

PLAGUE

PLAGUY ACTIVITIES

DECAMPING

FROM a notice posted in 1665: "Nicholas Hurst, an upholsterer, over against the Rose Tavern, whose maid servant dyed lately of the Sickness, fled on Monday last out of his house, taking with him several Goods and Household Stuff and was afterwards followed by one Doctor Cary and Richard Bayle with his wife and family, who lodged in the same house. Whereof we are commanded to give this Publick Notice, that diligent search may be made for them and the houses in which any of their persons or goods shall be found may be shut up by the next Justice of the Peace, or other of his Majesty's Officers of Justice! . . ."

GIBBETING

UNDER Mary Stuart, David Duly, tailor of Edinburgh, kept his wife "sick in the contagious sickness of pestilence four days in his house," and heard mass "among the clean people" without informing the town officers. Duly was condemned to be hanged before his own door. The rope broke, and he fell from the gibbet. Because he was a poor man with small children, "for pity of him the Provost, Bailies and Counsel banished the said David from the town all the days of his life, and not to come therein in the mean time under pain of death."

QUARANTINING

THE Dutch imposed a strict quarantine on all shipping from the East when plague swept across Europe in 1721. They went so far as to burn valuable cargo and required that sailors on suspected ships swim ashore naked.

DISPOSING OF THE DEAD

THE plague of Justinian, says Cartwright, "may have been the most terrible that has ever harrowed the world." At its height, 10,000 died daily. Grave digging was abandoned before this inexorable tide of death. Roofs were lifted from the towers of forts and the towers were then filled with corpses. "Ships were loaded with the dead, rowed out to sea, and abandoned."

CONTAGION BY LETTER

IN 1665

THE plagues that devastated Europe from 1400 to 1700 gave common folk and authorities alike a healthy fear of infection, a fear sometimes extending even to paper. Here is an excerpt from a letter written during the great plague of London: "Henceforth you must not look to be supplied with correspondence as you were wont. The plague is in the parish . . . and it grows very dangerous on both sides to continue an intercourse of Letters; not knowing what hands they pass through before they come to those to whom they are sent."

IN 1720

MALTA, which suffered a plague epidemic in 1675–1676 that took 8,732 lives, by 1720 instituted regulations that included the following: "Dispatches brought in by ships are not to be received unless they are first perfumed. The packets and letters are to be unpacked, disinfected by a double perfume and left exposed to the latter for twenty-four hours." Belief that contagion could inhere in paper still weighed heavily with the authorities when plague again visited Malta in 1813. Wood, in contrast to paper, was thought incapable of carrying contagion. Tablets of wood were used for writing wills, receipts, and other documents.

IN 1900

WRITING in 1961, a correspondent of the *British Medical Journal* notes that this "fallacy of epidemiological thought" was still alive at the turn of the century. He relates how his father, a ship's surgeon, was required to take the ship's papers ashore at Algiers before anyone was allowed to land. "He was rowed to the medical officer's office. The papers were then handed through an inspection window, and opened out with two pairs of metal forceps which had previously been disinfected by flaming."

LEPROSY

LEPERS IN FEUDAL JAPAN

FEUDAL Japan treated lepers with unspeakable barbarity. When begging could no longer suffice to keep body and soul together, they were abandoned in the streets, and sometimes at year's end they were rounded up and slaughtered. The samurai used the grisly occasion to practice their swordsmanship.

LEPERS IN FEUDAL ENGLAND

IN 1375 the porters stationed at the city's gates swore before London's mayor and recorder that they would "well and trustily" keep the gates and posterns, and "will not allow lepers to enter the city or to stay in the same . . . and if anyone shall bring any leprous person to any such gate or postern aforesaid, or if any leper or lepers shall come there and wish to enter, such person shall be prohibited by the porter from entering."

SEPARATIO LEPROSARUM

LEPERS in the Middle Ages were cast out of the world by ecclesiastical authority in a solemn ceremony called *separatio leprosarum.* His face covered by a black veil, the leper knelt before the altar. The officiating priest then sprinkled earth from a burial ground on the leper's head while intoning the fateful words, "Be thou dead to the world, but live again in God."

These words were a preamble to a long litany of prohibitions. "I forbid you to enter churches, or go into a market, or a mill or bakehouse, or into any assemblies of people. Also I forbid you to wash your hands or even any of your belongings in a spring or stream of water of any kind; and if you are thirsty you must drink water from your cup. . . . Also I forbid you ever henceforth to go out without your leper's dress [a black cloak and veil], that you may be recognized by others; and you must not go outside your house unshod. Also I forbid you wherever you may be to touch anything you may wish to buy." The leper was forbidden to reply to anyone "who may question you, except you step off the road to leeward." He must not travel the highway, and when on a path, he must not touch hedges or bushes on either side without first putting on gloves. To warn of his approach, he must carry a bell or a pair of clappers at all times.

LONDON EXPELS ITS LEPERS

KING Edward in 1346 signed a royal mandate "enjoining the exclusion of Leprous persons" from London. "Some lepers," says the edict, "endeavoring to contaminate others with that abominable blemish (that to their own wretched solace, they may have the more fellows in suffering), as well as in the way of mutual communications, and by the contagion of their polluted breath, as by carnal intercourse with women in stews and other secret places, do sicken persons who are sound. . . ." Lepers were given fifteen days to get out of town and "betake themselves to places in the country."

LICE AS A WEAPON OF WAR

THE role of lice in the pathogenesis of leprosy seems to have been well known among one primitive people. Henschen quotes a Batak warrior in the Dutch East Indies who tells how his people collected lice from the bodies of lepers and then spread them in the enemy's camp. He deplores the decline in the number of lepers and the ending of the native war. "For us natives life has now lost all excitement."

SMALLPOX BEFORE JENNER

MEDICAL PROGRESS ENCOUNTERS A GRENADO

OPPOSITION to inoculation could be ferocious in the first decades of the eighteenth century. Cotton Mather, who took up the cudgels for the practice in New England, discloses in his diary how a kinsman of his, a minister staying in Mather's home that he might be inoculated, was attacked with a "grenado" thrown into his chamber "around three o'clock in the morning." It failed to go off. Tied to the bomb was this message: "Cotton Mather, You dog, damn you: I'll inoculate you with this, with a pox to you!"

SMALLPOX AND VARIOLATION

. . . the old woman comes with a nutshell full of the matter of the best sort of smallpox and asks what veins you please to have opened . . . and puts into the vein as much venom as can lie upon the head of her needle. . . .
                    Lady Mary Montague in a letter from Adrianople, 1717.

On 8 July 1875, Boston merchant Joseph Barrell wrote to his friend Colonel Wentworth, "Mr. Storer has invited Mrs. Martin to take the small pox in his house; if Mrs. Wentworth desires to get rid of her fears in the same way we will accommodate her in the best way we can. I've several friends that I've invited, and none of them will be more welcome than Mrs. Wentworth." All over New England the more or less well-to-do were "taking the smallpox" to order at smallpox parties like Joseph Barrell's. Such parties were the occasion for much friendly socializing, and as one writer puts it, the participants "took their various purifying and sudorific medicines in cheerful concert, were 'grafted' together, 'broke out' together, were feverish together, sweat together, scaled off together, and convalesced together." And we are told that "many a pretty and sentimental love affair sprang up between mutually 'pock-fretten' New Englanders."

Available, too, were smallpox hospitals where patients paid from three to fifteen dollars for a week's lodging, food, care and inoculation. Daniel Sutton had a home of this sort in London. It was popular with the rich, and the enterprising operator pocketed 6,500 pounds in a single year. But these cheerful developments came after the disease had proved fatal to untold thousands and had disfigured many more. Half of Boston's 12,000 inhabitants contracted the disease in 1721. Of these, 844 died. Cotton Mather,* who learned of variolation as it was practiced in Africa from one of his slaves, tried to mobilize the physicians of the city for a campaign of immunization. Only Zabdiel Boylston responded. He inoculated his son, and then proceeded to inoculate 200 more Bostonians despite press, public, and outraged colleagues.

Opposition to variolation was fierce and vociferous on the Continent as well. "Smallpox is a visitation from God and originates in men, but cowpox is produced by presumptuous, impious man" was a typical outcry. American Indians, who had suffered so much from the ravages of the disease, knew better. An Indian tribe sent Jenner a belt and a string of wampum "in token of our acceptance of your precious gift, and we beseech the Great Spirit to take care of you in this world, and in the land of spirits."

INOCULATION.

THE subscriber respectfully informs the public that he has lately opened an Inoculation, at the pleasantly situated hospital in Glastenbury; Gentlemen and Ladies who wish to have the Small-Pox by this safe and easy method, may be boarded, and have faithful attendance paid them, by their obedient,
                    ASAPH COLEMAN.
March 23, 1797.

---

* A puritanical theologian who preached hell-fire and brimstone, Mather "backed into modernity."

Variolation was not to be generally accepted until well after 1750, and the favored treatment continued to be bleeding and purging. This newspaper advertisement of 1755 was typical of hundreds:

> **WANTED A NURSEMAID. None need apply who cannot bring a good character from their last place, and has had the Small pox.**

Two decades later, inoculation was the thing:

> **WANTED an Apprentice to an eminent Surgeon in full practice in the county of Suffolk. If he has not had the Small-Pox, it is expected he will be inoculated for it before he enters on business. Enquire of John Fox, at Dedham, Essex.**

The tide was turning, with the assistance, curiously enough, of Europe's royalty. In Russia, Catherine the Great had herself and her son inoculated. Frederick the Great induced an English physician, William Baylies, to introduce the practice into Prussia in the teeth of strong opposition from the Berlin medical fraternity. Organized resistance to inoculation in France collapsed with the death of Louis XV, a smallpox victim. His frightened successor, Louis XVI, lost no time in having the royal family inoculated. Maria Theresa of Austria was another victim of the disease who saw the light. Stricken at age fifty-two, she engaged a Dutch physician after her recovery to inoculate all the members of the imperial household.

A smallpox epidemic in Mexico in 1538 inspired this portrayal of the victims. (From the original in the Bibliothèque de Genève.)

ISOLATING THE VICTIMS

ATTEMPTS to isolate individual cases of smallpox were first made in Colonial America in 1667. In that year Northampton County, Virginia, proclaimed a warning to all families infected with smallpox to allow no member "to go forth their doors until their full cleansing, that is to say, thirtie dayes after thei receive the sd. smpox."

In 1721 HMS *Seahorse* arrived in Boston from the West Indies. She was challenged before docking because of a report of a sailor "sick with the smallpox." He was taken to a house near shore. The selectmen provided a nurse to care for him, with orders not to leave. A red flag reading "God have mercy on this house" was raised and two "prudent persons" were employed to stand guard and prevent entrance or egress.

BRITAIN VICTIMIZES THE INDIANS

SMALLPOX spread like wildfire through the Indian population of America shortly after the arrival of Cortés and his conquistadors. In at least one case, the disease was used as a weapon against the extremely susceptible natives. In 1763 Lord Jeffrey Amherst, a British general, ordered that blankets used by smallpox victims be distributed among Indians favoring the French in the French and Indian Wars.

SPAIN MAKES AMENDS

IN 1803 the corvette *Maria de Pita* sailed from La Coruna with ten doctors and twenty-two children, all of whom had been exposed to cowpox. The children, who were accompanied by mothers and nurses, were to keep the virus alive by successive inoculations during the crossing. They were declared children of the country by Venezuela, and the government undertook to take charge of their education. Says one historian, "Vaccination was the first important thing done for the Indians since the laws of Charles V."

IMMUNITY BY INSPIRATION

BEFORE Jenner, inoculation was widely practiced in the Near East. In China, direct contact was avoided. A powder made from the crusts shed by smallpox patients recovering from the disease was used as an inhalant. As with the usual technique, the patient would develop a mild case and enjoy immunity with little or no scarring.

EXILING THE INOCULATED

IN the smallpox epidemic of 1721 in Boston, of 6,000 affected, 900 died. In that same year a mass inoculation took place in Boston—the first in the English-speaking world. Fatalities were far fewer among these Bostonians than in the public at large. Nevertheless, the last six to be inoculated were in such great danger from violence at the hands of the mob, they had to be spirited away to an island in Boston Bay for safety. Had the inoculated been isolated, there would have been no danger of contagion and no reason for mob fury. But in many instances their mild cases did become foci of infection among those who had no immunity.

SAFEGUARDING AN INOCULATOR

IN 1768 Dr. Thomas Dimsdale was invited to Russia to inoculate Catherine the Great and her son, the Grand Duke Paul, against smallpox, a disease the sovereign regarded with horror and dread. To safeguard Dimsdale from the rage of her subjects should the procedure end disastrously, Catherine arranged for relays of horses to carry him all the way from St. Petersburg to the frontier. Catherine's inoculation was done in secret with variolous matter taken from a youngster named Alexander Markov. Nine days later, it was the Grand Duke's turn. The procedure in both cases was successful. Markov was ennobled and the dates of the royal inoculations were declared national holidays. In all, some 140 members of Catherine's court underwent the procedure.

INOCULATION UNDER STRESS

LADY Mary Montague had her daughter inoculated while four leading doctors looked on. They had been charged by the government to report their findings. In one of her letters Lady Mary said they were so hostile, she dared not leave the child alone with them.

CHOLERA

THE HORROR OF IT

EVERYWHERE cholera struck there was horror. When British troops were shipped from Bulgaria to the Crimea, cholera embarked with them. Those who died of the disease "were flung into the sea with weights at their feet, but the weights were too light; as the bodies decomposed they rose to the surface. The weights kept them upright, and they floated, head and shoulders out of the water, hideous in the sun."

HOW NOT TO TREAT IT

IN America during the epidemic of 1832 doctors resorted to laudanum, calomel, and bleeding. One Louisiana physician boasted that he had drawn "blood enough to float the *General Jackson* steamboat, and gave calomel enough to freight her." Another gravely proposed as the best method for checking choleraic diarrhea the plugging of the anus with a soft velvet cork. An English physician suggested that the "blood may be kept circulating by placing the patient on a board and keeping up a rocking, see-saw to and fro movement from 80 to 100 times a minute." The one decisive therapy—replacement of body fluids—was not employed before our own century.

A victim of Vibrio cholerae. *From a woodcut by Posada.*

CHOLEROPHOBIA IN ACTION

CHARLES Greville notes in his diary for 1 April 1832 that the London populace refused to believe that an epidemic then in its early stages was indeed cholera. "Anti-cholerites," as they were called, declined to cremate victims of the disease directly after death and otherwise frustrated the recommendations of the authorities. Greville describes an incident in which "a patient who was being removed with his own consent had been taken out of his sedan chair by the mob and carried back [to his dwelling], the chair broken, and the bearers and surgeon hardly escaping with their lives."

Distrust of the medical profession because of grave snatching persisted into the cholera years. The belief was abroad that the cholera hospital had been founded for the express purpose of providing bodies for dissection. When a boy's corpse was found buried without its head, a crowd gathered, forced open the hospital gates, carried away a number of patients, and encouraged others to leave. Four troops of hussars were needed to restore order.

OF CHOLERA AND PUMP HANDLES

DURING an epidemic of cholera in London in 1854, John Snow, a pioneer in inhalation anesthesia and obstetrician to Queen Victoria, carefully mapped the incidence of the disease. He concluded that most of the victims had drunk water from the Broad Street pump, which piped in supplies from the Thames. Parish officials were convinced by Snow to remove the pump handle. The epidemic quickly dwindled.

GIVING CHOLERA THE SLIP

TURGENEV'S mother had so great a fear of cholera she is said to have been borne around the grounds of her very extensive estate in a glass-enclosed sedan chair.

SCURVY

"TERRIBLE HAVOC" AT SEA

ON September 1740 Commodore George Anson began his mission to "annoy and distress" the Spaniards in South American coastal waters. He sailed with six ships and a total complement of 1,955 men. A little short of two years later he returned with only the flagship and 904 survivors of the original crew. Scurvy had killed 1,051 men, whose symptoms described by Anson included lassitude, gum lesions, joint pain, ulcers, mental changes, convulsions, and sudden death.

DR. JOHN WOODALL HAD THE ANSWER

IN his *The Surgeon's Mate*, Dr. John Woodall insists that "the Chirurgeon must not faile to perswade the Purser in all places where they touch in the Indies to provide themselves of the juyce of oranges, limes or lemmons. . . ." Before Woodall, Admiral Sir Richard Hawkins found citrus fruit to be a specific against scurvy. And James Lind drove the point home with the first dietetic experiment on record aboard HMS *Salisbury* in 1746. Fifty years later the British Admiralty began victualling their ships with antiscorbutics.

THE CHINESE HAD THE ANSWER IN 1405

DURING the reign of Emperor Lung Lo, enormous nine-masted "treasure ships" were launched. Each was equipped with tubs in which vegetables were grown. These were stored on the lower decks.

TAKING NO CHANCES WITH SCURVY

IN 1845 Sir John Franklin's third polar expedition left England with a complement of 129 men. To prevent scurvy, his two ships carried 9,300 pounds of lemon juice in kegs. Every man aboard was required to drink an ounce daily—in the presence of an officer.

GOLDEN TUBERS

DURING the Klondike gold rush, scurvy was prevalent in the camps of the sourdoughs. The only readily available source of vitamin C was the humble potato, and an enterprising few found it more lucrative than prospecting. They cornered the market and hoarded the supply until desperate sufferers gladly exchanged gold for potatoes, weight for weight.

A "CURE" FOR SCURVY IN 1521

WHEN Magellan landed off the coast of Guam, the natives swarmed aboard his flagship, stealing everything but "the paint off the deck." At daybreak Magellan attacked the native village in an effort to obtain fresh food and water. Pigafetta in his memoirs notes that some of the sick on board begged the landing party to bring them a few buckets full of the natives' guts as a sure cure for scurvy.

THE SWEATING SICKNESS

FLUID REPLACEMENT AND INSPIRATION SAVES MARGARET ROPER

WHEN Sir Thomas More's daughter Margaret fell victim to the sweating sickness, all despaired of her life. Her fond father went to chapel to pray, "Where incontinent came into his mind that a clyster should be the only way to help her." It was administered "unto her sleeping." She awoke and miraculously recovered.

A KING GETS OUT OF TOWN

THE sweating sickness (*Sudor Anglicus*) struck England on six separate occasions and northern Europe once. It has never been heard of again—fortunately, for it was virulent and deadly. Du Bellai, French Ambassador at the English court, wrote in 1528, "One of the filles de chambre of Mlle Boleyn was attacked on Tuesday by the sweating sickness. The King left in great haste, and went a dozen miles off. . . . This disease is the easiest in the world to die of. You have a slight pain in the head and at the heart; all at once you begin to sweat. There is no need for a physician: for if you uncover yourself the least in the world, or cover yourself a little too much, you are taken off without languishing. It is true that if you merely put your hand out of bed during the first 24 hours . . . you become stiff as a poker."

ONE DOCTOR TAKES ON A DELUSION

THE delusion that those afflicted must perspire for twenty-four hours without pause undoubtedly killed many who might otherwise have recovered. Patients were put to bed under piles of blankets and furs, windows were tightly shut, and sickrooms heated by roaring fires. Hecker mentions a doctor of Zwickau who went from house to house dragging patients out of their beds and into the cool air with his own hands.

168

YELLOW FEVER

DR. RUSH GIVES SOME ADVICE

WHEN the devastating yellow fever epidemic of 1793 struck Philadelphia and environs, Benjamin Rush stayed on and ministered to the sick without rest. Despite the therapeutic carnage his treatment entailed, he became a popular hero. On one occasion his coach was stopped at Kensington by a crowd of hundreds who begged him to visit their homes and care for their sick. Rush stood up in his curricle and addressed the throng. "I treat my patients successfully by bloodletting and copious purging with calomel and jalop, and I advise you, my good friends, to use the same remedies." Someone shouted, "What, bleed and purge everyone?" "Yes!" cried the doctor. "Bleed and purge all Kensington!"

SHOOTING DOWN YELLOW FEVER

DURING the epidemic in Philadelphia, citizens kept vinegar-soaked handkerchiefs to their noses, hung bags of camphor around their necks, and carried lengths of tarred rope on their persons. "Those who could locked themselves indoors and chewed garlic while they went from room to room whitewashing interior walls." Others burnt gunpowder in their rooms, and then more and more took to shooting from windows. So many citizens were wounded, the mayor forbade the practice.

YELLOW FEVER, THE CENSUS, AND HOLY SCRIPTURE

THE yellow fever epidemic of 1712 in New York was attributed by large numbers of the faithful to a census taken the previous year. "For the Lord had spoken to Moses, saying only thou shalt not number the tribe of Levi, neither take the sum of them among the children of Israel." So widespread and obstinate was this belief that the governor of New York was defeated in his efforts to take a census of the colony's population in 1713.

TYPHUS

TYPHUS AND THE BLACK ASSIZES

IN 1577 a Black Assize was convened at Oxford to hear the case of Rowland Jencks, accused of treason and of profanation of the Protestant religion. Jencks, condemned to have his ears cut off, survived for thirty-three years, but the gaol fever he introduced into the courtroom carried off the Chief Baron of the Exchequer, a sergeant-at-law, five justices of the peace, two sheriffs, one knight, and most of the jury. The 1577 Black Assizes was followed by five others. The toll at the last of these, in London's Old Bailey, included the Lord Mayor, an alderman, two judges, an under-sheriff, the jury, and many lesser court personages.

GAOL FEVER AND EARLY AIR-CONDITIONING

LONDON'S ancient Newgate Prison was a notorious breeding ground of typhus. Its fearsome crowding and lack of hygienic facilities were ideal for the body louse, carrier of the causative microorganisms. In its rat-infested cells, more men died of typhus (also known as gaol fever or putrid fever) than through the execution of the law. A ventilator system devised by Stephen Hales reduced deaths from gaol fever to a considerable extent. It featured a rooftop "windmill" that carried air to the interior.

FIGHTING TYPHUS ON SHIPBOARD

EMIGRANT ships in the first decades of the nineteenth century were notorious for their unhealthful conditions. Pervasive filth of every description along with fearful overcrowding made ship's fever (typhus) a prevalent scourge on shipboard. Action taken by the authorities to ameliorate the situation was not calculated to change matters much. It was decided to fine a ship's master ten dollars for every corpse found on board his vessel after it made port.

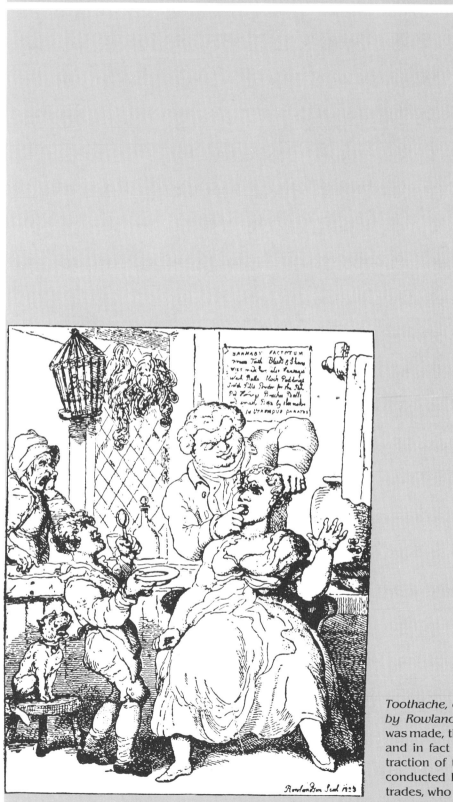

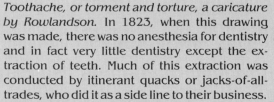

Toothache, or torment and torture, a caricature by Rowlandson. In 1823, when this drawing was made, there was no anesthesia for dentistry and in fact very little dentistry except the extraction of teeth. Much of this extraction was conducted by itinerant quacks or jacks-of-all-trades, who did it as a side line to their business.

AFFLICTIONS —
MAJOR AND MINOR

GLUTTONY AND BIBULOSITY

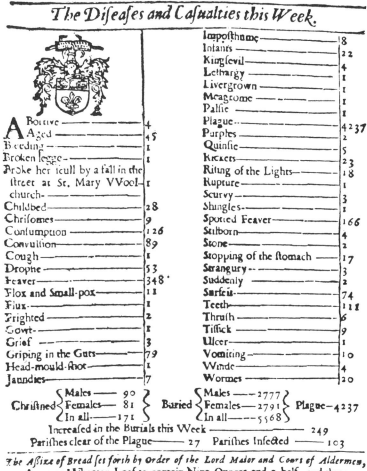

The Diseases and Casualties this Week.

Abortive	4	Impostume	8
Aged	45	Infants	22
Bleeding	1	Kingsevil	4
Broken legge	1	Lethargy	1
Broke her scull by a fall in the street at St. Mary VVoolchurch	1	Livergrown	1
		Meagrome	1
		Palsie	1
Childbed	28	Plague	4237
Chrisomes	9	Purples	2
Consumption	126	Quinsie	5
Convulsion	89	Rickets	23
Cough	1	Rising of the Lights	18
Dropsie	53	Rupture	1
Feaver	348	Scurvy	3
Flox and Small-pox	11	Shingles	1
Flux	1	Spotted Feaver	166
Frighted	2	Stilborn	4
Gowt	1	Stone	2
Grief	3	Stopping of the stomach	17
Griping in the Guts	79	Strangury	3
Head-mould-shot	1	Suddenly	2
Jaundies	7	Surfeit	74
		Teeth	111
		Thrush	6
		Tissick	9
		Ulcer	1
		Vomiting	10
		Winde	4
		Wormes	20

Christned	Males — 90	Buried	Males — 2777	Plague—4237
	Females — 81		Females — 2791	
	In all —— 171		In all —— 5568	

Increased in the Burials this Week —————— 249

Parishes clear of the Plague —— 27   Parishes Infected —— 103

The Assize of Bread set forth by Order of the Lord Maior and Coart of Aldermen, A penny Wheaten Loaf to contain Nine Ounces and a half, and three half-penny White Loaves the like weight.

The London Bill of Mortality for 15–22 August 1665 lists seventy-four deaths from "surfeit," a polite term for overeating. Said Addison in the *Spectator*, "When I behold a Fashionable Table set out in all its Magnificence, I fancy that I see Gouts and Dropsies, Fevers and Lethargies, with other innumerable Distempers lying in Ambuscade among the dishes."

The diseases and casualties during the plague year. A bill of mortality for the week August 15 to 22, 1665. During this week 171 children were christened, but 5,568 persons died, and 4,237 of these deaths were attributed to the plague.

174

ZEALOUS TRENCHERMEN, COMBUSTIBLE ALCOHOLICS

THIRTY-THREE DISHES, ONE MEAL

TO illustrate the persistence in England of the heroic banquets of medieval times, Mead catalogs the incredible menu of a great feast at Knole in Kent, 3 July 1636. Listed are nine varieties of meat, seven of fish, and four of fowl. Only one vegetable is mentioned: stewed potatoes.

1. Rice pottage
2. Barley broth
3. Buttered pickrell
4. Butter and burned eggs
5. Boiled teats
6. Roast tongues
7. Bream
8. Perches
9. Chine of veal roast
10. Hash of mutton with anchovies
11. Great pike
12. Fish chuits
13. Roast venison in blood
14. Capons
15. Wild ducks
16. Salmon, whole hot
17. Tenches, boiled
18. Crabs
19. Tench pie
20. Venison pasty of a doe
21. Swans
22. Herons
23. Cold lamb
24. Custard
25. Venison, boiled
26. Potatoes, stewed
27. Salad
28. Redeeve pie, hot
29. Almond pudding
30. Made dishes
31. Boiled salad
32. Pig, whole
33. Rabbits

AVERSION THERAPY FOR A GOURMAND

ABERNETHY (1764–1831), celebrated in his time as an innovative surgeon, seems to have practiced an early type of aversion therapy. To reform an obese and overfed alderman with whom he dined, he had the footman place a large bowl on a sideboard, into which the servant was to throw surreptitiously a like quantity of whatever he served his master. After dinner, the stout trencherman was invited to look into the bowl—a nauseous mess of mock turtle, turbot, roast beef, turkey, sausages, cakes, wine, ale, fruits, and cheese.

DEATH BY FIRE(WATER)

CREDIT for the "discovery" of the spontaneous combustion of chronic alcoholics usually goes to the French surgeon Le Cat (1700–1768), but mention of the phenomenon occurs as early as 1604. The scientific legend Le Cat helped perpetuate survived right into the second half of the nineteenth century. Charles Dickens makes an alcoholic in his novel *The Bleak House* a victim of spontaneous combustion, and in the preface to that work he says, "I do not wilfully or negligently mislead my readers, and I took pains to investigate the subject." He cites some thirty cases, in one of which, attested to by Le Cat, a man convicted of murdering his wife in Rheims in 1725 was ultimately acquitted when the cause of death was found to be spontaneous combustion brought on by excessive drinking.

THREE TIPPLERS AND A TEETOTALER

DUKE OF NORFOLK (1746–1775)

THE convivial duke would on occasion become immovable in his chair at his London club. He would then request that a bell be rung three times—the signal for four servants to enter with a kind of litter, consisting of four equidistant belts fastened together by a transverse one. Slipping the litter under him, the servants "removed his enormous bulk, with a gentle swaying motion, up to his apartment."

HENRI MARIE RAYMOND DE TOULOUSE-LAUTREC (1864–1901)

TOWARD the end of his short life, Toulouse-Lautrec drank to excess on the principle that "one should drink little but often." To discourage his addiction to drink, his family provided him with a bodyguard, "but his will dominated that of his protector, whom he brought home on one occasion completely inebriated."

ALGERNON CHARLES SWINBURNE

FORD Madox Ford's grandfather, the painter Ford Madox Brown, was "the most benevolent of human beings." A good friend of Swinburne's, he had a tape inscribed with his address sewn onto the poet's lapel. The precaution was necessary. Brown was frequently roused by a cabman with the announcement, "I've got your master very drunk in my keb." A very fuddled Swinburne would be dumped in the upstairs bathtub, where he was dosed by the servants with strong coffee and smelling salts. Certain hackney coach drivers made a good living in those spacious times by cruising about late at night and driving intoxicated gentlemen home.

JOSEPH LIVESEY

LIVESEY was prostrated with rheumatic fever and was told by his doctor that his only hope of recovery was to drink brandy. The sick man, a leader in the English temperance movement and founder of the first total abstinence magazine in 1834, heaved himself up in bed and roared, "I will not drink the stuff! . . . If I am to die, I will die now!" Livesey lived to the age of ninety, unsullied by the cup that cheers.

GOUT—THREE VICTIMS, ONE BENEFICIARY

DICING AND GOUT

HORACE in his Seventh Satire, Book II, tells of old Volanerius, "the jester." He was so badly afflicted with gout in his fingers he could not throw the dice, so he hired a man to cast for him.

GOUTY? DINE WITH AN M.D.

CHARLES V was a victim of gout, a family affliction. So disabling did he find the disorder that he wisely abdicated the throne and retired to a life devoted to mending clocks, overseeing a small estate, and entertaining the local nobility. His son, Philip II, seeking to avoid the family curse and his father's fate, devised an ingenious solution. At his side sat a physician, an ever-present safeguard against imprudence and a reminder that he was not to overindulge.

SUICIDE VIA GOUT

GOUT-STRICKEN Septimius Severus (A.D. 146–211) was elevated to the purple in 193. Virulent attacks of his disorder were pretexts for plots by palace cabals and the military for his overthrow. His courage and steadfastness brought him through these trials, but the thanklessness of his sons when he was prostrated with pain was too much to bear. He deliberately indulged in the dietary heedlessness that ultimately proved fatal.

GOUT—THE REMUNERATIVE DISEASE

GOUT, like bladder stone, seems to have been particularly inclined to make martyrs of Englishmen. Sidney Smith was one, but he could joke about it. Said he, "it is the only enemy that I do not wish to have at my feet." It was Smith who reported that the physician Warren "left behind him 100,000 pounds with the following account of how he acquired that princely sum: 'Aurum catharticum, 20,000 pounds; aurum diureticum, 10,000 pounds; aurum podagrosum, 40,000 pounds; aurum apoplecticum, 20,000 pounds; aurum senile et nervosum, 10,000 pounds.' "

MENTAL ABERRATIONS

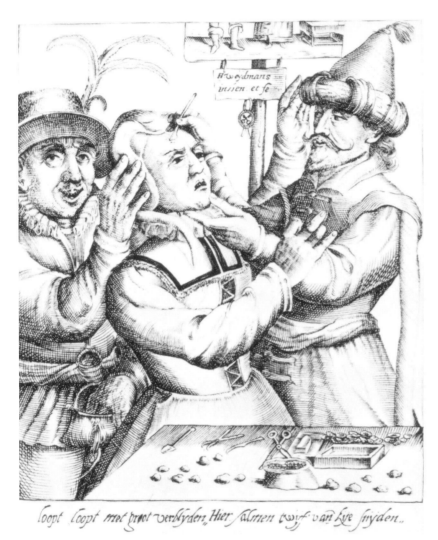

loopt loopt met groot verblyden, Hier salmen twyt van kye snyden.

In the sixteenth and seventeenth centuries it was widely believed that "stones in the head" were the cause of actual or incipient dementia. To cure it, a superficial incision would be made in the scalp by the operator, who would palm one or more small stones, usually with the aid of a confederate who stood behind him. Trepanned skulls dating from Neolithic times may indicate that primitive man believed that malign spirits could thus be liberated. Was the stones-in-the-head superstition a twisted survival of that belief?

An operation for stones in the head. Engraving by H. Weydmans, early seventeenth century. Reproduced from Medicine and the Artist (Ars Medica) *by permission of the Philadelphia Museum of Art.*

BEHEADING A SOMATIC DELUSION

FRIEDRICH Schiller, the dramatist, had an early career as a physician. In a letter he speaks of his treatment of a madman who believes he had two heads. Schiller set up an artificial head on the patient's shoulder and then struck it off, a procedure that would not be out of place in modern psychotherapy.

CURE BY TERROR

THE treatment advocated by Benjamin Rush for the mentally ill was draconian, to say the least. A strong believer in the effectiveness of terror, he recommended pouring cold water down the patient's sleeves, "so that it may descend into the armpits and down the trunk of the body" for fifteen to twenty minutes. In the "well cure," cold water was poured into an empty well at the bottom of which the patient lay bound and helpless. Despite his misguided methods, Rush was among the first to advocate occupational therapy for the mentally ill, and among the first to offer them a measure of sympathy and kindly interest.

SERENDIPITOUS COLLAPSE THERAPY

THE widely held belief in the eighteenth and nineteenth centuries that the mentally ill were rarely afflicted with pulmonary tuberculosis seems to have had a basis in fact. One investigation suggested that the straitjacket, once extensively employed in mental institutions, reduced lung capacity in much the same way as an artificial pneumothorax.

DR. ANDREW BOORDE OFFERS A TREATMENT FOR LUNATICS

". . . it apperyd of late dayes of a lunatycke man named Michel, the which went many yeres at lybertye, and at last he did kyll his wyfe and his wyfe's suster, and his own selfe wherefore I do advertyse every man the whiche is madde . . . to be kepte in savegarde, in some close house or chamber, where there is lytle lyght. And that he have a keper the whiche the madde man do feare. . . . Also the chamber . . . that the madde man is in, let theere be no paynted clothes, nor paynted walles, nor pyctures, for suche thynges makethe them full of fantasyes. . . . And use fewe wordes to them, excepte it be for reprehensyon, or gentyll reformacyon yf they have any wytte to understande. . . ."

A MADMAN WHO WASN'T "KEPTE IN SAVEGARDE"

THE Rev. John Ashbourne enjoyed a reputation for treating the mentally deranged in his own home. One of his patients waylaid him, "stab'd him in the Neck with a Pitch-fork, which ran clean thorow." The madman finished the job by stabbing his victim seventeen times with a knife.

HE ANTICIPATED PINEL

AS physician in charge of the Hospital of St. Mary of Bethlehem (Bedlam), Edward Tyson (1650–1708) did much to humanize treatment of the inmates by emphasizing therapy rather than punishment. He welcomed women nurses and set up a wardrobe fund for his impoverished charges. His great innovation was the introduction of postinstitutional treatment with periodic home visits.

GEORGE III GETS A CRACKBRAINED TREATMENT FOR INSANITY

IN 1788 George III was given the then-orthodox treatment for madness—hot poultices applied to the shaven head "to draw out the humours."

MADHOUSES—PUBLIC AND PRIVATE

It's a mad world. Mad as Bedlam.
      Charles Dickens in David Copperfield

Special institutions for the insane began to appear during the sixteenth century. But as a general rule, the mentally and emotionally disturbed were permitted their liberty as long as they were docile. When no longer controllable by family and friends, they were institutionalized.

In London, the Hospital of St. Mary of Bethlehem (Bedlam), practiced an "open-door policy." Patients presumed to be recovered from states of violence, agitation, or torpor were allowed to leave. For the year 1707 we read that "distracted persons who went out cured in the year ending at Easter" numbered fifty-nine. In that period Bedlam buried twenty-four and "brought into this Hospital under Cure" 142. Discharged patients had a band of tin fixed around the left arm, which served both as a badge of madness and a license to beg. About their necks they wore an ox horn on a string, "which when they came to a house for alms, they did wind, and then did put the drink given them into this horn, whereto they did put a stopple."* These "Tom O'Bedlams," while generally well-treated, were likely to have their valuable begging licenses—their armlets—stolen by vagrants.

One of the principal sights of London, Bedlam could boast of gate receipts totaling 400 pounds a year. For two pence a sightseer could view the chained lunatics in their cages and encourage them to entertain by prodding them or by imitating their lunacies. Milder patients were allowed to mingle in an open area, and here, too, the spectators had a jolly time by provoking with mocking gestures and ridicule. So objectionable did the conduct of sightseers become that the Governors ordered in 1776 that "the doors be kept locked on public holidays against all visitors." Later it was further ordered "that the admission of visitors be henceforth only by ticket and that accredited visitors be accompanied by an attendant."

When not abused by sightseers, inmates had to deal with their keepers, many of them brutal and sadistic. It was not to be wondered at that private madhouses flourished though they were often far from adequate and sometimes no better than Bedlam itself. One madman escaped from such a place at Bethnal Green "dragging with him along the road to Aldgate the post of the bed to which he had been chained."

The private madhouse was a natural outgrowth of the practice of taking an occasional patient into one's home, a practice that seems to have begun with Helkiah Crooke, physician to James I. In 1630 he charged 200 pounds a year for "Physick, Diet, Clothes, Lodging, washings

---

* "Poor Tom, thy horn is dry," says Edgar in *King Lear*.

and all things necessary," including "two Men Servantes." By 1700 private madhouses were numerous, prosperous, and competitive: "I do hereby give notice, that I can accommodate any distempered Person with such conveniency as is fit for their Recovery, having had much practice and success that way, and can place them in an excellent Air nere the City, fit for that purpose; and with the greatest security and delight to patients; there being no better way for their Recovery."

As for therapy, a "Cantharides plaister" aplied to the head was a much favored treatment. Daniel Oxenbridge, a colleague of Mayerne and Harvey, treated a Mrs. Miller by diet, clysters, leeches, fresh cyder drinks, warm herb baths, and the application of "warm Lungs of Lambs" to her shaven head. To Goodwife Jackson "being poor," he gave only a scruple of "Glass of Antimony" in beer every other day, with occasional "Bleeding and Sleepers."

Dr. Willis at Home, by Thomas Rowlandson. Willis maintained a private asylum. He treated George III during the king's first porphyria attack and used a straitjacket when his royal patient was unruly. In Rowlandson's caricature, restraint is by `winding sheet."

OCCUPATIONAL HAZARDS

SILVER MINING IN COLONIAL PERU (FIFTEENTH CENTURY)

PALEOPATHOLOGICAL studies have revealed that silver mining as conducted by the Spanish conqueror "killed more Indians than all disease epidemics combined." Heavy iron or bronze bars were used to extract the ore, "and the air was thick with dust and metal vapors." Often climbing 500 to 1,000 feet on woven cowhide ladders and carrying fifty-pound packs of ore on their backs, the miners succumbed to cave-ins, falls, black lung, osteoarthritis, and chemical poisoning. This last was the product of the lead and mercury used in the refining process. Ironically, the first chairs in medicine at San Marcos University owed their funding to revenues of a mercury mine "where numberless Indians died."

CLEANING CESSPITS IN MODENA (1700)

RAMAZZINI was moved to write his pioneering work on occupational diseases when he observed "a cleaner of jakes" at work in his own house in Modena. "I took a narrow View of his Eyes and found them very red and dim; upon which I asked him if they had any usual Remedy for that Disorder? He replied their only Way was to run immediately Home and confine themselves for a Day to a dark Room, and wash their Eyes now and then with warm Water. . . . After this I took notice of several Beggars in the City, who, having been employed in that Work, were either very weak-sighted or absolutely Blind." According to Ramazzini, vaults for receiving human excrement were cleaned every third year.

WORKING CONDITIONS IN A COTTON MILL (1839)

A VICTORIAN observer gives this account of a visit to a cotton mill. "The place was full of women, young, all of them, some large with child, and obliged to stand twelve hours each day. Their hours are from five in the morning to seven in the evening, two hours of that being for rest. . . . The heat was excessive in some of the rooms, the stink pestiferous, and in all an atmosphere of cotton flue. I nearly fainted. The young women were all pale, sallow, thin. . . ."

CHOPIN SHOWS DOCTORS THE DOOR

Great men in less enlightened times took their medicine—often worthless, sometimes fatal—without a murmur. Not so Chopin. Said he after three eminent physicians had come to see their tubercular patient for a consultation, "One sniffed at my spittle, the second tapped to make me spit, and the third felt and listened as I spat. The one said I was a dead man, the second that I was on the verge of death, and the third that I should undoubtedly die." They recommended blisters and bleeding. Chopin showed them the door.

Death and the Notables. From Der Doten Dantz, *Mainz, 1492.*

EMINENT INVALIDS

LOUIS XIV TAKES A SECRET ELIXIR

FOR more than seventy-seven years the Sun King survived the care of his physicians. An operation for anal fistula did not disturb the royal gravity. Operated on at seven, Louis insisted on holding his levee at the usual hour of eight. Earlier assaults on what must have been an iron constitution included a "purgative soup," which acted eight times in eleven hours. Nonetheless, His Majesty only felt "somewhat fatigued" but retired early. In his last illness, gangrene progressed from foot to knee and from knee to thigh. The perplexed and desperate court doctors turned in their helplessness to an empiric from Provence named Brun, the sole proprietor of a secret wonder-working elixir. The moribund monarch took two doses and soon felt better. Saint Simon in his memoirs tells us that the whole court hailed the miracle, "especially the ladies, to whom Brun was an angel descended from heaven." Next day the king was dead and Brun well on his way back to Provence.

FREDERICK THE GREAT DISCOVERS THE VIRTUES OF FRESH HERRING

HIMSELF a valetudinarian with persistent gastrointestinal difficulties, Frederick freely medicated and prescribed for his sister Wilhelmina and his brother Ferdinand, chronic invalids both. Their physicians were not only under his constant supervision, but were also required to report in detail on their patient visits. Frederick's competence as self-prescriber is amusingly revealed in this journal jotting by his personal physician, Zimmerman: "Yesterday several strong stools had dispelled for a moment all the King's bad humor. 'A new remedy,' says his Majesty, 'has just arrived, which I mean to try at noon; this remedy,' added he, 'is fresh herrings.' I congratulated his Majesty on his new remedy, and begged him not to forget rhubarb and glauber salts."

GOYA TURNS LEAD POISONING TO GOOD ACCOUNT

IN 1792 Goya experienced a sudden overwhelming assault on his nervous system. He suffered from dizziness, mental confusion, impaired hearing and speech, tinnitus, and partial blindness. He had been in daily contact with a toxic lead compound, sometimes grinding it and inhaling its fumes. Ramazzini had observed that painters suffer from palsy of the limbs, cachexia, blackened teeth, unhealthy complexions, melancholia, and the loss of the sense of smell. He traced the cause to red and white lead and the mercury in cinnabar. Goya's palette also included toxic lead chromate and mercury-based pigments. After many months Goya recovered, and a new Goya emerged. Up to the time of his illness, he had painted charming portraits and pastoral scenes. Now the "humane and bitter social observer, the scourging and despairing delineator of vice and cruelty" took over.

ALEXANDER POPE COMPARES HIMSELF TO A SPIDER

FRAIL, feeble, "protuberant before and behind," Pope compared himself with good humor to a spider. "He was always wrapped up in fur and flannel, besides wearing a boddice of stiff canvas." He was so weak and infirm, he was unable to dress or undress himself.

PIRANESI BENEFITS FROM HIS MALARIA

COULD Piranesi's haunting drawings of prisons have their origin in the malaria from which he suffered? *The Dark Brain of Piranesi* suggests that the disease "increased the artist's perception to the point of erethism, and almost to torment, thereby making possible on one hand the dizzying energy, the mathematical intoxication, and on the other, the crisis of agoraphobia and claustrophobia combined, the anguish of captive space from which the 'Prisons' certainly resulted."

H. G. WELLS MAKES THE MOST OF HIS DIABETES

SOMERSET Maugham, who described Wells as "fat and homely," was curious to discover the secret of his success with women. "I once asked one of his mistresses what especially attracted her to him. I expected her to say his acute mind and sense of fun; not at all; she said that his body smelled of honey." Wells was diabetic.

SCHUBERT LEAVES A SYMPHONY UNFINISHED

G. R. Marek in his biography of Schubert poses the following question: Was the "Unfinished" unfinished because its composition coincided with Schubert's realization in shame and bitterness that he had been infected with syphilis? "He would not, he could not, turn back to it, the composition created at the very time of the inception of the disease. The reminder struck too sharply. Such a victory over himself he could not manage. . . . He gave it up and forever."

NIKOLAI VASILYEVICH GOGOL HAS ICE WATER POURED OVER HIS HEAD

WHATEVER therapy the frail and sickly author of *Dead Souls* required, it probably wasn't hydrotherapy, but a typical hydropathic treatment is what he got. According to his recent biographer, Henry Troyat, Gogol was seized bodily by his doctors "and thrust into a tub of hot water, while a servant poured ice water over his head. He was then put naked to bed, and Dr. Klimentov applied a half-dozen leeches to his nose."

FORD MADOX FORD HAS ICE WATER POURED OVER HIS FEET

WHAT ailed Ford was perfectly clear to his doctors at the Kaltwasser-Heilenstadt (cold water sanitorium) on the Rhine. Defective circulation, they said. Solution? Force the blood to the head by heating that organ and back to the feet by freezing the extremities. In *Return to Yesterday*, the novelist says, "Three times a day I had alternately a boiling shampoo and a fliessende Fussbad—a footbath of ice water forced against the feet in a stream running 90 miles an hour."

THE QUEEN OF TLATELOLCO SUFFERS THE CONSEQUENCES OF UNTREATED HALITOSIS

PRE-COLUMBIAN Mexican chronicles relate the story of Moquihuixtli, ruler of Tlatelolco, who repudiated his wife because he found her breath insufferable. The queen's brother, infuriated by the insult, declared war on his fastidious brother-in-law, defeated him in battle, annexed his kingdom, and took his life.

CATHERINE THE GREAT IS FITTED FOR A BRACE

AT age seven, the German princess who was to become Catherine the Great, ruler of all the Russias, was stricken with fever and delirium. After three bedridden weeks, "her body had taken on the form of a Z," with the right shoulder higher than the left, the backbone curved, and the left shoulder hollow. A morning massage with the spittle of a young girl who had not had breakfast was prescribed by the local executioner, who had been summoned as soon as Catherine could sit up. He then fitted her with "a kind of strait-jacket," which was not to be removed except in cases of dire necessity. The executioner came daily to adjust the brace, and did so good a job that years later Catherine would attribute her queenly posture to his orthopedic expertness.

HERBERT SPENCER WAS A HYPOCHONDRIAC

WHEN out driving in his victoria, Spencer would suddenly cry out to his coachman, "Stop!"— even in the thick of traffic. He would then take his pulse. If the pulse rate was normal, the drive was continued; if not, the philosopher was driven home.

TOULOUSE-LAUTREC REMAINS UNREPENTANT

IN 1899 two male nurses seized Toulouse-Lautrec outside his studio and took him to a sanitarium. His friends had convinced his mother to have him committed for an alcoholism cure because he had become prey to hallucinations and had had a severe attack of delirium tremens. His comment when the officiating doctors permitted him to leave on condition that he be kept under strict surveillance: "[Here are] more people who believe that illness and the sick were created for their benefit."

EDVARD MUNCH HAD A FINGER PHOBIA

MUNCH (1863–1944), the Norwegian painter, sustained a gunshot wound in his left hand as the result of an unfortunate love affair. Henceforth, the sight of human hands—his own as well—was to be unendurable. He wore gloves constantly, and when he did his self-portrait, a stand-in posed for the hands. He is quoted as saying, "there is nothing more naked or more disgusting than fingers."

TYCHO BRAHE HOLDS BACK HIS WATER

ON the 13 October 1601 Tycho Brahe, the great astronomer, was a guest at Baron Rosenberg's in Prague. Kepler records what happened. Brahe "held back his water beyond the demands of courtesy. When he drank more, he felt the tension in his bladder increase, but he put politeness before his health. When he got home he was scarcely able to urinate." There follows Kepler's description of wakeful nights, extreme dysuria, anuria, delirium, and death.

As a student, Tycho Brahe fought a duel with another Danish youth, in the course of which Brahe's nose was sliced off. The missing nose part—the bridge—was replaced by a gold and silver alloy shaped to fit. Brahe carried with him a small case the size of a snuffbox, which contained an "ointment of glutinous composition." This he frequently applied to his nose.

RENOIR DEFIES OSTEOARTICULAR DISEASE

PIERRE Auguste Renoir (1841–1919) began to experience the first symptoms of polyarthritis at about age fifty, when his reputation as a painter of genius was at last conceded everywhere. He settled in warm Provence, and the story of his life thereafter was one of slow aggravation of his disablement. In his last years he painted sitting in a wheelchair with his brush tied to his fingers.

SWINBURNE REFUSES TO BE MADE A MAN OF

SWINBURNE was obsessed with flagellation, a monomania no doubt fostered by the floggings the poet received as a schoolboy at Eton. His friends were, of course, aware of his aberrant tastes and decided to "make a man of him" by engaging the services of the celebrated actress Adah Menken. The attempted seduction was a fiasco, and Miss Menken returned her ten-pound fee as unearned. Her comment: "I can't make him understand that biting's no use!"

ROUSSEAU EXPOSES HIS BUTTOCKS

AT age eight Rousseau was spanked by the sister of his guardian, M. Lambercier. In his *Confessions* he dates the perversion of his sexual desires to that event. "I invoked, imaginatively, the aid of the opposite sex, without as much as dreaming that a woman could serve any other purpose than the one I lusted for." In his teens, trying again to experience that early erotic satisfaction, Rousseau exposed his buttocks in dark alleyways, hoping that a passing woman might satisfy his desires.

PAUL VERLAINE SAMPLES THE HOSPITALS OF PARIS

WITH his unkempt beard, scarf, and walking stick (he had hydrarthrosis of the knee), Paul Verlaine (1844–1896), slave of the muse and absinthe, could be seen by his contemporaries limping from one cafe to another. Homeless and poverty-stricken, his preferred places of refuge were the Paris hospitals. His favorite was the Hôpital Broussais, where he always found a friendly welcome and where the same bed and small bedside table was waiting for him. Here he could compose his poems during the long afternoon hours.

LULLY SELF-INFLICTS A FATAL BLOW

JEAN-BAPTISTE Lully, the French composer, was in the habit of beating time when conducting by striking the floor with his staff. He died of blood poisoning in 1687 after striking himself on the foot at a rehearsal.

GEORGE II HAS A DISLOCATED DIGIT

QUACK doctor "Spot" Ward got his big chance when George II, afflicted with a dislocated thumb, called him in for consultation. After examining the royal digit, Ward set it back in place with a sudden wrench and jerk. His reward—the royal favor and a coach and pair, together with the privilege of driving in St. James's Park.

PAGANINI PROFITS FROM MARFAN'S SYNDROME

FOLK belief has ascribed Paganini's astounding virtuosity on the violin to his purported association with the Devil. Dr. Myron R. Schoenfeld, a cardiologist writing in the *Harvard Magazine*, attributes Paganini's satanic gift to something far more mundane—Marfan's syndrome. "The hyper-extensible 'spider' fingers of his hand permitted an incredible range of mobility on the fingerboard. Those on the right allowed him to brace the bow solidly against the edge of his hand, and the looseness of the right wrist and shoulder joint gave his arm a pliancy that lent itself to broad, acrobatic bowing."

RICHELIEU SWALLOWS A CURE

LIKE so many of his royal and noble contemporaries, Cardinal Richelieu suffered from the ministrations of his doctors and the nostrums of folk healers. When Louis XIII's great minister was *in extremis*, an ancient peasant woman was brought in. She proceeded to minister her remedy—four ounces of horse droppings in a pint of white wine. Richelieu's tuberculosis osteitis did not respond. Still, this desperate therapy was in the best style of the day. The extended listing of excremental cures in the *London Dispensary* of 1649 would not have raised many eyebrows even a century later. And it is only a little over a hundred years ago (1862) that John Hastings bought out his pamphlet on *The Value of Excreta of Reptiles in Phthisis and Some Other Diseases*.

MARCEL PROUST OBSERVES AN APPLE BLOSSOM

PROUST claimed he could breathe freely only at night. His days were given over to sleep, his nights to writing. Indoors he was comfortable only with the mercury a few degrees below ninety; outdoors he wore "a thick twill overcoat with numerous heavy linings." His apartment was padded with cork from floor to ceiling, and the windows were never opened. There were occasions when he would send his chauffeur Odilon out into the country to fetch a few apple blossom branches. He would gaze at them through a glass door so the scent would not provoke an asthmatic attack.

GEORGE GORDON STRIKES A BYRONIC POSE

IN the late eighteenth and early nineteenth centuries, "wan, hollow-chested young women and pallid, rachitic young men" paraded themselves as victims of the "romantic" disease, tuberculosis. "When I was young," wrote Gautier, "I could not have accepted as a lyrical poet anyone weighing more than 99 pounds." As Susan Sontag points out in *Illness as Metaphor*, debility became languor, exhaustion, spirituality. To eat heartily was considered rude, to look sickly made one glamorous. Byron made a public show of dining on biscuits and soda water, but was caught out on one occasion gorging himself on potatoes and mutton at a public house.

LOUIS XI HAD A NOSE FOR SMELLS

BURTON, in the *Anatomy of Melancholy*, says that Louis XI "had a conceit that everything did stink about him. All the odoriferous perfumes they could get would not ease him, but he smelled a filthy stink."

NAPOLEON IS DEFEATED BY EPILEPSY

IN middle life, Napoleon was plagued by a variety of disorders, one of which—epilepsy—on one occasion caused the Little Corporal acute embarrassment. The emperor had invited Mlle George, a popular actress, to share his bed. In media res, Napoleon suffered a seizure. Mlle George screamed, and the imperial household burst in. Mlle George was not seen again in the royal precincts.

—AND LOSES HIS BATTLE WITH PROSTATITIS

THE ills that most discomfitted Napoleon were prostatism and hemorrhoids. In the saddle all day at the Battle of Ligny, he suffered from prolapsed and thrombosing piles and was unable to clinch his victory by pursuit of the enemy. In the Russian campaign, Napoleon's polyuria must have been aggravated by the extreme cold, and the "mysterious illness" referred to by some historians may have been nocturia.

JOHN RUSKIN SCORNS THE MARRIAGE BED

RUSKIN'S marriage of six years was not consummated. In a letter to her parents, Effie Ruskin reveals that her husband had told her that "he imagined women were quite different from what he saw I was, and that the reason he did not make me his wife was because he was disgusted with my person." Some biographers surmise that Ruskin was put off by his wife's pubic hair.

SIR JOSHUA REYNOLDS CONTRACTS A HEARING DISABILITY

REYNOLDS used an ear trumpet. His hearing had been impaired because of long hours spent in a drafty corridor of the Vatican, where Reynolds was copying a Raphael. In consequence, his estimate of Raphael's genius was somewhat muted. As Goldsmith put it:

> *When they talk'd of their Raphaels, Correggios, and stuff,*
> *He shifted his trumpet and only took snuff.*

SAMUEL JOHNSON APPRAISES THE EFFECTS OF AN APHASIC ATTACK

PROMINENT in Johnson's medical history were recurrent asthma, a tendency to melancholia, dropsy, and what concerns us here — right-sided hemiplegia with aphasia and agraphia. On one occasion in his seventy-fourth year, he woke and sat up, and "after feeling a confusion and indistinctness in his head lasting about half a minute, had the alarming shock of finding himself aphasic." Fearing that his mind would be permanently affected, he knelt and prayed that his sanity might be spared. He then tested his mental powers by translating his prayer into Latin.

POPE PIUS II HAS HIS HEAD WARMED

JEROME Cardan, the most celebrated physician of his time, suggested dropping certain medicated waters onto the patient's coronal suture from a height. His object was to keep the brain at normal temperature and its substance firm and dense. Pope Pius II, taking the medicinal waters at Petriolo in Tuscany in 1460, had the warm sulfurous waters poured through a pipe onto the crown of his head for a period of twenty days.

PHILIP V HIRES A CASTRATO

DERANGED Philip V of Spain was convinced that the singing of Farinelli, a vocal virtuoso, was the perfect medicine for his frequent depressions. To ensure the singer's remaining at court, he settled a pension of 14,000 pieces of eight on him and undertook to keep a coach for him at the royal expense.

WILLIAM III GETS A DEATH SENTENCE BY POST

WILLIAM III of England corresponded under assumed names with eminent physicians all over Europe. One of his letters, in which he let himself be known as a parish priest, reached Fagon, Louis XIV's physician. Fagon's reply: "Prepare for death."

BOSWELL RECEIVES SOME WELCOME COUNSEL

WHEN Boswell, womanizer extraordinary, was traveling abroad and fell into a mood of deep depression, he sought the counsel of the eminent professor Dr. Hahn of the city of Utrecht concerning his sexual propensities. Said Hahn, "Women are necessary when one is accustomed, or retention will influence the brain."

THOMAS BABINGTON MACAULAY SUFFERS A SLIGHT INDISPOSITION

A CHILD prodigy, Macaulay was widely read when scarcely out of babyhood. Asked by a concerned friend of the family how his stomach-ache did, little Thomas, aged four, replied, "Thank you, madam, the agony is abated."

CHOPIN SOWS PANIC

CHOPIN, a victim of tuberculosis, suffered terribly from the public's attitude toward the disease, which was one of unreasoning fear amounting to mania. Fits of coughing coupled with the presence of a physician were enough to prompt a Majorcan hotel owner to put him out on the street. He could get no conveyance out of town, and had finally to hire a broken-down butcher's cart to carry him to Palma. There he had a hemorrhage. No passenger ship would allow him on board, and he was obliged to travel to Barcelona in a freighter transporting a cargo of pigs. At his hotel, the landlord, aware that he was spitting blood, demanded payment for all his room's furniture and decorations because, by law, they had to be burnt.

SIR EDWIN LUYTENS MAKES ILLNESS PAY

OSBERT Sitwell once asked Sir Edwin Luytens, the celebrated architect, whether any other of his twelve brothers and sisters shared his genius. "Any talent I may have," he replied, "was due to a long illness as a boy, which afforded me time to think, and to subsequent ill health, because I was not allowed to play games, and so had to teach myself, for my enjoyment, to use my eyes instead of my feet. My brothers hadn't the same advantage."

T. H. HUXLEY WITNESSES A FATEFUL AUTOPSY

WHEN the great biologist was a boy of thirteen or fourteen, older student friends took him to observe an autopsy. "Most unfortunately sensitive to the disagreeables which attend anatomical pursuits," Huxley was so upset, he says, that for years he "suffered from occasional paroxysms of internal pain, and from that time my constant friend, hypochondriacal dyspepsia, commenced his half-century of co-tenancy of my fleshly tabernacle."

EMILY DICKINSON HAD AN EYE AILMENT

FROM measurements of a daguerrotype of Emily Dickinson when the poet was seventeen, Dr. Martin Wand concluded that she suffered from "a prominent right extropia of at least 15 degrees." This abnormality, in which the eye turns out instead of demonstrating a forward alignment, leads to eye strain, blurring of vision, reading difficulties, headaches, and pain from sunlight. According to Dr. Wand, these difficulties may account in part for the poet's reclusiveness and may explain references in her letters to "a calamity" and "a woe, the only one that ever made me tremble."

THE REV. RICHARD BAXTER CONFESSES HIS SINS

IN his history of his life and times, the Rev. Richard Baxter ingenuously confesses the sins of his youth. One was lying; the other he describes as follows: "I was much addicted to excessive gluttonous eating of apples and pears, which, I think, laid the foundation of that weakness of my stomach which caused the bodily calamities of my life."

BEN FRANKLIN BATHES IN A "SHOE"

IN his old age, Franklin found leisure for reading and relief from the pains of kidney stone by taking long hot baths in his shoe-shaped copper tub. He sat on the heel, stretched his legs along the vamp, and set his book on the instep.

TIMOTHY DWIGHT GOES ON A DIET

WHEN a student at Yale, Timothy Dwight (1752–1817) reduced his diet to the barest minimum to save time for his studies and sharpen his intellect. He dined on exactly twelve mouthfuls, and resisted other meals with similar Spartan rigor. Finding, however, that he had "less clearness of apprehension than was desirable," and suspecting the few morsels of meat he was accustomed to eat as the cause, he began to confine himself to vegetables alone, while continuing to adhere to his customary quota of mouthfuls. After Dwight suffered several successive and severe attacks of colic, his dismayed father took the skeletal scholar home, presumably to die. He lived to serve as president of Yale.

JOHN KEATS DIAGNOSES

ONE night in 1821, Keats returned home, felt feverish and got into bed. His head had hardly touched the pillow when he coughed slightly. A friend, Charles Armitage Brown, saw him carefully examine a single drop of blood that had fallen on the sheet. To Brown Keats calmly said, "It is arterial blood. I cannot be deceived in that color; that drop of blood is my death warrant—I must die."

JOHN HUNTER MISDIAGNOSES

HUNTER, founder of modern experimental and surgical pathology, believed that gonorrhea and syphilis were different manifestations of the same infection. Everything, he thought, depended on the infection site. While syphilis developed if the virus attacked the skin of the penis, gonorrhea arose in the mucous membrane of the urethra. To prove his point, Hunter injected the skin of his own penis with pus from a patient he believed to be a victim of gonorrhea. If his theory was valid, symptoms of syphilis would develop. They did. Unfortunately for Hunter and medicine, his patient must have had both diseases, a possibility Hunter had not counted on.

FLIMFLAMMERY

In Elizabethan England palliards or clapperdudgeons were beggars who excited compassion by means of artificial sores made by binding corrosives like arsenic or ratsbane to the flesh. The skin was first made raw by application of a mixture of crowsfoot, spearwort, and salt. The finished product was then covered with a foul and bloody cloth, easily turned up to reveal the horrible wound to passersby. Others of the begging fraternity were the counterfeit cranks, who pretended to have the feared "falling sickness," Abraham men or bogus madmen, and dommerers or mutes.

A paillard or clapperdudgeon, from an etching by Callot.

ARTFUL DODGES

MALINGERING

In Milan. The duke of Osana, governor of Milan, was dismayed by the great number of beggars, many of them sham cripples, infesting his city. To every cripple appearing in the Cathedral Square at midday on the day of the Holy Cross, announced the duke, half a filippo would be given. On the appointed day, the duke had a rope drawn across the square some three feet from the ground. In plain view was a cartload of the promised coins. Excitedly tossing away bandages and crutches, hundreds made the leap. The duke thereupon gave all those who had not jumped a filippo and sent the rest to the galleys.

In London. Robert Shakesberry, counterfeit crank, was tried twice by the London courts in 1547. The first time around he fooled his judges: "Robt Shakysberie being butt a boy and dyseased with the palsey or some other dysease wherewith his bodie shakethe verie sore shal lykwyse furthwith departe out of ye cytie uppon payne of whypping if he made defaute." Robert made the mistake of repeating his crime, was discovered, and condemned to be whipped through the streets of London "at cart's tail."

INSOMNIA

ONLY Thomas Edison could have invented his eccentricities. On occasion he almost starved himself to death because he believed that food poisons the intestines. The putting on and off of one's clothes, he contended, produces insomnia, so he often slept in his. A less inventive but more rational approach to the problem of sleeplessness was adopted by Count Keyserlingk, insomniac patron of Bach. During his wakeful nights, the count listened to music expressly written for him by the composer and played for him by his private harpsichordist, Johann Gottlieb Goldberg. The pieces came to be called the "Goldberg Variations."

TENSION

MATISSE attributed healing power to his art and maintained that he had cured his friends Carco and Marquest by leaving them in a room filled with his works. In his *Notes of A Painter* he says, "What I dream of is an art of balance, of purity and serenity, devoid of troubling or depressing subject matter, an art which might be for every mental worker, be he business man or writer, like an appeasing influence, like a mental soother, something like a good armchair to rest from physical fatigue."

PROLAPSUS UTERI

EURYPHON, a contemporary of Hippocrates, was a leader of the Cnidian School, which borrowed its name from the site of one of the temples of health sacred to Aesculapius. Soranos (second century A.D.) attributes to him the novel treatment of suspending the patient with a prolapsed uterus from a ladder to which her feet were tied.

STERILITY

IN 1849, at the age of twenty-eight, Flaubert made a tour of the Orient. The following is from a letter he wrote to a friend: ". . . some time ago a santan [ascetic priest] used to walk through the streets of Cairo completely naked except for the cap on his head and another on his penis. To urinate he would doff the penis cap and sterile women who wanted children would run up and put themselves under the parabola of his urine and rub themselves with it."

MUSCLE TENSION

A STRONG cigar introduced midway into the patient's rectum was employed by some American surgeons as a muscle relaxant in the first half of the nineteenth century. Smoke was sometimes blown into the rectum for the same purpose, and injections of distillates of tobacco were in use as well. Recognition of the relaxant properties of tobacco came early. Regner de Graaf (1641–1673) describes his enema tube "as not unlike the pipes used by the English for introducing tobacco fumes into the bowel."

FEAR OF DENTISTRY

WHEN Queen Elizabeth I on one occasion was experiencing the torture of toothache, the Privy Council was convened to convince Her Majesty to have the offending tooth pulled. They failed. Enter the bishop of London, who volunteered to have one of his own teeth extracted so the queen could observe the operation and satisfy herself that the operation was comparatively painless. Accordingly, out came the bishop's tooth, and Her Majesty consented to the extraction.

CONCEPTION

THE author of the pseudo-Hippocratic treatise, *On the Nature of the Infant*, advises a Greek dancer, a slave of a woman of his acquaintance, how to avoid a pregnancy that would mar her shape and interfere with her activities. He suggests that she take several leaps into the air, so that heels touch buttocks. When this is done several times, he assures her, the seed will drop out of the uterus to the ground, producing an audible thud.

HIDDEN BLEMISHES

IN biblical times prospective brides were not able to hide bodily defects with impunity. Before the wedding was celebrated, it was the proper thing for the wife-to-be to submit herself to a thorough physical examination by her groom's relatives in the communal bathhouse — or at least it was so recommended by the Talmud.

EYE LOSS

PRINCE Christian of Schleswig-Holstein had a large collection of glass eyes, begun when he lost one of his own in a hunting accident. He was fond of showing off one bloodshot item. "I wear it," said he, "when I have a cold."

INDIGESTION

BOSWELL, in his journal, tells us that he met at court the Marquis Cavalcabo, an Italian nobleman of ancient family. "I was sadly troubled with weakness of the stomach and relaxation of the nerves," the marquis told Boswell, "but I have cured myself by taking ice. The water, Sir, when it is mixed with food, makes it soft, and the chill of the ice gives elasticity to the fibres of the stomach, and you digest as though you had millstones in your belly."

NIGHTCAPS

FOR Thomas Elyot, author of the *Castel of Helth* (1541), the four humors—hot and moist, hot and dry, cold and moist, cold and dry—must be kept in strict balance if bodily health is to be maintained. He warns his readers of the dangers of keeping the head too warm, "wherby the brayne, which is naturally colde" is deleteriously affected by hot vapors ascending from the stomach. Heavy and elaborate headgear is therefore to be avoided. And as for nightcaps, just punch a few holes in them.

TUBERCULOSIS

RECOURSE to the animal kingdom for medical purposes had its finest hour when Dr. Thomas Beddoes of Shiffnal, Shropshire, England, began his practice of taking cows into the sickrooms of his tubercular patients to purify the air with their sweet breath. A firm believer in the treatment of disease by inhalation of chemical mixtures, he established the Pneumatic Institute in 1798 with Humphrey Davy as his assistant. It was at the Institute that Davy discovered the anesthetic properties of nitrous oxide.

John of Gaddesden (1280–1361) was more rational. His prescription for a consumptive's diet: "As for food, the best is the milk of a young brunette with her first child; which should be a boy; the young woman should be well-favored and should eat and drink in moderation."

PAINS OF CHILDBIRTH

GUSTAV Mahler read to his wife from the works of Kant while she was in labor. What may seem gross lack of feeling on the part of the composer may have been wisdom. Kant, in the words of Twain's characterization of the Mormon bible, is "chloroform in print."

RESPIRATORY PROBLEMS

IMMANUEL Kant, the celebrated German philosopher, was fond of taking long walks, but always ventured out alone, accompanied only by his faithful servant Lampe, who trailed behind with an umbrella. Kant's reasoning was as simple as his philosophical works were abstruse. If he had a companion, the companion would talk, obliging Kant to reply. Replying would cause him to breathe through his mouth. Breathing through his mouth would invite coughs, hoarseness, colds, and pulmonary derangements. Q.E.D.

DEHYDRATION

THE bushmen of the Kalahari Desert are compelled by their arid environment to conserve both their energy and their body moisture. In the heat of the day "they may lie in shallow pits lined with pulp moistened with their own urine, the evaporation of which helps them keep cool and prevents their own dehydration."

SENESCENCE

JAMES Thurber remarks in the *Paris Review Interviews* that Frank Harris once boasted he'd live to be a hundred. "When I asked him what the formula was, he told me it was very simple. He said, 'I've bought myself a stomach pump and one hour after dinner I pump myself out.'" Harris died in 1931, at seventy-five.

A more sensible prescription was followed by the duke of Alva, who died at age seventy-five in 1582. In his old age he kept two wet nurses by whom he was nourished. John Caius, physician and author of a work on the sweating disease, was fed in the same manner when he was senile.

TIRED BLOOD

IN her medical school days, Gertrude Stein was convinced she was in precarious health. Something, she felt, was wrong with her blood. Having made her own diagnosis, she proceeded to adopt her own treatment—boxing with a professional welterweight. Her neighbor living below reported that the "chandelier in my room used to swing and the house echoed with shouts of, 'Now give me one on the jaw! Now give me one in the kidney!' "

POISONOUS SKATE WOUND

THE French anthropologist Claude Lévi-Strauss encountered a colony of diamond hunters deep in the vast recesses of the Brazilian jungle. They held the belief that the wound inflicted by the tail of a poisonous skate (*Raja ocellata*), a fish abounding in the region, could be cured by having a woman pass water on it. Lévi-Strauss remarks that since the women in the area "are nearly all peasant prostitutes, this ingenious remedy often brings in its train a particularly virulent form of syphilis."

LOSS OF SEXUAL POTENCY

ACCORDING to N. Lewis, who was stationed in Naples in 1944 with the occupying army, certain pharmacies in that city were frequented by middle-class women who there receive injections called *iniezione reconstituenti* for "keeping sexual powers at their peak." Lewis says the injection needles were often not too clean and that the buttocks of many women who avail themselves of this service were covered with hundreds of scars.

PEDICULOSIS

AMONG the peasantry of medieval France, delousing was a ritual widely indulged in. In Ladurie's study of the village of Montaillon, we are told that "In bed, by the fire, or by the window, Beatrice used to delouse Pierre, an act which combined rudimentary hygiene with affection."

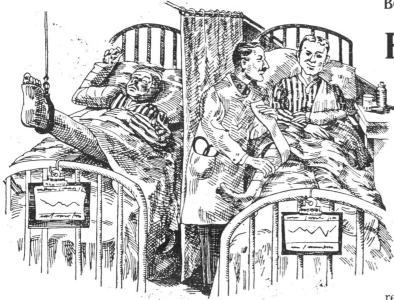

BOGUS WOUNDS

PRINCE Friederich Karl of Prussia sustained serious internal injuries when his plane was shot down over England in World War I. Once he was safely in a hospital behind the lines, British Intelligence arranged to have a bilingual English officer masquerade as a wounded German. He and the prince occupied adjoining beds, and each day the surgeon on duty carried out from behind a screen a supposed dressing of the bogus German. How much, if any, information was extracted from Prince Friederich is not recorded.

ILLNESS OF INDETERMINATE ETIOLOGY IN MALES

A SHAPELY leg can accomplish wonders, as this excerpt from the medieval chanson de geste, *Aucassin and Nicolette*, testifies;

> *A pilgrim once I saw*
> *Native he was of Limousin*
> *He was sick with a great sickness*
> *When you passed before his bed*
> *You raised up your train*
> *And your pelisse of ermine*
> *Your chemise of white linen you lifted*
> *So that he saw your shapely leg.*
> *Now the pilgrim was healed*
> *Lustier than he was before*
> *And he rose from his bed*
> *To return to his homeland*
> *Safe and well he was, his health amended.*

Eve's debt this daughter doubly satisfied;
In sorrow she brought forth, in sorrow died.
                    From a parish register of 1778

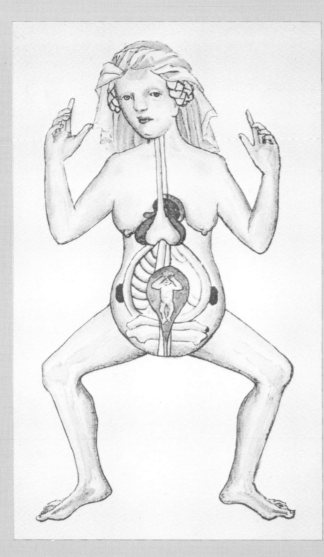

Gravida from a miniature painted c. 1400.
Courtesy Yale University Library.

XIII

A CHILD IS BORN

CONCEPTION AND AFTER

IS SHE OR ISN'T SHE—TESTING FOR PREGNANCY

THE URINE DIVULGES

HERE are two tests dating from the middle of the sixteenth century, which appeared in popular medical books of the time.

"If a woman desires to know whether she be with child or not, let her make water in a clean Copper or Brazen Vessel at night when she goes to bed and put a Nettle into it; if the Nettle have red spots in the morning, she is with child, else not."

"Some also make this tryal of conception: they stop the woman's urine in a glass or vial for three days, and then strain it through a fine linen cloth, and if they find small living creatures in it, they conclude that the woman has certainly conceived." (Another source refers to the "small living creatures" as "minute living animalcules looking like lice.")

THE NECK REVEALS

THYROID enlargement is a common occurrence during gestation, a fact known to physicians of ancient Rome. Catullus refers to the daily measurement of the neck in suspected pregnancy. The same procedure appears in eighteenth-century medical literature: "A girl is a virgin when a thread which has been stretched from the tip of her nose to the end of the saggital suture at the point where it joins the lambdoidal can then encircle her neck." A test devised by a certain Rabbi Gamaliel and recorded in the Talmud is far less rational but far more ingenious. He seated two slave women, a virgin and a nonvirgin, in turn on a barrel of wine. The breath of the deflowered woman smelled of wine; the breath of the virgin did not. Presumably the intact hymen choked off the vinous odor.

THE NEEDLE TELLS

IN Hungary it was the custom for a woman to stick a sewing needle into a picture of the Virgin and to leave it there undisturbed for nine days. If the needle was unrusted at the end of that time, the woman in question had not conceived; if rusted, she was pregnant.

THE MIDWIVES KNOW

CECILY Mann, "a spinster of Ingleston," was charged in 1613 with assaulting John Evans on the public highway and snatching his purse. She pleaded benefit of pregnancy. The twelve matrons appointed to examine her found no evidence of gravidity and so testified under oath. Cecily was hanged.

BOY OR GIRL?

1300 B.C.

MORE than three millennia ago, an Egyptian scribe recorded the following in what has become known as the Berlin papyrus: "Another test for a woman who will bear or a woman who will not bear. Wheat and spelt; let the woman water them daily with her urine. . . . If they grow, she will bear; if the wheat grows it will be a boy; if the spelt grows, it will be a girl. If neither grows, she will not bear." We now know that the estrogenic hormones in urine can speed up various germination processes in seeds, cuttings, and plants. It has been said that the test "seems to be one of the most striking examples of intelligent anticipation" in the history of biology and medicine.

CIRCA A.D. 300

LABOR pains were said by Talmudic scholars to be more severe in the case of a female infant than a male. Prediction was also based on the ability of the husband to withhold ejaculation until after the wife's orgasm. Should he do so, he would procreate male children only. According to Talmudic opinion, the newborn emerges in the position the sexes assume during intercourse, so that the female infants would be expected to be delivered in the occiput posterior position.

42 B.C.

ACCORDING to Pliny, Livia, the wife of Nero, seeking to determine the sex of her unborn child, placed an egg in her bosom. In due time the egg hatched and produced a cockerel. The omen proved right — Tiberius, an undoubted male, was born to the royal pair.

CIRCA 1200

MICHAEL Scot, court astrologer to Frederick II of Hohenstaufen, invented a "chiromantic" method of determining the sex of the unborn. The parturient woman is asked to hold out her hand. If she extends her right, a boy was to be expected; if the left, a girl. Aristotle and after him Hippocrates and Galen believed that the right side was concerned with the male sex and the left with the female. Avicenna wrote that sperm reaching the left cavity of the uterus would generate a female, the right, a male.

MATTERS MAINLY OBSTETRICAL

ROYAL DELIVERY UNDER TWO KINGS

LOUIS XIII was delivered in the presence of the princes of the blood, each of whom stepped forward and presented himself to the king-to-be even before the umbilical cord had been cut. The ritual was necessary to establish the legitimacy of the royal infant.

Louis XIV had his mistresses delivered by court doctors so he could observe their manipulations from behind a screen.

BEING BORN AMONG THE CHEROKEES

IN most American tribes, a kneeling or squatting posture was commonly used during parturition. To correct an abnormal position of the fetus, the Cherokee would have four women grasp the arms and legs of the mother, lift her into the air and shake her until the correct position was assumed. A comparable drastic procedure was followed by the Nez Percé.

Violent movement was also employed for the relief of protracted labor. Indians of the Canadian plains tossed the mother in a blanket, while among the Apache tribes it was the practice to tie a rope under the armpits of a woman in labor and then raise her off the ground by throwing the free end over a tree branch. Thus suspended, she was tossed up and down. The ancient Greeks used a similar contrivance, and classical sources reveal that shaking the bed of the mother-to-be was not an uncommon practice.

OBSTETRICS IN THE DARK

BY the middle of the eighteenth century, physicians were beginning to attend women in childbirth, but prudery made their ministrations both difficult and dangerous. Operations were conducted under bed-clothes, often in darkened rooms. Sometimes a protective sheet would be extended from patient to doctor and tied around the latter's neck. Even the most qualified doctors sometimes blundered.

William Smellie once caused a serious hemorrhage in one of his patients by dividing the umbilical cord in the wrong place. He retied the cord and pacified the assisting midwife by assuring her that what he had done was a method for preventing convulsions. He confessed later that he was never more frightened in his life.

A SECRET BOON—OBSTETRIC FORCEPS

FOR almost one hundred years the obstetric forceps remained the carefully guarded property of the Chamberlen family. Consisting of two curved pieces of iron shaped like spoons and united at a pivot joint, it was a simple device that could remain secret so long only because of the strenuous precautions adopted by the Chamberlens. The instrument, locked "in a massive wooden chest trimmed with gilt," was transported under guard to the lying-in chamber, which was barred to everyone but the operator. It is said that the patient herself was blindfolded. Tradition has it that a group of patriotic Englishmen got up a purse for purchase of the forceps and were presented with only one blade, a dodge that the ineffable Hugh Chamberlen apparently repeated in Holland. A contemporary obstetrician put it well: "He who keeps secret so beneficial an instrument . . . deserves to have a worm devour his vitals for all eternity. . . ."

CESAROTOMY IN UGANDA AND SIEGERSHAUFEN

IN 1879 the English explorer and physician R. W. Felkin witnessed a Caesarian section performed by natives in Uganda. According to his account, both mother and infant survived, a formidable accomplishment when one considers that for over 2,000 years in the Western world only postmortem operations were performed. However, the Ugandan feat was duplicated by at least one European and a layman at that. In 1500 Jacob Nufer, a sow gelder of Sigershaufen, driven to desperation by the failure of midwives and lithotomists to deliver his wife, opened her abdominal and uterine walls with the razor of his trade and removed the infant safely. The mother made a complete recovery. Nufer probably controlled bleeding with hot irons, the common practice of the time.

"FALSE LABOR"

MARCO Polo may have been the first to describe the practice of couvade, which he encountered among the aboriginal hill tribes of China's interior. The custom is not unknown in the West, and seems to have been practiced in the Béarn region of France. A kind of male childbirth, couvade requires that the husband take to his bed, wailing and moaning, while the wife gives birth unobserved and in silence. The husband may even be confined to his bed for a period after the birth. He may avoid certain foods and follow other taboos observed by pregnant women of the community. It is thought that the custom was designed to frustrate the demons of puerperal fever.

DOCTORS, MIDWIVES, AND WET NURSES

That Rowlandson should include a nursery in his England Dance of Death is not as perverse as it may appear. In the seventeenth century, wet nursing was perceived as tantamount to infanticide. In Rowlandson's century—the eighteenth—it was still a significant cause of infant mortality, the free use of sedatives being not the least of the contributing factors.

The Nursery, from Rowlandson's Drawings for the English Dance of Death.

MIDWIVES AND MIDWIFERY

Also the mydwyfe muste instruct and comfort the partie, not onely refreshing her with good meate and drinke, but also with sweete woordes, gevying her good hope of a speedful deliveraunce, ecouraging and so gevying her patience and tolleraunce . . .

Thomas Raynalde, The Byrthe of Mankynde, *1540*

In the Middle Ages law and tradition demanded that childbirth be the exclusive province of women. Dr. Wertt of Hamburg was burned at the stake in 1522 for impersonating a midwife. Apparently he had wanted to study obstetrics at first hand. This extract from a midwife's license, dated 2 August 1588 at London, shows how uncompromisingly the Dr. Wertts of the time were kept at arm's length. "ITEM that you shalbe secrete and not open anye matter appertayninge to your office in the pnce of anye man unlesse necessarye or gret urgent causes shall contrayne you soe to doe."

A more enlightened attitude toward women in childbirth was not fostered by the biblical injunction, "In sorrow thou shalt bring forth children. . . ." So literally was the divine dictum taken that Agnes Simpson was tried before the king of Scotland in 1591 as a heretic, condemned as a witch and burned alive because she had helped a lady of rank seek relief from pain during the birth of her sons.

The respected status and competence of the French midwife in the 16th century is amply demonstrated by a medicolegal report of May 15, 1545, translated by the eminent medical historian, Erwin H. Ackerknecht. It concerns Mariette de Garrigues, aged 15, "said to have been raped and deflowered and devirginized." The midwives Jeanne de Mon, Jeanne Verguire and Beatrice Laurade, by the order of the Judge of Espere in Béarn, "examined and observed everything in the light of three candles." They state that they "touched with our hands and examined with our eyes, and turned over with our fingers. And we found that neither was the vulva deformed nor the curunculae displaced, nor the labia minora distended, nor the perineum wrinkled, nor the internal orifice of the uterus opened, nor the cervix uteri split, nor the pubic hair bent, nor the hymen displaced, nor the breasts wilted, nor the margin of the great labia changed, nor the vagina enlarged, nor the membrane that connects the curcunculae returned, nor the pubis broken, nor the clitoris in any way damaged. All this we, the above-mentioned midwives, state as our report and direct judgement."*

* Copyright © 1950 Ciba-Geigy Corporation. With permission from Ciba Symposia, by E. H. Ackerknecht, M.D.

MIDWIFERY TAUGHT AT HOME

SMELLIE, "master of British midwifery," treated the gravid poor of London in their own homes in return for permission to bring his pupils along. He trained no fewer than 900, a number of them women, at a time when London had no maternity hospital offering the means for clinical instruction. To "dulcify the asperities of the male physique," Smellie wore a "loose washing night-gown" when treating his patients. To this he added a bonnet to cover his wig.

MIDWIFERY IN THE SEVENTEENTH CENTURY

A REMARKABLE midwife was Catherine Schraders, who practiced her art for fifty-two years in the Netherlands. She made notes after each delivery, and published them in her *Memory Book of the Women*, a work of 544 pages. Her results were striking in an age when asepsis was unknown. In 4,000 deliveries, Mrs. Schraders lost only fifteen mothers and ninety children. She discusses one case in which labor lasted three days. Ultimately the infant died, and Schraders attempted to bring down an arm. She finally amputated it, "and after some terrifying moments" with her hook, delivery took place. Neither the mother nor family members saw the amputated limb. The resourceful midwife had hidden it in her sleeve. The mother survived, "healthy and undamaged."

THE BIZARRE OCCUPATION OF "MAMMER"

IN the villages of seventeenth-century Europe, the mammer was an individual employed to relieve mothers who produced milk too copiously or whose children did not suckle well. His job was to remove excess milk by suction. Villages with populations of differing religious loyalties might have both a Protestant and Catholic mammer.

WILLIAM HUNTER SAYS NO TO OBSTETRIC FORCEPS

HUNTER, displaying a pair of old and rusted forceps, had this to say: "This is how the forceps of the good midwife looks. The more rust there is on them, the better the midwife, for he rarely uses them. Birth is a natural process with which the doctor should interfere as little as possible." This laissez-faire doctrine seems to have been adopted by Sir Richard Croft, and it got him into deep trouble. After fifty-two hours of labor, his patient, Princess Charlotte, only child of George IV, suffered a stillbirth. The princess died soon after. The princess's narrow pelvis had placed Croft firmly on the horns of a dilemma. A Caesarian would have been fatal for the mother. Dismemberment of the fetus, the only true solution, would have been regicide once removed. Guilt-ridden Croft put a bullet through his head.

MIDWIFELY SUPERSTITIONS

TO stop hemorrhages before or after delivery, a thread should be bound around the mother's fifth toe. The placenta should not be buried near water because the newborn in his childhood would always wish to play near rivers and lakes and might drown. During labor, doors, closets, and drawers should be allowed to remain wide open. The placenta should be buried deeply because if a dog or cat should dig it up, the newborn would grow up to be a vagrant.

OBSTETRICS BY PROXY

THE prohibition against the presence of men during delivery suffered a blow in the seventeenth century when surgeons were permitted to assist midwives at the Hôtel Dieu in Paris. But old pruderies died hard. Queen Charlotte was delivered by a midwife while William Hunter was in attendance. The great anatomist, however, was seated in an antechamber and from that undignified distance relayed his advice to the midwife.

WET NURSING

"Everything takes after the dam that gave it suck.
  Where had'st thou thy milk?
      James Ford, "The Lovers' Melancholy" (1628)

For the poor, the baby farmer; for the well-off, a wet nurse—sometimes several wet nurses. Louis XIII went through four, Henry IV and Louis XV no fewer than eight. Royalty could afford to be choosy, and the ideal nurse was hard to find. Ambrose Paré, surgeon to four kings of France, described her thus: "She must have a capacious chest and rather large breasts, not flaccid and pendant, between hard and soft . . . the child presses the end of his nose to the breast; finding it too hard he is irritated and refuses to suckle, and he sometimes becomes snub-nosed."

Laurence Sterne, in *Tristram Shandy,* has great fun with Paré's prescription. "Paré convinced my father . . . that the firmness and elastic repulsion of the organ of nutrition . . . tho' happy for the woman was the undoing of the child, inasmuch as his nose was so snubbled, so rebuffed, so rebated, and so refrigerated thereby, as never to arrive *ad munsuram suam legitimam,"* whereas "by sinking into it as into so much butter, the nose was comforted, nourished, plumped up, refreshed, refocillated, and set a-growing forever."

Sterne notwithstanding, choosing a wet nurse was a serious matter. There was the matter of the nurse's sex life, for example. Intercourse "troubled the blood," observed French physicians of the seventeenth century, and caused the wet nurse's milk to smell. Among the rich and powerful separation of nurse from husband was not difficult, since she "lived in." But even under such circumstances, she had to watch her step. Louis XIII dismissed one of the dauphin's nurses because she had been observed talking to her husband. For the conscientious parent, the wet nurse's personality and character were important too, since it was widely believed that she passed on her vices and virtues along with her milk.* An Italian cleric condemned the practice of wet nursing in these words: "Though he be your own child, and you be pretty-mannered and discreet, yet sometimes you give him to be nursed by a sow . . . and when he comes home you say: 'I know not whom you resemble! You are not like unto any of us!' You mark not where the cause lies— and it serves you right."

* The primitive notion that mother's milk can shape character was alive and well in the nineteenth century, and undoubtedly has its adherents today. Litwack, in his *Been in the Storm So Long,* quotes an elderly South Carolinian (1885): "We gave our infants to black wenches to suckle and thus poisoned the blood of our children, and made them cowards . . . it will take 500 years, if not longer, by the infusion of new blood to eradicate the hereditary vices imbibed with the blood— milk *is* blood—of black wet nurses."

A manuscript dating from the twelfth century attests to the antiquity of the belief in the character-forming potency of mother's milk. It recommends that the nurse be as much like the mother as possible,"not angry or sad or lazy and stupid" because such qualities are passed on to the nursling. The breasts should be firm and not too large, lest they "smother the child when they cover her nose." But the very real fear of defilement from "bad" milk is best conveyed by the story of the Countess Yde, related by G. G. Coulton in his *Life in the Middle Ages.* The countess suckled her three sons, one of whom became a duke; the second, a crusader, was crowned king of Jerusalem. The third remained a mere count, the victim of an unfortunate misadventure in the nursery. It seems that on one occasion when the countess was at mass, "one of the three brothers, awakening, wailed sore and howled; wherefore the maiden called a damosel and bade her suckle the child." When the countess heard of it, "all her heart shook; for the pain that she had she fell upon a seat; sore gasped her heart under her breast. . . . Swiftly she flew, all trembling with rage and caught her child under the arms: the child of tender flesh, she caught him in her hands, her face was as black as coal with the wrath that seethed within. . . . There on a mighty table she bade them spread out a purple quilt, and hold the child: there she rolled him and caught him by the shoulders, that he delayed not to give up the milk that he had sucked. Yet ever after were his deeds and his renown less, even to the day of his death."

PRENATAL INFLUENCES AND TERATOLOGY

Folk belief insists that congenital malformations arise not in utero but as the result of maternal fright or other extraneous cause. Lazarus Johannes Baptista Colloredo is regarded as a classic case of parasitic teratism. Born in Genoa in 1617, he was a normal child except in one particular. From his abdominal wall there hung a monster with one thigh, a torso with hands and arms and a well-developed head. Colleredo, who apparently fathered several children, was exhibited all over Europe, and seems to have lived a normal life span.

INFLUENCING THE UNBORN

BEAUTIFUL PICTURES

READ uplifting books, look at beautiful pictures, think spiritual thoughts was the advice in the folder that came with every bottle of the popular paregoric Castoria of our great-grandmother's day. In Evelyn Waugh's *Work Suspended* Lucy says of her mother's pregnancy, "D'you know, before I was born, so Aunt Maureen says, my mother used to sit in front of a Flaxman bas-relief so as to give me ideal beauty."

A WHITE HOUSE

RABBI Akiba, says the Talmud, was questioned by the king of the Arabs. "I am black and my wife is black, and she bore me a white son; shall I kill her because of unfaithfulness?" Rabbi Akiba asked the king, "Is your house white or black?" The king replied, "It is white." Rabbi Akiba said, "She looked at the house and therefore bore you a white offspring. This also happened to Jacob, our Father." The King thanked Rabbi Akiba.

A SKELETON

ACCORDING to one early source, Phaillus gazed so intently at the bronze skeleton that Hippocrates had consecrated in the Temple of Aesculapius, that dreaming later of the skeleton's hideousness he became ill and expired.

UGLY M.D.'S

AT the University of Louvain in the seventeenth century, no one was admitted to the doctorate in medicine who had a facial deformity because "he could trouble the imagination of pregnant women, who might give birth to monsters resembling these physicians." The superstition is as old as Leviticus, in which a ban on priests with broken noses is advised because women remembering their appearance at the altar might retain that memory and give birth to a teratoid infant.

CHOCOLATE

IN one of her letters, Mme de Sévigné (1626–1696) assures her correspondent that the Marquise de Coëtlogen "took too much chocolate, being pregnant last year, and she was brought to bed of a little boy who was black as the devil."

POLAR BEARS

THE poet and essayist Helen Bevington visited the zoo when pregnant. She tells how a woman came up to her at the polar bear cage and put her hands tightly across Bevington's eyes. "Stay away from the bears, dear," she begged earnestly. "You mustn't stare at them like that. You'll mark your unborn child."

FRIGHT

WALTER Warner (d. 1640) was a mathematician and philosopher who had some tentative notions about the circulation of the blood. He was born with only one hand. Says Aubrey, ". . . his mother was frighted, which caused his deformity, so instead of a left hand, he had only a stump with five warts upon it, instead of a hand and fingers."

TALL TALES AND TERATOLOGY

A BLESSED EVENT FOR A HERMAPHRODITE

HERMAPHRODITES were exploited as circus freaks well into the eighteenth century. In Fielding's play *Pasquin*, a child exclaims when told the family was to go to London, ". . . and then we shall see Fanbelly, the strange man-woman they say is with child . . . and the rope dancing and the tumbling." From the Fugger News Letters we learn that a Landsknecht attached to an Italian regiment "on going to bed one night complained to his wife that he had great pains in his belly and felt something stirring herein. An hour thereafter he gave birth to a child, a girl." A hermaphrodite, he was able to "suckle the babe with his right breast only and not at all on his left where he is a man. He also has the natural organs of a man for passing water." His daughter was christened with military fanfare, and many noble ladies stood sponsor for the infant. We report with regret that the marriage was dissolved by the clergy.

A RAFT OF RABBITS

MARY Tofts of Godalming was so badly frightened by a rabbit when she was pregnant, that instead of a human child, she presented her husband with a total of 15 bunnies. With a surgeon of Westminster Hospital testifying that the rabbit birth had occurred in his presence, the miraculous accouchement was soon the talk of the town and all London was agog. Sent by George I to investigate, a German physician claimed to have seen a rabbit part on the lady's person but was nonetheless somewhat skeptical. It remained for Sir Robert Massingham to expose the cheat. He showed that Tofts had concealed the rabbits about her person, a stratagem made easy by the practice of performing delivery under a sheet.

AN OVIPAROUS WOMAN

IN 1638, in the presence of four neighbors, Anna, wife of Gudbrand Erlandson, gave birth to an egg. In external appearance, as well as in the nature of its white and yolk, it was very like a hen's egg. Toward evening of the same day, Anna was delivered of a second egg in the presence of the same four neighbors. Both mother and witnesses testified that the pains of parturition in both cases exceeded by far those she had suffered in bringing forth her eleven children. A learned report of the event speculates that the egg was not of uterine origin but was expelled via the intestines.

AN UNFORTUNATE HOUSEWIFE OF WALES

MARGARET Gryffith, housewife, in 1588 grew "a hideous prong of packed and layered keratin" from her brow. For her contemporaries, the growth was unquestionable evidence of adultery. She was denounced from the pulpit, avoided by her neighbors, and "made readie to be seene" as a warning and example as far away as London.

FROM A FLORENTINE DIARY OF 1514

"20 OCTOBER. A Spaniard came to Florence who had with him a boy of thirteen, a kind of monstrosity, whom he went around showing everywhere, gaining much money. Instead of being only one boy, there were two, attached to one another in an extraordinary way. . . . The boys do not seem greatly troubled."

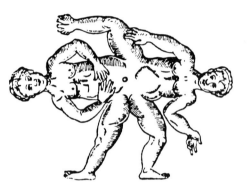

PARÉ'S MEDUSA

A CAPUT Medusa—a monster with a human head encrusted with snakes instead of hair and beard—was said by Paré to have been found in a hen's egg. A treatise on monsters referring to this bizarre phenomenon offers an explanation: either a madman had had intercourse with a hen, or a hen had mated with a rabid rooster after ingesting male semen, menstrual blood, and the eggs of a snake!

JONATHAN SWIFT AND THE MONSTER-MONGERS

PEPYS wrote that he was "big with child to see any strange thing." He managed to see many, because there always have been "monster-mongers and other retailers of strange sights" to divert the population of London. Among the most fascinating were midgets and dwarfs, the latter being of miniature size but burdened with various structural abnormalities—humpbacks most frequently. Altick in his *Shows of London*, demonstrates that Swift's imagination must have been stimulated by London's freak shows, and particularly by exhibitions of giants and dwarfs. Gulliver in Brobdingnag is carried about in a box just as dwarfs were in Swift's day. John Evelyn speaks of a Swiss dwarf, thirty-one inches high, "a little manikin that was lately carried about in a box" to be exhibited in taverns and the homes of the well-to-do.

Hunchback with walking stick. An etching by Callot.

Cripple with wooden leg and crutch. An etching by Callot.

The history of childhood is a nightmare from which we have only recently begun to awaken.

Lloyd DeMause

Found in the Street, London, 1868. An etching by Gustave Doré.

INFANTS WITHOUT PROMISE, CHILDREN WITHOUT CHILDHOOD

OVERLAYING AND OTHER BARBARITIES

OVERLAYING

VALENTINE'S servant in Congreve's *Love for Love* announces that a wet nurse is at the door with one of his children. Valentine responds, "Pox on her, could she find no other time to fling my Susan in my Face? Here give her this [gives money] and bid her trouble me no more; a thoughtless two-handed Whore, she knows my condition well enough [he is bankrupt] and might have overlaid the Child a Fortnight ago, if she had any forecast in her."

Congreve's play appeared in 1695, in an age when "overlaying" or smothering an infant who shared a bed with parents or wet nurse was widely practiced—largely among the desperate poor. It has had a long history. A penitential of 850 declares, "If anyone overlays an unbaptized baby, he shall do penance for three years, if unintentionally, two years." Later the practice was regarded as homicide. By the fifteenth century it was punished by burning at the stake or burying alive.

OVERLAYING IN AMERICA

ABANDONMENT was not unknown in America, nor was overlaying. This letter sent to his absentee mistress by a southern plantation overseer reveals like a sudden lightning flash the same misery that was claiming so many little lives across the sea.

Marm

   i have just Received your leters 1 of the 4th and 1 of the 7th Your woman Jane had a child and at 2 weeks old overlyed it the rest of your servants are wel at present.

Respectfully
John A. Mairs

KEEPING NURSLINGS QUIET

WILLIAM Buchan, in his *Domestic Medicine* (1769), asserted that half the children who died in London each year were killed by laudanum, spirits, or proprietary sedatives. Among the latter was Godfrey's Cordial, a mixture of opium, treacle, and sassafras.

MAIMING

WET nursing was widely regarded as a form of infanticide—"overlaid and starved at nurse" was the stated cause of 529 deaths in the London bills of mortality for the years 1639–1659. A petition to the king drawn up by Thomas Coram, who was almost single-handedly responsible for the establishment of the London Foundling Hospital, refers to the "putting of unhappy foundlings to wicked and barbarous nurses, who undertake to bring them up for a small and trifling sum of money, do often suffer them to starve . . . or either turn them into the streets to beg and steal, or hire them out to loose persons by whom they are trained up in that infamous way of living and sometimes are maimed or blinded and distorted in their limbs in order to move to pity and compassion. . . ."

Like infanticide, maiming the young for the purpose of exciting compassion was a practice of ancient lineage. A chronicle of the year 1416 records that "III beggeres stole III childyr at Lenne, and of on thei put oute his eyne, the other thei broke his bak, and the thirde thei cut of his handis and his feete, that men schuld of pite gyve them food."

GETTING RID OF FOCI OF INFECTION IN 1620

IN January 1620, one hundred minors were "gathered up in divers places" and forcibly shipped to the American colonies, the Lord Mayor of London having been informed by the Privy Council that the ills and plagues of the city were caused by the swarms of homeless and starving children in the streets of the slum districts. The city contributed 400 pounds to rid itself of this pitiful human cargo.

LIFE AND DEATH ON SHIPBOARD

ON their way to Australia in four ships, nearly 300 emigrants, most of them children, succumbed to typhus, scarlet fever, and measles. At an inquiry ordered by the Colonial Secretary, one expert testified that the cause of the disastrous loss of life was damp. "It is understood that the decks were washed, an unhealthy practice strictly prohibited by instructions." One investigator was nearer the mark. He describes the medical examination passengers were obliged to undergo before sailing. "I passed before the surgeon for inspection. 'What's your name? Are you well? Hold out your tongue. All right.' He then addressed himself to the next person."

GIN-SOAKING THE YOUNG

TESTIMONY before a House of Commons investigating committee in 1833 turned up evidence that children from six to sixteen were frequenting public houses, where they commonly purchased a pennyworth of gin or rum. And liquor was available at every hand. Every fourth house in the St. Giles district was a gin shop where anybody could be "drunk for a penny, dead drunk for twopence, straw free." It was no secret that women brought children-in-arms into public houses where they were given sips of liquor to keep them quiet, and child abuse by gin-crazed parents was a recurring fact of life. M. Dorothy George, a student of life in the eighteenth century, cites the case of Judith Dufour, who "fetched her two-year-old child from the workhouse where it had just been 'new clothed.' She strangled it and left it in a ditch in Bethnal Green in order to sell its clothes." The one and fourpence she obtained was spent on gin.

PRIVATE INDIGNITIES, PUBLIC SCANDALS

When my mother died, I was very young,
And my father sold me while yet my tongue
Could scarcely cry, Weep, weep, weep!
So in your chimneys I sweep and in soot I sleep.
                                        William Blake

William Burges,
chimney sweeper, No. 36 Bolton
Street, Chorley, flatters himself in
having boys of the best size for such
branches of business suitable for a Tunnel
or Chimney, that it is now in his power to render
his assistance in a more extensive manner than he
usually has done. He also carries his boys from room
to room occasionally to prevent them staining or marking
any room floor with their feet.

A calling card of 1867

"CLIMBING BOYS"

S WEEPS were bound as apprentices as young as four years. Parents would take children to master sweepers and bind them over to the highest bidder "as they cannot put them to apprentice to any other master at so early an age." Shimmying himself up chimneys as narrow as nine inches square and as high as sixty feet, a sweep would have to show his head or brandish his brush above the chimney pot to prove he had done his job. He dislodged the soot as he climbed, emptying it into a bag. By the time he reached his teens, the sweep "might find himself not only a bandy-legged hunchback, but also a eunuch," the victim of a scrotal disease known as "chimney sweeper's cancer." Years of pressing knees against chimney walls deformed his legs and played havoc with his knee caps, while the ubiquitous soot brought inflammation of the eyes and skin disease.

SOME VICTIMS OF ADULT CARE

THE DUKE OF SOUTHAMPTON

THOUGH "a most lovely youth," the duke had two incisors that "grew out very unhandsome." His mother, Barbara Villiers, one of the many mistresses of Charles II, had him bound tightly to a chair so that the unbecoming teeth could be extracted. He lost his teeth, and with them, because of the acute pain, his understanding.

SWADDLED INFANTS

TIGHTLY wrapped as he was, the swaddled infant was a helpless bundle often treated cavalierly by his guardians. A brother of Henry IV of France was dropped accidentally while being passed from one palace window to another for his amusement. The fall killed him. A like fate overtook the little comte de Marle when his nurse and a gentleman-in-waiting played at tossing him from one window to another, sometimes pretending not to catch him. He fell, struck a stone below, and died.

As late as 1889, Jules Renard recorded in his journal this observation on swaddling as practiced among French farm laborers: "Once the child is born it is entirely swaddled up, even the arms, which are bound down. All you see is the head, purple and puffy." Fresh air and frequently changed clothes could have given swaddling at least a modicum of medical validity. But even in the time of William Smellie (1697–1763), the founder of scientific midwifery in England, the mother of the newborn babe was "covered up close in bed with additional clothes, curtains drawn and pinned together, every crevice stopped close, not excepting the keyhole, and blankets were fastened across windows." In this stifling atmosphere babies were rolled up tight in twelve feet of linen.

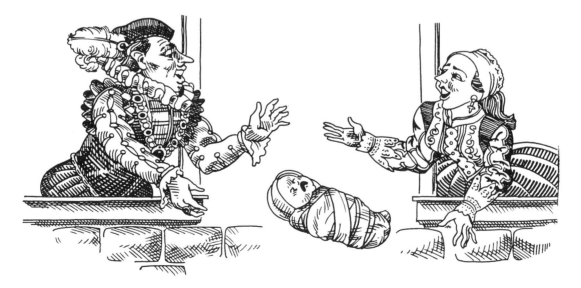

TWO SCHOOLCHILDREN

MARY McCarthy, in her *Memoirs of a Catholic Girlhood*, relates how she and her brother were put to bed by their guardians with their mouths sealed with adhesive tape to prevent mouth-breathing. Ether, which made her sick, "was used to pull the tape off in the morning, but a grimy, gray, rubbery remainder was usually left. . . ."

A BOY OF SIX

FROM the journals of W. F. Tolmie, who visited Paris in 1842, comes an account of his meeting with a famous phrenologist who showed him the skull of a boy of six. He attributed the child's death to masturbation. The parents, being wealthy, had spared neither trouble nor expense in their efforts to save him. According to the phrenologist, "Amativeness was excessive and the inferior part of the occipital bone corresponding to the organ was worn thin as a wafer and was perforated in one or two places." No doubt the parents had tried the criminal arsenal of restraints widely used right up to the turn of the century—partial circumcision, shackles and mittens for night-time wear, a cage to be placed around the genitals, even infibulation, which the medical profession recommended for stubborn cases. A comprehensive review article on infibulation in the *Bulletin of the New York Academy of Medicine* reproduces an engraving from a minatory book on self-pollution. In it a father is shown having his son swear on the hand of a skeleton that he would never be guilty of self-abuse because it meant certain death.

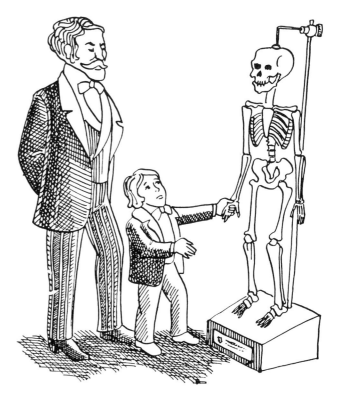

EDITH SITWELL

THREE hundred years after James I, orthopedic technology had vastly improved, but not the quality of parental wisdom. When Edith Sitwell's parents noticed that she stooped slightly and that her ankles were thin and weak, her purgatory began. She was incarcerated in a "bastille of steel," a devilish contraption that imprisoned legs and arms and even her nose, which was turned "very firmly to the opposite way which Nature had intended. . . ." Miss Sitwell avers in her delightful autobiography, *Taken Care Of,* that this satanic device "semi-atrophied" the muscles of her legs and back.

"MUN" VERNEY

FROM that treasure trove of seventeenth-century lore, the Verney Memoirs, we learn that little "Mun" Verney was sent to Utrecht to be cured of "crookedness" by a Dr. Skatt, who specialized in such cases. Mun was strapped into an iron and leather corselet from which he was released only once a week in order to have his shirt changed.

THE DUKE OF YORK

IN his memoirs, Robert Carey describes how Lady Carey, his wife, who had the guardianship of the duke of York from his fourth to his eleventh year, persuaded King James I not to put him in iron boots "to strengthen his sinews and joints." Carey's lady must have been remarkably resolute: "Many a battle my wife had with the King, but she still prevailed." She won out too when the king decided that the string under the duke's tongue should be cut because "he was so long beginning to speak."

CORSETING THE YOUNG

IN FRANCE

SENSIBLE Mrs. Thrale, the long-time friend of Samuel Johnson, describes the twelve-year-old sister of King Louis XVI as "not handsome but passable, if she was not so pinched in her stays as makes her look pale and uneasy to herself. All children through the Nation I perceive are thus squeezed and tortured during their early Years, and the deformity they exhibit at maturity repays the stupid Parents for their Pains."

IN AMERICA

TIGHTLY laced ladies of the last century were proud of their hourglass figures, won at considerable cost in impeded circulation, constricted lungs, and skeletal malformation. But their torture was self-imposed. Children, on the other hand, had no choice but to suffer from the injudiciousness of their parents. It was the custom, at least in the first decades of the century, to put them in stays at an early age and make them sit for hours strapped to a board so as to acquire a straight back. Oliver Wendell Holmes wrote of an aunt at boarding school:

> *They braced my aunt against a board,*
> *To make her straight and tall;*
> *They laced her up, they starved her down,*
> *To make her light and small;*
> *They pinched her feet, they singed her hair,*
> *They screwed it up with pins;*
> *Oh, never mortal suffered more*
> *In penance for her sins.*

IN ENGLAND

PERCIVAL Pott, a celebrated eighteenth-century surgeon, warred against the then prevalent practice of encasing children with "weak backs" in corsets. His colleague Abernethy took an unequivocal approach to the problem. A patient brought her young daughter to him, claiming the child had difficulty breathing after meals and when taking exercise. Picking up a pair of scissors, Abernethy slashed the youngster's stays from top to bottom. After walking about for ten minutes on the doctor's orders, she felt better. After another ten, she felt fine.

THE FATE OF FOUNDLINGS

"SADDLING THE SPIT"

IN England care of foundlings devolved on the parish. Of particular concern to overseers of the poor were illegitimate children, who more than others were likely sooner or later to become a burden on the parish treasury. Overseers kept a vigilant eye out for gravid nonresidents, and the pregnant poor were unceremoniously hounded out of the parish's precincts. An illegitimate child was often turned over to the parish with a lump sum to maintain it. Parish officers looked upon this payment (usually in the neighborhood of ten pounds) as a perquisite to be used for "saddling the spit," that is, arranging a parish feast. It was assumed that since the child's life would be short, the money might as well go for good cheer. No supposition was more on the mark. Of 307 foundings, 148 of them illegitimate, under four years of age received by twelve typical parishes in 1763–1765, 256 (83%) were dead by the end of 1765.

IN MEXICO, THE SHADOW LIFTS

IN Mexico the cuna (cradle) or foundling hospital accepted all "offspring of abject poverty or guilt" without question. After a month's stay, each baby was sent with an Indian nurse to the latter's village, where she and other paid nurses were under the supervision of a responsible person who was answerable for their good conduct. The children were brought back when weaned, but of the thousands admitted, rarely was a child left to grow up in the cuna. Adoption was the rule, and foundlings became favorite servants or were brought up as their own children by their guardians.

A FOUNDLING SURVIVES

NOT all the luckless babes were children of the poor. When Mme de Tencin had a child by her lover, the Chevalier Destouches, she had it conveyed secretly by a servant to the church of Saint-Jean-le-Rond. A passerby heard it wailing on the steps of the baptismal chapel and carried it to the Enfants Trouvés, or foundling hospital. Returning from a military campaign, the father traced the babe and deposited him with a wet nurse, the wife of a glazier. One wonders how many of the abandoned ones might have made a stir in the world had they lived. This one did. He grew up to be the celebrated philosopher, scientist and mathematician, Jean le Rond d'Alembert.

A TRAFFIC IN INFANTS

UNSAVORY characters from all over England were employed as conveyors of unwanted children and sometimes moribund infants to London's Foundling Hospital when it opened its doors in 1741. Despite the threat of heavy penalties, a similar traffic in infants brought thousands from the provinces to Paris. As late as 1860, police apprehended a woman who had carried no fewer than 192 babies to Paris in the space of seventeen years. She used a basket capable of holding four or five little ones.

"CHILDREN KILLED AT GOVERNMENT EXPENSE"

IN an effort to check the exposure and murder of unwanted babies, Napoleon decreed that hospices be set up in every French department, each to be equipped with a revolving box and bell so that those abandoning a child could do so without discovery. In the single decade 1824–1833, 336,297 infants were left at some 270 hospices, an index of the widespread destitution and despair. Mortality among the *enfants trouvés* was staggering. In 1818 the Paris hospice took in 4,779 babies. Of these, 370 died in the first three months and another 956 within the first year. Somebody suggested the hospices set up signs reading, "Children killed at government expense."

CHILDREN AT WORK

COTTON MILL WORKERS IN 1810

AN observer noted in his diary that the cotton mills at Lanark, Scotland, employed 2,500 workmen, most of whom were children "who work from six o'clock in the morning till seven in the evening, having in that interval an hour and a quarter allowed for meals; at night, from eight to ten for school. These children are taken into employment at eight years old, receiving five shillings a week; when older they get as much as half a guinea." Says the diarist (Bless him!), "Eleven hours of confinement and labour, with the schooling, thirteen hours, is undoubtedly too much for children. I think the laws should interfere between avarice and nature."

THE LONDON WORKHOUSE IN 1700

IN the reign of Queen Anne, the workhouse children, who were either vagrants or charges of the parish, were taught spinning wool and flax, sewing, knitting, winding silk, and making their own clothes and shoes. Here is a description by a contemporary of their daily round."The Bell rings at 6 a Clock in the morning to call up the Children, and half an Hour after, the Bell is rung for Prayers and Breakfast; at 7 the Children are set to work. . . . All the Children are called down for an Hour every Day to Read, and an Hour every Day to Write . . . at 12 a Clock they go to Dinner, and have a little time to play till One, then they are set to work again till 6 a Clock: They are rung to prayers, to their Supper, and allowed to play till Bed time." In all, a twelve-hour day, nine hours of which were devoted to labor.

The London Workhouse was well endowed; other parish workhouses were likely to be fearfully overcrowded. In 1774 the parish of St. Leonard's Shoreditch petitioned to buy ground for a new workhouse. They were obliged, they said, to place thirty-nine children in three beds, "by which means they contract disorders from each other."

APPRENTICESHIP IN THE EIGHTEENTH CENTURY

FROM the records of the Middlesex Sessions comes this not untypical case cited by M. Dorothy George in her *London Life in the Eighteenth Century:* "Sarah Wise was discharge from Samuel Elwick of St. James Clerkenwell. She had been put to him to learn the art and mystery of a hair-twister for the term of ten years and had served nearly five, during which he had given her only one stuff gown and one bays petticoat, and had not provided her with enough to eat and drink so that she had to beg from neighbors." Sarah said she was obliged to sleep in a very small flock bed,"and six of them lays therein, some at the foot and some at the head." At the time of the hearing, Sarah's master had been in Newgate gaol for six months, leaving her utterly destitute.

CHILDREN AT PLAY

THE slums of London in the middle of the eighteenth century were noisome rookeries of decay and disease, in which children lived lives of unbelievable squalor with no opportunity for regular play in healthful surroundings. Says Jerrold in *London, A Pilgrimage*, from which the drawing on this page is taken, "As the sun rises, the court swarms at once: for there are no ablutions to perform, no toilets to make—neither brush nor comb delays the outpouring of babes and nurslings from cellar and garret." Doré's picture of children dancing in a dim courtyard to the strains of a hurdy-gurdy is heartbreakingly eloquent. One sees not a single smile; all the little faces are dismayingly solemn as though these little ones are already resignedly aware of the fate that awaits them—deprived lives and an early death.

The Organ in the Court. by Doré.

The necessities of nature are so base and brutish that in obeying them we are apt to forget that we are the noblest creatures of the universe.

Sir Ferdinando Lapith in
Aldous Huxley's Crome Yellow

Harington's invention, described in his Metamor-*phosis of Ajax, A Cloacinean Satire, was in its essentials no different from the modern flush toilet. Yet more than two centuries were to pass before it was installed in the homes of the affluent.*

A fifteenth-century "house of easement." Sir John Harington's water closet (1586).

Sprinto non spinto.   More feard than hurt.

XV

BEFORE THE BATHROOM

HYGIENE—PUBLIC AND PRIVATE

LIFE WITHOUT PLUMBING

PEPYS'S PRIVY PROBLEM

IN the houses of the city's poor, privies were placed over an open cesspool, which was usually to be found at the foot of the basement stairs. Provision was rarely made for emptying and cleaning, and cesspools were often leaky and overfull, foci of infection and danger to neighboring houses when, as sometimes happened, they overflowed. From Pepys's *Diary:* "October 20th 1660. This morning one came to advise me where to make me a window into my cellar . . . and going down into my cellar to look I stepped into a great heap of ———, by which I found that Mr. Turner's house of office is full and comes into my cellar, which do trouble me."

AT HOME

CLOSE stools were de rigueur in the homes of the well-to-do right through the eighteenth century. They were padded and fitted with a lid and handles so they could be carried about when necessary. An American visiting England was invited to dinner at the home of friends. He observed with astonishment in a corner of the dining room "a certain convenient piece of furniture to be used by anyone who wants it. The operation is performed very deliberately and undisguisedly, as a matter of course, and occasions no interruption of the conversation."

"FACILITIES" IN THE HOME OF A RICH MERCHANT

ORIGO tells us that an inventory taken of the household effects of Francesco di Marco Datini (d. 1410), a well-to-do merchant of Prato, Italy, reveals no mention of latrines, though they existed in some Florentine houses of the period. In both the chief guest room and the hall, however, there was an iscranna forata, or commode. For washing, there were "two basins for washing the feet and one round barber's basin." An assortment of different kinds of towels included five thick ones "for rubbing the head." Rubbing was much used as a substitute for washing and was thought healthful.

ON THE SEATS OF THE MIGHTY

A FIFTEENTH-CENTURY guide for serving men urges them to cover the seat of the privy with thick green woolen cloth and to have a care for their masters' comfort by having sufficient cotton stuff available when needed. The castle privy or "garderobe" was constructed in the thickness of the walls or under a stone staircase, and opened directly into a ditch or the castle moat, a dangerous circumstance in time of siege.

NASTY DOINGS AT COURT AND ELSEWHERE

COURTIERS AND OTHERS IN FRANCE

"IN the neighborhood of the Louvre, in several parts of the court, on the great stairway, and in the passageways, behind doors, and just about everywhere, one sees a thousand ordures, one smells a thousand intolerable stenches caused by the natural necessities which everyone performs there every day."

The Dutch-born sister-in-law of Louis XIV writes to a friend that "there is one dirty thing that I shall never get used to: the people stationed in the galleries in front of our rooms piss into all the corners. It is impossible to leave one's apartments without seeing somebody pissing."

COURTIERS IN ENGLAND

AT Oxford, to which the court had fled to escape the plague in 1665, the courtiers, "gay in their apparell, but nasty and beastly in their habits, left excrements in every corner, in chimneys, studies, cole-houses, cellars."

A MEMBER OF PARLIAMENT

AUBREY says that Sir William Fleetwood, Recorder of London, was overtaken in Cheapside by a sudden looseness near the Standard. "He turned up his breech against the Standard and bade his man hide his face; for they shall never see my Arse again sayd he."

THE SECRETARY TO HIS MAJESTY'S NAVY

SLEEPING one night at a stranger's, Pepys found himself in need of a chamber pot because, as he thought, of "some fresh damp linen" that he had put on. He felt in the dark for the necessary article, but there was none, and so, he says,"I was forced in this strange house to rise and shit in the chimney twice, and so to bed and I was very well again."

A NINETEENTH-CENTURY POET

THE consequences of a paucity of conveniences was still evident in Byron's time. It seems he was barred from Long's Hotel in Bond Street because "on a cold and wet night he deemed the hall to be a less inclement place than an uncovered yard."

FEAR OF WATER IN HIGH PLACES

IT was said of Queen Elizabeth I that she took a bath every month "whether she needed it or no." The unwholesome habits of her successor to the throne, James I, excited comment even in his own insalubrious day. Like most of his countrymen—but with less excuse— he had only a nodding acquaintanceship with water. "His skin was als softe as tafta sarsnet, which felt so because he neuer vasht his hands onlie rubb'd his finger ends slightly with the vett end of a napkin."

VERMIN AND SANCTITY

THE day following his murder, the mortal remains of Thomas à Becket were prepared for burial. Under mantle and surplice was a lamb's wool coat, under that the cowled robe of the Benedictines, and under that a shirt. Next to the skin was a hair cloth covered with linen. As the martyr's body grew cold, "the vermin boiled over like water in a simmering cauldron, and the onlookers burst into alternate tears and laughter."

BATHING THE DUKE OF NORFOLK

THE eleventh duke of Norfolk was never thoroughly laundered except when drunk. It was then that his servants could get him into his bath without his being aware of it. Samuel Johnson expressed the prevailing indifferent attitude when he said he hated "immersion." Shown a private cold bath by a prosperous draper, he urged his proud host to "let well enough alone and be content." Johnson's biographer would have approved. A dismaying mid-February entry by Boswell in his journal reads,"Washed my feet for the first time this winter."

SPITTING, GENTEEL AND UNINHIBITED

GENTEEL

AMONG the precepts of the Syon Rule written for the nuns of Syon Abbey in medieval times are these: "none shal jutte up on other wylfully, nor spyt up on the stayres, goyng up or down, nor in none other place repreciably, but yf they trede it out forthwyth."

Cornelia Adair, traveling in 1874 with her English husband, records in her diary that she was struck with the good manners of an American Indian chief who spat into his hand rather than on the carpet.

UNINHIBITED

"OTHE spitting!" cries Margaret Hall in her account of travels in America c. 1830. "It seems to increase daily." At a dinner party given by the Secretary of the Navy in Washington, her dancing partner began clearing his throat. "This I thought ominous. I said to myself, Surely he will turn his head to the other side. The gentleman, however, had no such thought, but deliberately shot across me. I had no courage to examine whether or not the result landed in the flounce of my dress." Frances Trollope, visiting America at about the same time, again and again refers with scorn to the backwoods habit of expectorating in public places. She speaks of "the loathesome spitting" at table, "from the contamination of which it was absolutely impossible to protect our dresses."

"OPENING HEADS"

EIGHTEENTH-CENTURY ladies were very partial to exotic and often towering hair creations, structures built up with false locks, pomatum, and wool padding—a veritable paradise for *Pediculus capitis.* Removing these monstrosities was called "opening the head," a process often postponed for weeks.

TEATIME ABOMINATIONS

IN Boswell's *Life,* Samuel Johnson has a characteristic fling at the French and (by the way) at the Scots. "The French are an indelicate people; they will spit upon any place. At Madam X's, a literary lady of rank, the footman took the sugar in his fingers and threw it into my coffee. I was going to put it aside, but hearing it was made on purpose for me, I e'en tasted Tom's fingers. The same lady would needs make tea a l'Angloise. The spout of the tea pot did not pour freely; she bade the footman blow into it. France is worse than Scotland in everything but climate."

ONE TOWEL, ONE STUDENT BODY, ONE TUB OF WATER

ROBERT Southey writes of hygienic conditions in the boarding school he attended. "There was a washing tub in the playground, with a long towel on the rail beside it. This tub was filled every morning for the boarders to perform their ablutions, all in the same water, and whoever wished to wash his hands and face in the course of the day, had no other. I was the only boy who had any repugnance to dip his hands in this pig trough."

STRIGILI

LAVACRVM
OCEANVM VEL
LABRVM

ORCEOLVM

CACCAB

TRVLLA BAL-
NEARIA

SOLIV

Die Badstube. Woodcut by Albrecht Dürer, Nuremburg, 1496. Reproduced from Medicine and Art (Ars Medica) *by permission of the Philadelphia Museum of Art.*

KEEPING CLEAN

. . . let us abhor uncleanliness, which neither nature nor reason can endure.

Sir John Harington*

One of the amenities brought back by the Crusaders was the *hammam,* or Turkish bath, which, in the East, was a marble affair, luxurious and commodious. European baths were wooden tubs, big enough, however, to accommodate several bathers. There were no less than thirty-two public baths in Paris as early as the thirteenth century, providing both steam baths and tubs. The latter, usually equipped with a carpet of linen for splinter protection, commanded a higher price.

Engravings of the period demonstrate that bathing, music making, eating, and friendly gossiping all went on at the same time. Mixed bathing was the rule at first, but abuses were inevitable and were not long in coming. In England most baths had become brothels in all but name by the middle of the fourteenth century. "Stews" (sweating baths) and "bordello" (room), originally innocent terms, began to take on the meanings they have today. In France pressure from the church banned mixed bathing, but abuses were rife: "Men make a point of staying all night in the public bath, and women at the break of day come in, and through 'ignorance' find themselves in the men's rooms."

Henry VIII banned mixed bathing and decreed that anyone operating a "Hot-house or Sweating-House for the Ease and Health of Men . . ." who have not found surety to the Chamberlain "for their good and honest Behavior" were to pay a fine of twenty pounds. The use of the words "Health and Ease" is significant, a reminder that steam baths were widely believed to be effective against venereal disease. One historian remarks that "few cures for the Pox or Clap can have been as harmless as this one."

By 1600, the heyday of the public bath was over, but the practice lingered on. Pepys, writing in 1664, remarks, ". . . my wife being busy in going with her woman to a hot-house to bathe herself, after her long being within doors in the dirt, so that she now pretends to a resolution of being hereafter very clean." He adds wryly, "How long it will hold I can guess."

In England the public bath was succeeded by the bagnio, a kind of semi-therapeutic establishment in which bleeding, cupping, sweating, and lodging were available. The Duke's bagnio, perhaps the oldest in England, opened its doors in 1676. It was subsequently known as the Queen's bagnio. The *Tatler* ran this ad in 1709: "The Queen's Bagnio in Long Acre is made very convenient for both Sexes to sweat and bath privately every Day in the Week, and cupp'd to the last perfection (he having the best and newest instrument for that Purpose). It is sufficiently evident, that it exceeds all others, by being more and constantly frequented by the Nobility and Gentry. Pr. 5s for one single Person; but if two or more come together, 4s each. There is no entertainment for women after 12 o'clock at Night; but all Gentlemen that desire Beds, may have them at 2s per night."

Harington exhorted his countrymen to bathe daily, a recommendation that must have been greeted with considerable amusement. But when spa bathing was all the vogue in the latter half of the eighteenth century, fashion accomplished what mere regard for personal hygiene had failed to do.

---

* Harington, author of *The Metamorphosis of Ajax, a Cloacinian Satire,* urged daily bathing on his Elizabethan contemporaries.

Then I hastened to town. . . . As usual the atmosphere has proved a complete malaria to me. How indeed should it be otherwise, when it is a compound of fen-fog, chimney smoke, smuts, and pulverized horse dung! The little leisure I have is employed in blowing my nose, with interludes of coughing.

Robert Southey, Letters, 1808

Salus Populi Suprema Lex. An etching by George Cruikshank. Reproduced by courtesy of the Trustees of the British Museum. The sewers of London emptied into the Thames at the very spot from which the borough of Southwark was supplied with its water. In the year of London's cholera epidemic, 1832, Cruikshank depicted John Edwards, owner of the Southwark pumping house, enthroned on a close stool with a chamber pot on his head.

XVI

ENGLISHMEN BELEAGUERED:
TAINTED AIR,
PUTRID WATER,
DOCTORED MEAT

ENGLISH STREETS BEFORE VICTORIA

Though all ill savours do not breed infection,
Yet sure infection commeth most by smelling.
                    From the Flos Medicinae *of the*
                              School of Salerno

Down the middle of English streets ran a gutter or kennel into which garbage and refuse were tossed to fester in the hot sun. As Swift put it,

> *Now from all parts the swelling kennels flow,*
> *And bear their trophies with them as they go:*
> *Filths of all hues and odours seem to tell*
> *What street they sailed from by their sight and smell . . .*

In this ripe and odoriferous garden pigs rooted at their own sweet will despite law, ordinance, and fines. In the time of Edward I (1239–1307) a law was enacted stating that "he who shall wish to feed a pig, must feed it in his own house." Any swine found wandering ad libitum might be taken and butchered on sight. But justice was tempered with mercy — the owner was free to purchase the dead pig for four pence, one penny for each foot. Similar regulations were instituted in towns of any size, and Cambridge in 1445 allowed no swine in the streets between 7 A.M. and 6 P.M. By 1700 stray pigs were no longer a public nuisance, but in country districts they remained an annoyance for parish authorities. In the records of the township of Bradford occurs this resolution: "May 1798. Resolved, that public notice be given by handbills and by cryer, that from after the twelfth of May next, the owner of such pig or pigs as are found at large will be indicted for the same by the constable of the town."

While for a long time English streets were safe for English pigs, they could be dangerous for the unwary pedestrian. "Gardy-loo" (*gardez l'eau*) was a universal warning cry in the seventeenth and eighteenth centuries when every variety of household slops was flung from windows and doors. Like London, Edinburgh was notorious for the state of its streets. There the sounding of the ten o'clock bell from the tower of St. Giles was the signal for emptying night soil and household rubbish into the street, and "Gardy-loo!" was heard on every hand in every alley and by-way. The hurrying pedestrian's anguished cry, "Haud yer han!" was not always well-timed. Conditions were no better in other major towns. When Pope Paul V visited Spain in 1594, he found the stench in the streets intolerable. Houses were built without privies and chamber pots were emptied from windows. As in England and Scotland, passersby were given warning, but "*Agua va!*" (beware, water!) was no more effective than "Gardy-loo!" Frequent accidents finally produced a law forbidding the use of windows for waste disposal and obliging the householder to throw offal from doorways only, and then only during stated hours. Penalties were harsh—four years' exile for the householder, six years' exile and a public whipping for a servant.

For Englishmen, remedies were late in coming. Disraeli's law defining a bad smell as a nuisance was not adopted until 1875, and "Gardy-loo!" was still to be heard as late as the first decades of the nineteenth century.

A NOTE ABOUT THE POT-DE-CHAMBRE

THE humble chamber pot developed out of a medieval device made of glass which had a funnel-like mouth and a narrow neck. Many a physician when uroscopy held sway must have found it very convenient for visual inspection and a quick diagnosis. It had the advantage of enabling the user to do what was needful while remaining snug in bed. Similar in shape was the *bourdalone*, named for a verbose Jesuit whose sermons were of inordinate length. Though confined to their pews, proper ladies could answer the calls of nature with discretion and without interrupting Father Bourdalou's flow of eloquence. The lowly chamber pot first appears in the fourteenth century. Early pots were of the plain earthenware or pewter variety, but with the introduction of porcelain, many were things of beauty, decorated with colored glazes and handsomely shaped. Before Waterloo and after, patriotic Englishmen favored pots with the image of Napoleon on the "target area," while the fun-loving might prefer those featuring a staring eye, beneath which were the lines

Use me well and keep me clean,
And I'll not tell what I have seen.

LONDON STREETS AND LONDON AIR

"COLDS KILL MORE THAN PLAGUES"

LONDONERS knew the lethal consequences of coryza-induced complications. According to a popular home remedy medical book of 1770, the secret of cold prevention lay in avoiding "obstructed perspiration" brought on by changes in the weather, wet clothing, wet feet, night air, damp houses, sudden transitions from heat to cold, and damp beds in inns and guest houses. Aubrey tells us that Lord Bacon was done in by a damp bed. The great philosopher, statesman, and man of science was feeling chilled after performing an ingenious experiment in refrigeration. He had tried to preserve a hen by stuffing it with snow. Taken to the Earl of Arundel's house in Highgate, "he was putt into a good bed warmed with a Panne, but it was a damp bed that had not been layn-in in about a yeare before, which gave him such a colde that in 2 or 3 dayes he dyed of Suffocation."

THE CONSEQUENCES OF SEA COAL

BUT it was sea coal rather than dampness that was the chief culprit. So called because it was carried to London by ship from Scotland, sea coal was harder than peat but much softer than anthracite. It gave off incredible volumes of smoke, corroding the lungs and blackening the skin. The first attempt to curb the nuisance was a smoke-abatement law enacted in the reign of Edward I in 1273. It prohibited the use of sea coal as detrimental to health, and a violator was prosecuted, condemned, and executed in 1307.

AIR POLLUTION—NO RESPECTER OF RANK

ELEANOR, queen of England, was driven in 1257 from Nottingham Castle by the noxious fumes of sea coal burning in the furnaces of the city below. Three hundred years after Eleanor, the London Company of Brewers, loyal citizens all, offered to burn wood instead of coal in the brew houses nearest Westminster Palace because they were aware that the queen "findeth herselfe greatly greved and anoyed with the taste and smoke of the sea-cooles."

JOHN EVELYN HAD AN ANSWER

"THOU didst swear to me upon a parcel-gilt goblet . . . by a sea-coal fire," says Mistress Quickly in Henry IV, so we know sea-coal was a common household fuel in Shakespeare's day. And Elizabethan brewers, silversmiths, dyers, salt and soap boilers and lime burners all added their quota of noxious fumes to the heavy pall that hung over London. One hundred and fifty years after Elizabeth, Smollett could refer in *Humphrey Clinker* to the "gross acid of sea-coal, which is a pernicious nuisance to lungs of any delicacy of texture." And in 1810 an American observer wrote that Londoners have "a sort of a dingy, smoky look; not dirty absolutely . . . but the outside garments are of a dull dark cast, and harmonize with mud and smoke."

One man came forward in 1661 with a plan to clear London's polluted air by turning the destruction wrought by the Great Fire into an asset. His efforts—and his failure—have a modern ring. He was John Evelyn, diarist and sometime secretary of the Royal Society. In his pamphlet addressed to the king, *Fumifugium, or Inconvenience of the Aer and the Smoake of London Dissipated*, he urged that all enterprises using sea coal be moved outside the city limits. This "cure," as he called it, would enable "Men to breath a new Life as it were, as well as London to appear a new City."

A French version of a "London particular," by Daumier.

LONDON WATER

WHERE SALMON ONCE SWAM

IN the summer of 1858, a season of hot sun and little rainfall, the Thames began to shrink from its shoreline, revealing outlets for discharging sewage into the river. Sewage and sun together produced a mephitic miasma, referred to by Londoners as "The Great Stink." Parliament debated whether to move out of town and finally compromised by having clothes soaked in chloride of lime hung over all the windows and doors.

"OH, GOD! WHAT I SAW!"

CHARLES Kingsley wrote to his sister,"I was yesterday over the cholera districts of Bermondsey and Oh, God! What I saw! People having no water to drink—hundreds of them—but the water of the common sewer which stagnates, full of . . . dead fish, cats and dogs, under their windows." An outbreak of cholera in 1848–1849 had killed 14,000 in London alone.

TYPHOID FEVER AT HIGH TIDE

DRAINAGE in London in the eighteenth century was primitive, and deaths arising from sewage contamination were commonplace. Conditions in the slum districts were worst, especially before improvements in the sewage system were made in 1770, but even in comparatively affluent areas "water used to be three or four feet deep in cellars; and servants used to punt themselves along in washing tubs from the cellar-stairs to the beer barrels to draw beer daily."

CONSUMER PROTECTION IN MEDIEVAL ENGLAND

STINKING PIGEONS

JOHN Russel, who had exposed "37 pigeons for sale, putrid, rotten, stinking and abominable to the human race . . . to the scandal, contempt and disgrace of all the City," was pilloried and the pigeons burnt beneath him.

DOCTORED MEAT

"THE vij day of Marche rode a butcher round about London, his face toard the horse's taylle, with half a lamb before and another behind, and veal and a calf borne before hym, upon a polle, rawe."

In this quotation from a London resident writing in 1553–1554, the butcher's misdemeanor is not specified, but it is more than likely that he was guilty of the practice of blowing air into his meat products. The Oxford English Dictionary quotes from a sixteenth-century Scottish writer, who complains that butchers "blaw the flesh, and cause it seme fat and fair."

CORRUPT WINE

IN the 1400's, a London court indicted John Penrose, vintner, because "he had sold corrupt wine . . . not good or wholesome for mankind." He was condemned to drink "a draught of the same wine which he sold to the common people; and the remainder of such wine shall be poured on the head of the same John; and that he shall foresewar the calling of vintner in the city of London forever."

You that would last long, list to my song,
Make no more coyle, but buy of this oyle.
Would you be ever faire? and yong?
Stout of teeth and strong of tongue?

Would you live free from all diseases?
Doe the act your mistris pleases;
Yet fright all aches from your bones?
Here's a med'cine, for the nones.
                    Ben Jonson, Volpone II, 2

The Quack Doctor, from Thomas Rowlandson's Drawings for the English Dance of Death.

XVII

QUACKERIES, CURE-ALLS, AND OTHER DELUSIONS

A GAGGLE OF QUACKS

A CUP OF CURE

FRANCIS Anthony (b. 1550) was a dedicated Paracelsian whose cure-all, *aurum potabile*, brought him an international reputation. It was prepared by the reaction of vinegar of wine with finely powdered gold, and its rationale was based on a simple syllogism: Metals are the most important of all remedies. Gold is the noblest of the metals. Therefore it must be the noblest of all medicines. John Evans, a minister, published a tract entitled *Universal Medicine* about 1640, basing it on somewhat similar reasoning: since antimony purifies gold, the noblest of metals, it must also purify the human body. He held that drinking from a cup made of antimony would cure most diseases. He offered the cups for sale, even permitting them to be taken home for a free trial. His theories were condemned by the Royal College of Surgeons and his tract was ordered destroyed by the Archbishop of Canterbury.

SARAH MAPP, BONESETTER EXTRAORDINARY

MRS. Sarah Mapp lived in Epsom but drove into London twice weekly to see her patients in her coach and four, liveried footmen and all, to see her patients. Like many empirics, Mapp had skill, and despite her repulsive appearance was popular with the public. On one occasion her carriage was stopped by a crowd who mistook her for one of the king's ugly and unpopular mistresses. Rising in wrath, she put her head out the coach window and cried, "Damn your bloods! Don't you know me, I'm Mrs. Mapp the bonesetter." The mob made way for her with laughter and cheers. It was the public's easygoing attitude that probably paralyzed the College of Physicians, which had the right to forbid the practice of medicine within seven miles of the city to anyone who lacked a license issued by it. That right was rarely exercised.

CURING A FALSE "PHYSITIAN"

A FALSE "physitian" of 1382 who claimed to cure the sick with a parchment of talismanic power was led on an unsaddled horse through the streets of London. Accompanied by trumpets and pipes, he was obliged to ride backward with the tail of the horse in his hands. Hung from his neck were the parchment and a whetstone "for his lies." A urine flask hung before him and another at his back.

A NOSTRUM MAKER GETS HIS COME-UPPANCE

S OLD widely in Newcastle, England, in the heyday of the nostrum, the Balm of Gilead consisted largely of brandy, then a cheap commodity costing only a few shillings a quart. It was advertised for women troubled by "weak and shattered constitutions, hypochondria, horrors of the mind, intemperance, debauchery and inattention to the necessary cares of health." Many customers apparently took the balm ad lib, and many a formerly temperate wife became a confirmed tippler. One day a band of outraged husbands waylaid the maker, roughed him up, tossed him in a blanket, and told him to get out of town.

BETTER A QUACK THAN NOTHING

I N the sixteenth century and later they were called wanton good-for-nothing vagabonds and worse by the professional fraternity, but the services of itinerant ocultists, lithotomists, and hernia operators were accepted faute de mieux. The Code of 1582 for the city of Worms stated that "such lithotomists, oculists and teeth-pullers who are skilled and who do not administer medicine internally, which does not belong to their art . . . shall be tolerated." In London the Barber Surgeons Company examined and licensed for lithotomy, couching of cataracts, etc. The licensee had to call in a member of the company for consultation and pay him a fee. Mathias Jenkinson was "examyned concernyge his skill in the arte of surgery and was lycensed to cut for the Hernia or Rupture and to couch the cataract, to cut for wry neck and the harelip, provided he call the present Masters of this Company to every such case. . . ."

THE ANODYNE NECKLACE

FEW charms against disease have had a longer life than the anodyne necklace. An early advertisement (1718) reads: "The Anodyne Necklace for children's teeth, women in labour, and distempers of the head, price 5s. Recommended by Dr. Chamberlen . . ." This was Hugh Chamberlen of the obstetrical-forceps family—good businessmen all! In its heyday the necklace was reputed to cure, among other disorders, gout, rheumatism, and venereal infections. When last heard of (about 1850) it was advertised for only the cutting of teeth in children. That's progress.

GRAHAM'S "CELESTIAL BED"

JAMES Graham, originator and purveyor of the Elixir of Life, a lifetime supply of which cost one hundred pounds, converted a spacious mansion overlooking the Thames into a "Temple of Health." Married couples who slept in its "Celestial Bed," a grand affair standing on glass legs and fitted with costly curtains, were assured beautiful progeny and childless couples were promised offspring. The fee: fifty pounds per night. The twelve-by-nine foot bed, which Graham claimed cost 10,000 pounds to build and equip, could be tilted after coition so that conception might be assisted. Graham was canny enough to exploit the then current electricity rage: "The chief principle of my Celestial Bed is produced by artificial lodestones. About 15 cwt of compound magnets are continually pouring forth in an ever-flowing circle." Graham was also a firm believer in the restorative power of Mother Earth. During one hour daily the public was invited to view him and his beauteous Goddess of Health buried in warm earth up to their chins. The goddess was Emma, afterwards ex-wife of Sir William Hamilton and a favorite of Lord Nelson.

A GIFT FOR COUCHING

COUCHING of cataracts was a quack specialty. George Bertisch in his book on the care of the eyes (1583) excoriates the practitioners of the art: "Nor is there any lack of old women, vagrant hags, therica sellers, tooth-pullers, ruined shopkeepers, rat and mouse catchers, knaves, tinkers, hog-butchers, hangmen, bum-bailiffs, and other wanton good for nothing vagabonds . . . all of whom boldly try to perform this noble cure." He was not exaggerating. William Reed, who started life as a tailor, ended as a titled oculist to weak-eyed Queen Anne. "Dr." Grant, another protégé of the queen, began as a tinker and graduated into preaching before finding his true vocation. George II had better luck than Anne. At least Charles Taylor, appointed royal oculist, had a nodding acquaintance with medicine, having been an apothecary's assistant. Among his patients were Gibbon and Handel.

France not only had its share of quack oculists—they persisted longer. In the 1820s, M. de la Chanterie, "célèbre médecin oculist," was leaving handbills in cafés and restaurants listing the names and addresses of those he had successfully operated on for cataract. The bills ended with the plea, "Please spread this information as widely as possible."

THE HEALING TOUCH—THEY ALL HAD IT

XIPE TOTEC

XIPE Totec, the Aztec god of spring, was associated with skin diseases. On his feast days, his priests, in the flayed skins of victims sacrificed on the altar, would run through the city, touching with healing hands all those with lesions of the skin.

A native artist shows a priest being vested to represent Xipe Totec.

270

VALENTINE GREATRAKES

"GOD almighty heal thee for his mercy's sake," so went the prayer offered by Greatrakes as he stroked the sick back to health. One convinced witness of his cures maintained that Greatrakes's body was composed "of some particular ferments, the effluvia thereof being introduced, sometimes by a light, sometimes by a violent friction, restore the temperament of the debilitated parts, regenerate the blood, and dissipate all heterogeneous ferments of the bodies of the diseases, by the eyes, nose, mouth, hands and feet."

MRS. UTTERBECK

MARK Twain tells of a "faith doctor" named Mrs. Utterbeck whom his mother often visited. "Her specialty was toothache. She would lay her hand on the patient's jaw and say, 'Behave!' and the cure was prompt."

ST. JOHN LONG

LONG invented a lotion capable of distinguishing between sound and diseased tissue that he applied to the head, neck, and arms of his patients, the great majority of whom were female. The applications— always administered in the presence of a third person— sometimes resulted in burning excoriations, and Long was found guilty of contributing to the death of one patient and fined 250 pounds. Supported and protected by his fashionable clients, Long continued to pursue his profitable ministrations.

HANGED FELONS

TO ensure their good health, children were brought to the gallows in eighteenth-century London to be stroked by the hands of executed criminals. Sterile women would visit the gallows secretly, lift the arms of the dead man, and stoke their bellies to make them fruitful. Elsewhere in England, the hands of hanged felons were applied to the affected parts to cure goiters and bleeding tumors. Even the gallows tree was considered therapeutic. A bag of gallows splinters worn around the neck was believed effective against chills and malarial fever.

A HEALER NAMED NEWTON

A FALL on the ice when she was sixteen mysteriously paralyzed Olivia Langdon, who was to become the wife of Mark Twain. Bedridden for two years, she was visited by a procession of doctors who held out little hope for even partial recovery. As a last resort, her family called in a healer named Newton whose power derived, as he himself put it, from "some subtle form of electricity proceeding from my body." He threw up the shades, opened the windows, prayed, put his arm around the patient's shoulders, and said, "Now we will sit up, my child." After a few moments, he said, "Now we will walk a few steps, my child," and she did. His fee? Fifteen hundred dollars.

EMPEROR VESPASIAN

ACCORDING to Tacitus, the emperor cured the maimed hand of a citizen by exerting gentle pressure on it with his foot. Belief in the curative power of the royal person was to have its finest hour in the practice of "touching for the king's evil."

ELISHA PERKINS

PERKINS practiced the laying on of hands at one remove with his patented metallic rods. Good for all painful conditions, the rods were especially effective in sedating violent mental patients, and in cases of gout, pleurisy, crippling rheumatism, and "inflammatory tumours." Perkins believed passionately in his tractors, and when the yellow fever epidemic of 1799 struck New York, he traveled to that city to halt it with his tractors. Within weeks he was dead of the disease.

KING CHARLES II

IT was revealed to Arise Evans, who had a fungous nose, that "the King's Hand would Cure him: and at the first coming of King Charles into St. James's Parke he kiss'd the King's hand and rubb'd his Nose with it; which disturb'd the King, but cured him."

MAIMONIDES AND FRANÇOIS DE PARIS

THE poor of Cairo, Christian and Muslin as well as Jewish, once brought their severely ill to the old synagogue of Maimonides, leaving them "in the basement under the prayer room for one or two nights so as to absorb the healing power of Reb Moshe." Here, in his *Story of My Life*, relates how he happened on a woman, apparently ill, who was lying on a grave in a Prague cemetery. The caretaker explained: "A rabbi buried here was so good when alive and his good works are so well known, sick persons are brought here to lie on his grave in hope of a cure."

After the death of De Paris, a pious Jansenist, curious happenings were observed at his grave in the St. Medard cemetery. At first visited by only a few, who announced miraculous cures, his grave was soon resorted to by ecstatic crowds of the halt, the sick, and the blind. It was here that the niece of Blaise Pascal recovered from an apparently incurable disease of the eyes. A royal decree signed by Louis XIV, who was no friend of the Jansenists, finally closed the gates of St. Medard, prompting a wit to post thereon this verse:

> *In the King's name, it is forbidden*
> *For God to work his miracles here.*

TOUCHING FOR THE KING'S EVIL

God give you better health and more sense. . . .
　　William III upon touching a scrofulous petitioner

Touching for the King's Evil—scrofula—had its basis in the belief that the monarch, owing his kingship to divine inspiration, possessed supernatural powers. The custom, which has been traced back to eleventh-century France, crossed the Channel with William the Conqueror. It was Henry VII (reigned 1485–1509) who began the practice of touching a scrofulous sore with a freshly minted gold noble. On it was pictured an angel surrounded by the legend *Per Crucem Tua Salva-Nos-Chr' — Redempt'* (By thy Cross save us, Redeemer Christ).* The medal was given to the sufferer, who wore it thereafter on a ribbon around his neck.

A proclamation of 1626 fixed the times for healing and required each petitioner to present a certificate from the minister and churchwardens of his parish attesting that he had not already been touched. Here is one:

> *Mem: that the Minister and Ch. Wardens of Stoke upon Trent in the County of Safford gave unto Cethar. Fluit, ye daughter of Arthur Fluit and Mary his wife of the parish aforesaid upon the third day of May in the year of our Lord God one thousand, six hundred eighty and Four a Certificate under their hands and seals in her to her obtaining of his Majestie's sacred touch for the healing of the Disease called the King's Evil.*

The crowds beseiging the king must have been enormous. Between the date of his restoration and his death, it is said that Charles II touched nearly 100,000 of his subjects. John Evelyn, in his diary, mentions the ceremony in 1684 when "There was so greate a concourse of people with their children to be touch'd for the Evil that six or seven were crush'd to death by pressing at the Chirurgeon's doore for tickets." Old parish records reveal that the sick were often speeded on their way with money from the public treasury. Entries like these are common:

1641—"Given to John Parkin wife towards her trauell to London to get cure of his Matie. for the disease called Euill which her son Thom is visited withall—0.6.8."

1678—"Ann Thornton to have Xs for goeing to London to be touched for the euvill."

* Shakespeare refers to the medal in *Macbeth:*

> *How he solicits heaven,*
> *Himself best knows; but strangely-visited people,*
> *All swoln and ulcerous, pitiful to the eye,*
> *The mere despair of surgery he cures;*
> *Hanging a golden stamp about their necks,*
> *Put on with holy prayers. . . .*

In France, Louis XIV was touching the scrofulous as often as eight times a year, on most major religious holidays. After the ceremony, the Sun King washed his hands three times, in vinegar first, next in plain water, and last in orange water. Remember, he had no gold coin between himself and morbidity! Louis XV, his successor, who had appeared in public with a new mistress at three separate ceremonies, was advised not to officiate, presumably because his moral turpitude would vitiate the potency of his touch.

No doubt among the thousands of English people who came to be touched there were malingerers intent on pocketing the gold coin. One interpreter of the practice says, "Exactly how great a proportion of the patients were cured, to what extent such patients were genuinely scrofulous, and how far they suffered from other diseases readily curable by suggestion, it is difficult to say." Eczema or psoriasis could easily have been misdiagnosed by doctors of that era of still primitive medicine, a fact which would account for the large number of "indisputable" cures that were reported.

In any case, the belief died hard. The blood-stained shirt and drawers worn by Charles I at his execution were exhibited in a London church for "touching" by the scrofulous as late as 1860.

The Manner of His Majesties Curing the Disease,
CALLED THE
KINGS-EVIL.

Part of a broadside announcing the touching ceremony for the King's Evil.

DOING WITHOUT DOCTORS—
THE QUEST FOR PANACEAS

UNICORN'S HORN

AT first used as a specific against poison, unicorn's horn dipped into fluids or ground into powder was later prescribed for epilepsy, impotence, sterility, the plague, smallpox, and other ills. Fashioned into a drinking cup, the horn was thought to impart healing properties to water and wine. In 1598 a German traveler in England wrote,"We were shown here (at Windsor Castle), among other things, the horn of a Unicorn, of about eight spans in length, valued at about 100,000 pounds!" Elephant or norwhale ivory was undoubtedly the "unicorn's horn" sold by Dutch traders in the Orient well into the nineteenth century.

Legend had it that only a young virgin of noble birth could capture the fabulous unicorn with the therapeutic horn. Seeing her, the unicorn would approach, lay his horn in her lap, and fall asleep.

SKULL SCRAPINGS

FROM the Middle Ages to the end of the eighteenth century, anything associated with the gibbet was thought to have medicinal value. Hangmen prospered from the sale of the noose, offered in tiny lengths. Scrapings from the skull of hanged criminals was another source of revenue. Usnea, as it was called, was officially listed in the pharmacopoeia until the nineteenth century, and its external application in nervous and wasting diseases was accepted medical practice.

CLAY

IN the Middle East in medieval times geophagy, or clay eating, as a specific for the plague was widely indulged in, taken as advised by Galen, with water and vinegar. The clay in question was Armenian bole, a clayey earth with a deep red color caused by its iron oxide content. It was used both for prevention and treatment, and was smeared over the entire body, or on the buboes alone. Armenian bole was known in Europe as well. When plague struck Avignon, Guy de Chauliac, physician to Pope Clement VI, recommended "consoling the bodily humors" with it.

UNICORN'S HORN PLUS

ONE of the panels of the celebrated Bayeux Tapestry depicts William the Conqueror seated between Bishop Odo and Robert of Mortan. Before them kneels a servitor holding a bowl of wine. He is probably William's *prae-gustator*, or taster, charged with the duty of tasting the royal victuals before his master partook of them. Charles VIII of France carried vigilance to its ultimate. When he feasted at the Palazzo San Marco in Rome after his invasion of Italy, four physicians tasted the wine into which "the chamberlain dangled a unicorn's horn on a golden chain before His Majesty raised it to his lips." Such precautions were not misplaced in the age of the Borgias. It is said that the formidable Caterina Sforza sent Pope Alexander VI a poisoned letter. It was enclosed in velvet and slipped into a tube to protect the ambassadors who carried it.

TLALOC FOR COLDS

WHEN respiratory diseases attacked the Aztecs, they turned to the great rain god Tlaloc for aid and comfort. Belief in the god's powers persisted into this century. In 1964, the National Museum of Anthropology began uprooting the centuries-old statue of Tlaloc near Tetzcoco for transportation to Mexico City. Fearful that the outrage would affront the god and bring drought and disease, hundreds of angry peasants tore down winches and roughed up museum workers.

TAR WATER

WHILE on a visit to Rhode Island, Bishop Berkeley learned of the virtues of tar water, used in that colony as a preventive against smallpox. Berkeley's modified recipe called for a gallon of cold water to a quart of tar* to be mixed well and allowed to stand for three days. The supernatant fluid was poured off and the resulting product was guaranteed to cure all the ills that man is heir to. Said Oliver Wendell Holmes, "Berkeley died at the age of seventy; he might have lived longer but his fatal illness was so sudden that there was not enough time to stir up a quart of the panacea. . . ."

POCCIE LATTAIE

IRIS Origo speaks of secluded caves in the farming areas of Tuscany in which water drips from stalactite-like formations with shapes like cow's udders and women's breasts. To these caves farmers would bring their sterile cows to taste the water. Nursing mothers who were losing their milk came too, "bringing as gifts the seven fruits of the earth: a handful of wheat, barley, corn, rye, vetch, dried peas, and sometimes a saucer of milk." Ms. Origo believes this local superstition of *poccie lattaie* (literally, milk-bearing udders) probably had its origin in a very primitive form of nature worship.

MOTHER EARTH

IN the closing months of her life, Queen Elizabeth was in the habit of sitting on the floor after it had been well-cushioned. The Queen, whose dislike of physicians and their medicines was well known, may have embraced the folk belief that such contact with mother earth was salubrious for the sick. The concept no doubt flourished when most dwellings had earthen floors.

* Resin obtained from evergreen trees.

MIRACULOUS WATER

IN the Middle Ages the shrine of Our Lady of Walsingham was much frequented by pilgrims seeking cures, but the medical powers of St. Thomas of Canterbury were considered to be superior even to hers. On the pewter ampullae containing miraculous water that the pilgrims brought back from Canterbury was inscribed the motto *Optimus egrorum, medicus fit Thomas bonarum.* (For good people who are sick, Thomas is the best of physicians).

CAULS

THE piece of amnion that sometimes covers an infant's head at birth has from ancient times been credited with bringing good luck—"born with a caul, no misfortune befall." Cauls were especially valued as infallible preservatives against drowning. Ads offering cauls for sale were frequent, like this one from the London *Times* of 27 February 1813: "To persons going to sea. A child's caul in a perfect state, to be sold cheap. Apply at 5 Duke Street, Manchester Square, where it may be seen." The submarine menace during World War II revived the superstition, with British sailors parting with as much as fifteen and twenty pounds for the life-saving talismans.

THERIAC

MITHRIDATES VI of Pontus, the great antagonist of Rome, is said to have saturated himself with poison by degrees in order to foil attempts on his life. Defeated by Pompey and threatened by a mutiny of his own troops, he vainly tried to poison himself, and finally had to order a mercenary to dispatch him with a sword. After his death the formula for his antidote—mithradaticum—was discovered and was later developed into a pharmacologic monstrosity of some fifty to sixty-five ingredients called theriac. Shotgun pharmacy did not end there. One variation, the theriac of Matthiolus, used over 300 ingredients and weighed about thirteen pounds.

BEZOAR STONE

A CONCRETION found in the intestines of goats, bezoar stone was at first a highly valued specific against poisoning, and at five pounds an ounce in its powdered form, affordable only by the rich. It became in time a kind of universal antidote much prized by royalty. When Paré assured King Charles IX of France that his bezoar stone was valueless, a trial was proposed. A cook condemned to be strangled for the theft of two silver plates agreed to undergo the test in return for his freedom. He was given corrosive sublimate and immediately after, bezoar stone. Vomiting in his agony, and bleeding from ear, nose, and mouth, the wretched man took eight hours to die. According to some, the demonstration was lost on Charles. He contended the stone was counterfeit and that the genuine article would have worked.

EGYPTIAN MUMMY

TRAFFIC in the dried flesh of mummies started when Arab doctors began prescribing it in the tenth century. The grisly product was dug up from violated tombs by peasants and transported to Cairo and Alexandria, where merchants distributed it all over Europe. King Francis I of France carried a packet of powdered mummy with him at all times as "an emergency precaution." The trade in dead flesh was extremely lucrative, with a market value of eight shillings a pound in 1585. In that year John Sanderson, an agent residing in Egypt, brought up more than 600 pounds for export. Much of the mummy flesh was counterfeited, and Paré said that mummy was sometimes made "in our own France" from bodies stolen from the gallows.

FOILING DEMONS

AT NIGHT

DEMONS were thought to be particularly malevolent during the night, and for this reason it is still believed in Eastern Europe that exposure to night air is harmful. Extra care is taken to keep bedroom windows shut at night lest wandering demons afflict the sleepers. It is said that King Charles of Spain had his confessor and two friars sit beside his bed at night while he slept to guard him from the demons of the night.

AMONG THE BANTUS

AMONG the Bantus of southern Africa, sickness of the soul and sickness of the body are regarded as one. The cause may be either the presence of a demon or a sorcerer's spell. An important part of the healing ritual, which includes incantations, involves the use of emetics. The preacher leads his flock to the bank of a stream where the emetic potions are drunk and the demons expelled along with the vomitus.

IN THE MIDDLE AGES

IN medieval times, inquisitors examining women accused of witchcraft employed assistants known as "prickers," who discovered areas of anesthesia by jabbing suspects with pins or needles. Nevi and pigmented spots were suspect as well, and polymastia and polythelia, as devices for feeding "familiars," were abnormalities sure to bring their possessors to the stake or the torture chamber.

Weightlessness and weight not in accordance with the natural proportions of the body were also of interest to the witch-hunters. Fearful folk from all over Europe came to the city of Oudewater in Holland, the site from the beginning of the sixteenth century to the late eighteenth of an official "weighing house." An official certificate testified that the holder was absolved from the stigma of having unnatural weight.

FRUSTRATING THE EVIL EYE

One by one, by the star-dogged moon,
Too quick for groan or sigh,
Each turned his face with a ghastly pang,
And cursed me with his eye.
        Coleridge, The Ancient Mariner

The belief that the eye in certain persons can inflict evil and disease by a mere glance has persisted for millennia among primitive peoples and advanced cultures alike. One of the most ancient documents, an Akkadian inscription dating back to the reign of Ashurbanipal c. 700 B.C., contains an incantation against the evil eye. Here are some more recent means to frustrate it.

Certificaet van weginghe
in der stede Wage tot Oudewater

Door den bedienaer der stede Wage tot Oudewater wordt aan een yegelycken mits desen cont gedaen ende gecertificeert dat

in der stede Wage heeft gewogen / 73 ponden sodanige gewichte, als men ordinaris aldaer is gebruyckende, accorderende dit gewichte wel met de natuerlycke proportiën des Lichaems.

Ende also men gehouden is de waerheydt getuygenisse te doene so is hiervan afgegeven dese open briefe van certificatie omme den gewogene daermede te dienen in tijdt en wijlen sulckx nodig en te rade wesen mochte.

Sonder arghlist, des 't oirconde voorsien van der Stede Zegel

Also gedaen in den jare ons Heeren Duysent negen hondert negen ende vijftig op den / 5 Juli

IN ANCIENT ROME

A FAVORITE method for safeguarding a child from the evil eye was to tie a thread around his neck using three knots. One then spit three times on the ground. The soil mixed with spittle was placed on the child's lips and forehead with the middle finger.*

IN MEDIEVAL EUROPE

THE manipulation of the fingers in the form of a horn (*corne*) by extending the first and fourth fingers and closing the thumb over the remaining two was a common protection against the evil eye in Spain and Germany. The horned hand was often used in the form of an amulet to protect the home, or suspended from a necklace to protect the wearer. In Italy this manual sign (*mano fica*) is commonplace.

IN MODERN ITALY

A CUSTOM prevalent in the south of Italy is to frustrate the evil eye by touching the testicles by means of a hand in one's pocket. Mussolini was said to be addicted to this practice.

---

* The *digitus infamus*. This use of the middle finger, like that of the *mano cornute*, described above, is in accord with the ancient heathen belief that obscene gestures offer protection against the evil eye.

283

CHAPTER I

Adams N: *Dead and Buried.* New York, Bell, 1972.

Andrews W: *The Doctor in History.* London, 1896.

Ashton J: *When William IV Was King.* London, Chapman and Hall, 1896.

Bell WJ: Doctors' Riot, New York, 1788. *Bull NY Acad Med* 47:12, December 1971.

Birkett N: *The Newgate Calendar.* London, The Folio Society, 1951.

Bishop N: *Recollections of the Table Talk of Samuel Rigers.* University of Kansas, 1953.

Blunt W; *Sebastiano: Adventures of the Italian Priest, Sebastiano Locatelli.* London, J Barrie, 1956.

Boorstin DJ: *The Discoverers.* New York, Random House, 1983.

Cardan J: *The Biography of My Life.* New York, Dover, 1962.

Clendening L: *Source Book of Medical History.* New York, Dover, 1942.

Corcoran AC: *A Mirror Up to Medicine,* New York, Lippincott, 1961.

Cosman MP: Medieval medical practice: The dicta and the dockets. *Bull NY Acad Med* 49:1, January 1971.

Dale PM: *Medical Biographies.* University of Oklahoma, 1952.

Entralgo PL: *Doctor and Patient.* New York, McGraw-Hill, 1969.

Everitt G: *Doctors and Doctors.* London, Swan, Sonnenschein, Lowery, 1888.

Farmer L: *The Doctor's Legacy.* New York, Harpers, 1957.

Ficarra J: *Essays on Historical Medicine.* New York, Froben, 1948.

Griffith EF: *Doctors by Themselves.* Springfield IL, CC Thomas, 1965.

Haggard HW: *Devils, Drugs and Doctors.* New York, Harper & Brother, 1929.

Heiser V: *An American Doctor's Odyssey.* New York, Norton, 1937.

Helias PJ; *The Horse of Pride.* Yale University, 1978.

Hertzler AE: *The Horse and Buggy Doctor.* New York, Harper & Brother, 1938.

Hugall S: *Sailortown.* London, Routledge & Kegan Paul, 1967.

Hume EH: *Doctors East, Doctors West.* New York, Norton, 1946.

Illich I: *Medical Nemesis.* New York, Pantheon, 1976.

Jeaffreson JC; *A Book about Doctors.* London, Hurst & Blackett, 1904.

Kaufman MR: The doctor's image. *Mt Sinai J Med* 43:76, January–February 1976.

Kemble J: *Idols and Invalids.* London, Doubleday, Doran, 1933.

Ketton-Cremer RW: Doctor messenger Monsey. *London Mercury* 28:240, 1933.

King LS: *The Medical World of the Eighteenth Century.* University of Chicago, 1958.

Klein A: *The Empire City.* New York, Rinehart, 1955.

MacMichael M: *The Gold-Headed Cane.* London, The Royal College of Physicians, 1968.

Mitchell RJ, Leys MDR: *A History of London Life.* London, Longmans Green, 1958.

Mitford N: *The Sun King.* New York, Harper & Row, 1966.

Ober WB: *Boswell's Clap and Other Essays.* Southern Illinois University, 1979.

Origo I: *Images and Shadows*, London, J Murray, 1970.

Orleans Duchesse d': *Letters from Liselotte*, Kroll M (ed). New York, McCall, 1970.

Pottle FA (ed): *Boswell's London Journal, 1762–1763*. New York, McGraw-Hill, 1950.

Simond L: *Journal of a Tour and Residence in Great Britain during the Years 1810 and 1811*. London, 1817.

Tate WE: *The Parish Chest*. Cambridge University, 1969.

Timbs J: *Doctors and Patients*. London, Richard Bentley & Son, 1876.

Troyat H: *Chekhov*. New York, Dutton, 1986.

Turberville AS (ed): *Johnson's England*. London, Oxford University, 1933.

Turner ES: *Call the Doctor*. New York, St Martins, 1959.

Warbasse JP: Doctor Samuel Johnson and his court. *Med Lib Hist J* 5:2, June 1907.

CHAPTER II

Bayne-Powell R: *Eighteenth Century London Life*. London, J Murray, 1937.

Bloom U: *Victorian Vinaigrette*. London, Chivers Press, 1956.

Bragg M: *Speak for England*. London, Secker and Warburg, 1976.

Broughe JC: *Northwest Med* 58:1259, 1959

Dick OL (ed): *Aubrey's Brief Lives*. University of Michigan, 1962.

Duffy J: *Epidemics in Colonial America*. Louisiana State University, 1953.

Flemming P: *University College Hosp Magazine* 1:176, May 1926.

Gallagher T: *The Doctors' Story*. New York, Harcourt, Brace and World, 1967.

Garrison FH: The history of bloodletting. *NY State J Med* 97:432, 1913.

Glasscheib HS: *The March of Medicine*. New York, Putnam, 1964.

Hole C: *English Home Life, 1500 to 1800*. London, BT Batsford Ltd, 1947.

Holman DV: Venesection before Harvey and after. *Bull NY Acad Med* 31:9, September 1955.

Huizinga J: *Waning of the Middle Ages*. New York, St Martin's, 1924.

Kemble J: *Idols and Invalids*. London, Methuen, 1933.

La Wall CH: *4000 Years of Pharmacy*. Philadelphia, Lippincott, 1927.

Lewis WH: *The Splendid Century*. New York, William Morrow, 1954.

MacKinney L: *Early Medieval Illustrated Manuscripts*. University of California, 1965.

MacLaurin C: *Mere Mortals*. New York, GH Doran Co, 1925.

Miall B: *Master Johann Dietz*. London, Dutton, 1923.

Melicow MM: Evolution of urology. *Urol Surv* 18:199, August 1968.

Mossiker S: *Madame de Sévigné*. New York, Knopf, 1983.

Packard FR: Guy Patin and the medical profession in Paris in the 17th century. *Ann Med Hist*, vol 4, New York, Paul Hoeber, 1922.

Plumb JH: *Men and Centuries*. Boston, Houghton-Mifflin, 1963.

Pondoey GS: *Notes of a Soviet Doctor*. New York Consultants Bureau, 1959.

Powell JH: *Bring Out Your Dead*. University of Pennsylvania, 1949.

Roberts R: *The Classic Slum*. Manchester University Press, 1971.

Rosen G, Caspari-Rosen B: *400 Years of a Doctor's Life.* New York, Schuman, 1947.

Stephens JL; *Incidents of Travel in Yucatan.* New York, Dover, 1963.

Tallmadge GK: *Ciba Symposia* 9:748, November 1947.

Turner ES: *Call the Doctor.* New York, St Martin's, 1959.

Young HH; The renaissance of urology. *Bull Johns Hopkins Hosp* 27:327, 1916.

CHAPTER III

Anderson-Imbert E: *Spanish American Literature, VI.* Wayne University, 1969.

Arcinegas G: *Latin America, a Cultural History.* New York, Knopf, 1967.

Bremner MDK: *The Story of Dentistry.* London, H Kempton, 1946.

Butterfield WC: Patient and physician in 18th-century England. *Surg Gynecol Obstet* 134:843, May 1972.

Coulton GG: *Life in the Middle Ages.* Cambridge University, 1967.

Dalgetty AB: Auto-lithotrity: A record of 150 years ago. *Br Med J* 2:1329, 1936.

Duffy J: *The Healers.* New York, McGraw-Hill, 1976.

Epstein S: The case of Ellen French. *Angiology* 5:391, October 1954.

Farmer L: *Doctor's Legacy.* New York, Harpers, 1955.

Goldsscheib HS: *The March of Medicine.* New York, Putnam, 1964.

Graham H: *Surgeons All.* New York, Philosophical Library, 1957.

Jakobovitz I: The dissection of the dead in Jewish law. *Harofé Havri* 1:222, 1960.

Kahn M: History of the lithotomy operation, *Med Rec* 82:659, October 1912.

Lewis WH: *The Splendid Century.* New York, William Morrow, 1954.

MacLaurin C: *Post-Mortems.* London, Jonathan Cape, 1927.

MacQuitty B: *Victory over Pain.* New York, Taplinger, 1971.

Montaigne M: *Essays.* New York, Random House, 1946.

Murphy LJ: *The History of Urology.* Springfield, CC Thomas, 1972.

Norbury LEC: Proctology through the ages. *Ann R Coll Surg Engl* 4:65, February 1959.

Olson CC (ed): *Chaucer's World,* Columbia University, 1948.

Opuscula Selecta Neerlandicorum de Arte Medica, Amsterdam, 1943.

Putti V: Historic artificial limbs. *Am J Surg* 6:111, January 1929.

Remondino PC: *History of Circumcision.* Philadelphia, FA Davis, 1891.

Siegerist HE: *On the History of Medicine.* New York, M.D. Publications, 1960.

Stratton J: *Pioneer Women.* New York, Simon and Schuster, 1982.

Trease GE: *Pharmacy in History.* London, Balliere, Tindall & Cox, 1964.

Wakely T: *A Report of the Trial of Cooper v. Wakely for an Alleged Libel.* London, The Lancet, 1829.

Wheeler JB: *Memoirs of a Small-Town Surgeon.* New York, Frederick Stokes, 1935.

CHAPTER IV

Appleby H: *Pulse (Johannesburg)* 5:3, No. 415, 1949.

Baldick R (ed): *Pages from the Goncourt Journals.* London, Oxford University, 1962.

Beresford JD: *The Diary of a Country Parson.* London, Oxford University, 1971.

Brantôme S de: *Lives of Fair and Gallant Ladies,* New York, Liveright, 1933.

Burckhardt J: *The Civilization of the Renaissance in Italy.* New York, Random House, 1954.

Camp J: *The Healer's Art.* New York, Taplinger, 1977.

Clarke E (ed): *Modern Methods in the History of Medicine,* University of London, Athlone Press, 1971.

Clendening L: *Source Book of Medical History.* New York, Dover, 1942.

Cohn N: *The Pursuit of the Millennium.* New York, Harper and Row, 1961.

Colp C: *To Be an Invalid: The Illness of Charles Darwin.* University of Chicago, 1977.

Contenau G: *Everyday Life in Babylon-Assyria.* London, E Arnold, 1954.

Dawson WR: *Magician and Leech.* London, Methuen, 1929.

de la Barca CF: *Life in Mexico.* Fisher HF, & Fisher MH (eds). New York, Doubleday, 1970.

de Rios MD: *América* 33:28, April 1981.

Des Reaux GT: *Portraits and Anecdotes.* London, Oxford University, 1965.

Dewhurst K: *Dr. Thomas Sydenham.* University of California, 1966.

Dick OL (ed): *Aubrey's Brief Lives.* University of Michigan, 1962.

Edel L: *Stuff of Sleep and Dreams.* New York, Harper and Row, 1982.

Ficarra BJ: *Essays on Historical Medicine.* New York, Froben, 1948.

Graves R: *Goodbye to All That.* London, J Cape and H Smith, 1929.

Harrison GB: *A Second Jacobean Journal.* University of Michigan, 1958.

Hillesum E: *Diaries.* New York, Pantheon, 1984.

Holmes R: *Footsteps.* New York, Viking, 1985.

King-Hele D: *Doctor of Revolution.* London, Faber & Faber, 1977.

Mayor AH: *Prints and People.* New York, Metropolitan Museum of Art, 1971.

Prehoda RW: *Extended Youth.* New York, Putnam, 1968.

Sanders R: *Lost Tribes and Promised Lands.* Boston, Little Brown, 1978.

Segerburg O, Jr: *The Immortality Factor.* New York, Dalton, 1974.

Solomon HM: *Public Welfare, Science and Propaganda in Seventeenth Century France.* Princeton University, 1972.

Stephens JL: *Incidents of Travel in Yucatan.* New York, Dover, 1943.

Veith I: The medical world of Frederick the Great. *Calif Med* 115:3, 1971.

CHAPTER V

Brailsford D: *Sport and Society.* University of Toronto, 1969.

Briggs A: *A Social History of England.* New York, Viking, 1984.

Harrison GB: *A Second Jacobean Journal.* University of Michigan, 1958.

Lehmberg SE: *Sir Thomas Elyot, Tudor Humanist.* University of Texas, 1960.

Pottle FA (ed): *Boswell's London Journal, 1762–1763.* New York, McGraw-Hill, 1958.

Seltzer R: *Mortal Lessons.* New York, Simon and Schuster, 1976.

CHAPTER VI

Aberknecht EH: *Ciba Symposia* 11:1290, Winter 1950–1951.

Gimpel J: *The Medieval Machine.* New York, Holt, Rinehart & Winston, 1976.

Huxley A: *The Devils of Loudon.* New York, Harper and Brother, 1953.

Illich I: *Medical Nemesis.* New York, Pantheon, 1976.

Lewis WS (ed.): *The Yale Edition of Horace Walpole's Correspondence,* vol 18. Yale University, 1985.

Shapiro ED, Davis A: Law and pathology through the ages. *NY State J Med,* April 1, 1972.

Sterling W: Gynecology and obstetrics in the Old Testament and Babylonian Talmud. *Int Rec Med,* December 1960 and February 1961.

CHAPTER VII

Chesnutt MB: *A Dairy from Dixie.* New York, Houghton-Mifflin, 1949.

Fryer P: *Mrs. Grundy—Studies in English Prudery.* London, London House and Maxwell, 1964.

Haller JS, Haller RM: *The Physician and Sexuality in Victorian America.* University of Illinois, 1974.

Hughes MJ: *Women Healers in Medieval Life and Literature.* New York, Book for Libraries Press, 1968.

Rosenberg CE, Smith-Rosenberg C: *Sex, Marriage and Society.* New York, Arno, 1974.

CHAPTER VIII

Barker-Benfield GJ: *Horrors of the Half-Known Life.* New York, Harper and Row, 1976.

Bowers JZ: *Western Medical Pioneers in Feudal Japan.* London, Johns Hopkins Press, 1970.

Cleugh J: *Secret Enemy.* New York, Thomas Joseloff, not dated.

Creighton MS: *Dogwatch and Liberty Days.* Peabody Museum of Salem, 1982.

Fleming WL: Syphilis through the ages. *Med Clin North Am* 48:587, 1964.

Haller JS, Haller RM: *The Physician and Sexuality in Victorian America.* University of Illinois, 1974.

Himes NE: *Medical History of Contraception.* New York, Schocken, 1936.

Lévi-Strauss C: *Tristes Tropiques,* New York, Atheneum, 1974.

Lewis N: *Naples '44.* London, Pantheon, 1985.

McNeill WH: *Plagues and Peoples.* New York, Anchor, 1976.

Parran T: *Shadow on the Land.* New York, Reynal and Hitchcock, 1937.

Poynter FNL (ed): *The Journal of Thomas Yonge (1647–1721).* Connecticut, Anchor Books, 1963.

Rosebury T: *Microbes and Morals.* New York, Viking, 1971.

Sévigné Marquise de: *Letters,* Aldington R (ed). London, Routledge, 1937.

Tannahill R: *Sex in History.* New York, Stein and Day, 1982.

Tolley K: *Yangtze Patrol—The US Navy in China.* Annapolis, Naval Institute Press, 1971.

CHAPTER IX

Anderson-Imbert E: *Spanish American Literature.* Wayne University, 1969.

Baron AL: *Man against Germs.* New York, Dutton, 1968.

Bingham M: *Scotland under Mary Stuart.* New York, St. Martin's, 1975.

Blake JB: *Benjamin Waterhouse and the Introduction of Vaccine.* University of Pennsylvania, 1957.

Bowers JZ: *Western Medical Pioneers in Feudal Japan.* London, Johns Hopkins Press, 1970.

Brody SN: *The Disease of the Soul.* Cornell University, 1974.

Brown SH: Evolution of the medical advertisement. *Gen Mag Hist Chron* 31:1, October 1928.

Cartwright FF: *Disease and History.* New York, Crowell, 1972.

Cipolla CM: *Fighting the Plague in Seventeenth Century Italy.* University of Wisconsin, 1980.

Cyriax RJ: *Sir John Franklin's Arctic Expedition.* London, Methuen, 1939.

Duffy J: *Epidemics in Colonial America.* Louisiana State University, 1953.

Earle AM: *Customs and Fashions of Old New England.* Detroit, Singing Tree, 1968.

Glasscheib HS: *The March of Medicine.* New York, Putnam, 1964.

Gottfried RS: *Epidemic Disease in Fifteenth Century England.* Rutgers University, 1978.

de Gramont S: *Epitaph for Kings.* New York, Dutton, 1967.

Heaps L: *Log of the Centurion.* New York, MacMillan, 1973.

Henschen R: *The History and Geography of Diseases.* London, Longmans, 1966.

Hirschhorn N, Greenough WB III: Cholera. *Sci Am* 225:2, August 1971.

Langer WL: Immunization against smallpox before Jenner. *Sci Am,* January 1976.

Leasor J: *The Plague and the Fire.* London, Allen & Unwin, 1961.

Massingham H, Massingham P: *The London Anthology.* London, Phoenix House, 1950.

McNeill WH: *Plagues and Peoples.* New York, Anchor, 1976.

Mehta V: *Portrait of India.* New York, Farrar, Straus and Giroux, 1970.

Miller JC: *The Colonial Image.* New York, Braziller, 1962.

Newhall RH: *The Chronicle of Jean de Venette.* Columbia University, 1953.

Origo I; *The Merchant of Prato.* New York, Knopf, 1957.

Pelling M: *Cholera, Fever and English Medicine, 1825–1865.* London, Oxford University, 1978.

Plumb JH: *Men and Centuries.* Boston, Houghton-Mifflin, 1963.

Powell JH: *Bring out Your Dead.* University of Pennsylvania, 1949.

Rosenberg CE: *The Cholera Years.* University of Chicago, 1968.

Sanders M: *Intimate Letters of English Kings.* London, Museum Press, 1959.

Sigerist HE: *Great Doctors.* New York, Books for Libraries, 1933.

Silverman K: *The Life and Times of Cotton Mather.* New York, Harper & Row, 1984.

Stendhal (Beyle MH): *Travels in the South of France.* New York, Orion, 1970.

Stowe J: *The Survey of London,* Wheatley HB (ed), London, 1956.

Tuchman BW: *A Distant Mirror.* New York, Knopf, 1978.

Turberville AS: *Johnson's England.* London, Oxford University, 1952.

Wedgwood CV: *The Spoils of Time.* New York, Doubleday, 1985.

Winslow OE: *Destroying Angel.* Boston, Houghton-Mifflin, 1974.

Zinsser H: *Rats, Lice and History.* London, Routledge, 1942.

CHAPTER X

Allison MJ: Paleopathology in Peru. *Nat Hist* 88:74, February 1979.

Burton E: *The Pageant of Early Victorian England, 1837–1861.* New York, Scribners, 1972.

Congrés International de Rheumatologie (XVe): *Rheumatism in the World of Art and History.* Paris, June 1981.

Ellwanger GH: *Meditations on Gout.* Rutland, Vermont, 1968.

Evans J: *The Victorians.* Cambridge University, 1966.

Hassall WD: *How They Lived.* Oxford, Blackwell, 1965.

Hausman R, Dortu MG: *Lautrec by Lautrec.* New York, Galahad, 1964.

Hunter R, Macalpine I: The Rev. John Ashbourne and the origins of the private madhouse system, *Br Med J,* May 22, 1972.

Mead WE: *The English Medieval Feast.* New York, Houghton-Mifflin, 1931.

Orleans Duchesse d': *Letters from Liselotte,* Kroll M (ed). New York, McCall, 1970.

Ramazzini B: *Diseases of Workers.* New York, Hafner, 1964.

Rosen G: *Madness in Society.* New York, Harper & Row, 1969.

Sigerist HE: *Bull NY Acad Med* 12:597, November 1936.

Sigerist HE: *On the History of Medicine.* New York, MD Publications, 1960.

Wallace SL: A wit and his gout, the Reverend Sidney Smith. *Arthritis Rheum* 5:6, December 1962.

CHAPTER XI

Baxter R: *Life of Richard Baxter*. New York, American Tract Society, undated.

Bush RB: Disease and destiny—The imaginary world of Jean-Jacques Rousseau, *NY State J Med*, October 15, 1965.

Curtiss M: *Other People's Letters*. Boston, Houghton-Mifflin, 1978.

Dale PM: *Medical Biographies*. University of Oklahoma, 1952.

Ford FM: *Portraits from Life*. New York, H. Regnery, 1936.

Ford FM: *Return to Yesterday*. New York, Liveright, 1932.

Gay P: *The Bourgeoise Experience*, vol 1, Oxford University, 1984.

Henry D: Did eye ailments add to Emily Dickinson's woes? *NY Times*, December 18, 1979.

Hogwood C: *Handel*. New York, Thames and Hudson, 1985.

Kemble J: *Napoleon the Immortal*. London, John Murray, 1959.

Koestler A: *The Sleepwalkers*. New York, MacMillan, 1959.

de Lawrencie L: *Lully*. Ann Arbor, UMI Research Press, 1979.

Lewis WH: *The Splendid Century*. New York, William Morrow, 1954.

Loomer A: *Famous Flaws*. New York, Macmillan, 1956.

MacLauren C: *Post-Mortems*. London, Jonathan Cape, 1927.

Marek GR: *Schubert*. New York, Viking, 1985.

Maugham S: *Saturday Review*, April 11, 1953.

Muir F: *An Irreverent and Thoroughly Incomplete Social History*. New York, Stein & Day, 1976.

Nederland W: *Goya's Illness. NY State J Med*, 72:413, 1972.

Ober WB: *Boswell's Clap and Other Essays*. University of Southern Illinois, 1979.

Sitwell E: *English Eccentrics*. New York, Vanguard, 1957.

Sprigges SS: *Physic and Fiction*. London, Hodder & Stoughton, 1921.

Sutherland JR (ed): *The Oxford Book of Literary Anecdotes*. New York, 1975.

Timbs J: *Doctors and Patients, Anecdotes of the Medical World and Curiosities of Medicine*. London, R Bentley, 1876.

Troyat H: *Divided Soul—The Life of Gogol*. New York, Doubleday, 1973.

Woodhead AG: *Cambridge Hist J* 10:235, 1952.

Wykes A: *Doctor Cardano, Physician Extraordinary*. London, Frederick Muller Ltd, 1969.

Veith I: The medical world of Frederick the Great. *Calif Med* 115:78, 1971.

CHAPTER XII

Aydelotte F: *Elizabethan Rogues and Vagabonds*. New York, Barnes and Noble, 1967.

Canaday J: *Mainstreams of Modern Art*. New York, Holt, Rinehart & Winston, 1959.

Conot R: *A Streak of Luck.* New York, Seaview, 1979.
Everitt G: *Doctors and Doctors.* London, 1888.
Gartenberg E: *Mahler, The Man and His Music.* New York, Schirmer, 1978.
Hart R: *English Life in Tudor Times.* London, Wayland, 1972.
Jeaffreson JC: *A Book about Doctors.* London, Hurst & Blackett, 1861.
Ladurie EL: *Montaillou.* New York, Braziller, 1978.
Lévi-Strauss C: *Triste Tropiques.* New York, Atheneum, 1973.
Lewis N: *Naples '44.* New York, Pantheon, 1978.
Mellow JR: *Charmed Circle.* New York, Holt, Rinehart & Winston, 1974.
Steigmuller F: *Flaubert in Egypt.* New York, Little Brown, 1973.
Sitwell E: *English Eccentrics.* New York, Vanguard, 1957.
Swinnerton F: *A Galaxy of Fathers.* New York, Books for Libraries, 1966.

CHAPTER XIII

Ackerknecht EH: *Ciba Symposia* 11:1313, Winter 1950–1951.
Bayon HP: Ancient pregnancy tests. *Proc. Soc Med* 32:1527, September 1939.
Bevington H: *A Book and a Love Affair.* New York, Harcourt, Brace, Jovanovich, 1968.
Clair C: *Human Curiosities.* London, Abelard-Schuman, 1968.
Flack IH: *Eternal Eve.* New York, Doubleday, 1951.
Forbes TR; Early pregnancy and fertility tests. *Yale J Biol Med* 30:16, September 1957.
Forbes TR: *The Midwife and the Witch.* Yale University, 1966.
Ford CS: *A Comparative Study of Human Reproduction.* Yale University, 1945.
Forster R, Ranum O (eds): *Medicine and Society in France, Selections from the Annales,* vol 6. Johns Hopkins University, 1980.
Hitchcock J: A sixteenth century midwife's license. *Bull Hist Med* 41:75, January—February 1967.
Howard M: *Victorian Grotesques.* London, Jupiter, 1977.
Landucci L: *A Florentine Diary.* New York, Arno, 1971.
Litwack LF: *Been in the Storm So Long.* New York, Knopf, 1979.
Manner MJ: *Med Clin N Am* p. 207, July 1959.
Snapper I: Midwifery past and present. *Bull NY Acad Med* 39:503, August 1963.
Stage S: *Female Complaints.* New York, W.W. Norton, 1979.
Steinberg W: Gynecology and obstetrics in the Old Testament and the Babylonian Talmud. *Int Rec Med* December 1960 and February 1961.
Trewin ML: *Am J Surg* 98:758, November 1959.

CHAPTER XIV

Ashton J: *Social Life in the Reign of Queen Anne.* Detroit, Swinging Tree, 1968.
Blumenthal WH: *Brides from Bridewell.* New York, Greenwood, 1973.

Bogan L, Roget E (eds): *The Journal of Jules Reynad.* New York, Braziller, 1964.

Buchan W: *Domestic Medicine.* London, Thomas Kelly, 1824.

de Mause L: *The History of Childhood.* New York, Psychohistory Press, 1974.

Forbes TR: Mortality books for 1774–93 and 1833–35. *Bull NY Acad Med* 47:12, December 1971.

George MD: *London Life in the Eighteenth Century.* New York, Harper & Row, 1965.

Hunt D: *Parents and Children in History.* New York, Basic Books, 1970.

Hyland S: *Curiosities from Parliament.* London, 1955.

Jones KM: *The Plantation Society.* Indianapolis, Bobbs Merill, 1957.

Langer WL: Checks on population growth, 1750–1850. *Sci Am,* February 1972.

Mares FH (ed): *Memoirs of Robert Carey.* Oxford: Clarendon Press, 1972.

McCarthy M: *Memories of a Catholic Girlhood.* London, Heinemann, 1957.

Roelker NL: *Queen of Navarre—Jeanne d'Abret.* Harvard University, 1968.

Sitwell E: *Taken Care of.* New York, Atheneum, 1965.

Tolmie WF: My father. *Br Col Hist Q (Victoria),* 1937.

Tyson M, Guppy H (eds): *The French Journal of Mrs. Thrale and Doctor Johnson.* University of Manchester, 1932.

CHAPTER XV

Burckhardt J: *Civilization of the Renaissance in Italy.* New York, Random House, 1955.

Cobb R: *Paris and its Provinces 1792–1802.* London, Oxford University, 1975.

Manceroni C: *Twilight of the Old Order.* New York, A. A. Knopf, 1977.

Massingham H, Massingham P: *The London Anthology.* London, Phoenix House, 1950.

McLaughlin T: *Dirt.* New York, Stein and Day, 1971.

Origo I: *The Merchant of Prato.* New York, Knopf, 1957.

Orleans Duchesse d': *Letters from Liselotte,* Kroll M (ed). New York, McCall, 1970.

Pepys S: *Diary,* Wheatley HB (ed). New York, Random House, not dated.

Power EE: *Medieval English Nunneries.* Cambridge University, 1922.

Reynolds R: *Cleanliness and Godliness.* New York, Harcourt, Brace, Jovanovich, 1974.

Rye WB (ed): *England as Seen by Foreigners in the Days of Elizabeth and James I.* London, 1865.

Trollope F: *Domestic Manners of the Americans.* New York, Random House, 1949.

Turberville AS: *Johnson's England.* London, Oxford University, 1952.

Wright L: *Clean and Decent.* Boston, Routledge & Kegan Paul, 1960.

CHAPTER XVI

Aubrey J: *Brief Lives,* Dick OL (ed). University of Michigan, 1962.
Buchan W: *Domestic Medicine.* London, Thomas Kelly 1824.
Coulton GG: *Life in the Middle Ages,* Cambridge University, 1967.
Defourneaux M: *Daily Life in Spain in the Golden Age.* Stanford University, 1970.
Gimpel J: *The Medieval Machine.* New York, Holt, Rinehart & Winston, 1976.
Hunt P: *Fifteenth Century England.* University of Pittsburgh, 1962.
Massingham H, Massingham P: *London Anthology.* London, Phoenix House, 1950.
Salusbury GT: *Street Life in Medieval England.* London, 1948.
Sutherland J (ed): *The Oxford Book of English Talk.* Oxford, Clarendon Press, 1953.

CHAPTER XVII

Altick RD: *The Shows of London.* Cambridge, Belknap Press, 1978.
Ashton J: *Social England under the Regency.* Detroit, Singing Tree, 1968.
Bayne-Powell R: *Eighteenth Century London Life.* London, J Murray, 1938.
Brown SH: The evolution of medical advertisement. *Gen Mag Hist Chron* 31:1, October 1928.
Debus AG: *The English Paracelsians.* London, F Watts, 1965.
De Ries MD: *America* 33:28, April 1981.
Edelstein EJ, Edelstein L: *Asclepius, A Collection of Interpretations of the Testimonies.* Baltimore, 1946.
Gordon BL: Demonology and the eye. *Harofé Havri* 2:239, 1964.
Hibbert C: *Rome.* New York, WW Norton, 1985.
Kaplan J: *Mr. Clemens and Mark Twain.* New York, Simon and Schuster, 1966.
Linebaugh P et al: *Albion's Fatal Tree.* New York, Pantheon, 1935.
Nicholson MH: Ward's drop and pill and men of letters. *J Hist Idea* 29:177, April–June 1968.
Rousselot J: *Medicine in Art.* New York, McGraw-Hill, not dated.
Snow LF: *Ann Int Med* 81:1, July 1974.
Southerland J (ed): *The Oxford Book of English Talk.* London, Oxford University, 1953.
Tate WE: *The Parish Chest.* Cambridge University, 1969.